UNION MAIDS
NOT WANTED

UNION MAIDS NOT WANTED

ORGANIZING DOMESTIC WORKERS 1870–1940

DONNA L. VAN RAAPHORST

New York
Westport, Connecticut
London

Library of Congress Cataloging-in-Publication Data

Van Raaphorst, Donna L.
    Union maids not wanted: organizing domestic workers,
  1870-1940 / Donna L. Van Raaphorst.
      p.   cm.
    Bibliography: p.
    Includes index.
    ISBN 0-275-92288-X (alk. paper)
    1. Women domestics--United States--History. 2. Trade-
  unions--Domestics--United States--History. 3. Social classes--
  United States--History.   I. Title.
  HD6072.2.U5V36   1988
  331.4'8164046'09--dc19
  87-25899

Library of Congress Catalog Card Number: 87-25899
ISBN: 0-275-92288-X

First published in 1988

Praeger Publishers, One Madison Avenue, New York, NY 10010
A division of Greenwood Press, Inc.

Printed in the United States of America

∞
The paper used in this book complies with the
Permanent Paper Standard issued by the National
Information Standards Organization (Z39.48-1984).

10 9 8 7 6 5 4 3 2 1

To N.A.W., the dearest of friends.
Never a week passes that I don't
think of you and miss you, still.

Contents

Acknowledgments

Historical endeavors are, by their very nature, solitary ones. Our ruminations occur only with the events and personages of the past, who silently speak to us as we go about our work. The end product remains, as it must, the responsibility of our individual labors. Despite this fact, I have been most fortunate in finding those who would support me along my way. I am grateful to Ronald Sobel and Cuyahoga Community College for their generosity in allowing me access to college equipment for the purpose of revision. Marianne Lesniak made this entire volume possible through her endless hours of labor at the word processor. My editor, Alison Podel, made helpful suggestions along the way and gently prodded me on my path of progress. I am especially indebted to Robert P. Swierenga of Kent State University, who believed in this work in its dissertation form. Collectively, the Women Historians of Greater Cleveland were my own home base network of support. In particular, my gratitude goes to Bess Kaplan, Lois Scharf of Case Western Reserve University, and Marian J. Morton of John Carroll University. I shall remain eternally grateful to Edwin Burnes, an exceptional human being and the rudder of my soul for many years. To my dear friend Jane Mueller, I can only begin to express my appreciation. No person could possibly ask for a better friend than you have been to me. To Cheryl, my fifteen-year-old, and the truly great challenge of my existence, I can finally say this is behind us. I hope you will be proud, as proud as the remarkable person to whom this book is dedicated.

UNION MAIDS
NOT WANTED

1

Introduction

"my history books lied to me. They said **i** didn't exist."[1]

One of the most strikingly ironic facets of the topic under
study--domestic service--is the fact that it remains one of
the least studied, but most written about occupations. To
date there are only four full-length scholarly volumes which
deal with domestic service in U.S. history. Furthermore,
no detailed investigation has ever dealt with the issues
pertaining to collective action by these workers. Lucy
Maynard Salmon's pioneering examination, simply titled
Domestic Service, was the first comprehensive, academic,
historical investigation of this predominately female occupation. Not until 1978 with the publication of Seven Days
a Week: Women and Domestic Service in Industrializing
America, by David M. Katzman, would the subject be thoroughly treated again.[2]

Thoroughness and scholarship aside, thousands upon
thousands of articles in popular journals, magazines, and
newspapers attempted to confront what was variously labeled
the "servant question," the "servant problem," and the
"great American question."[3] That the quality and degree
of insight offered in such publications was of inferior
grade seems to have been generally recognized by many.
For example, in 1906 one author wrote:

> It is true that women have done a good
> deal of writing upon this subject, but
> their writing has consisted mainly of bitter
> complaining. And in so far as men have
> participated in the discussion, they have
> too often been writers for our popular Sun-
> day supplements.[4]

The most thorough early commentary on the literature was
provided by Salmon. She maintained that considerations
of domestic service could be broken down into four general
types, each providing its own particular point of view.
The first category included daily and weekly newspapers,
which offered characterizations of the helpless and ignorant
mistress of the home versus her presumptuous and insolent
maid. Second, there were the popular magazine articles.
Typically theoretical in character, they proposed remedies
for existing evils, yet lacked adequate consideration with
respect to causes. Third were the home departments of
religious and secular presses, along with household journals. They concentrated, almost exclusively, on the personal relationship between maid and mistress. Finally,
there evolved commonly accepted proverbs about service
generating from conversations among mistresses and among
maids.[5]

Table 1.1

Number and Percentage of Females
Employed as Servants, 1870-1940[1]

Year	Women Service Workers in Private or Public Housekeeping [1]	Women Service Workers in Private or Public Housekeeping [1] as Percent of all Women in the Labor Force or Gainfully Occupied
1940	2,831,874	21.8
1930	2,146,360	20.0
1920	1,356,531	15.7
1910	1,593,586	21.4
1900	1,430,656	26.9
1890	1,302,704	32.5
1880	970,257	36.7
1870	901,954	47.0

[1]Includes charwomen and cleaners, and the following workers whether or
not in private families: cooks, housekeepers, stewards, and hostesses;
servants; and waitresses.

Source: Janet M. Hooks, Women's Occupations Throughout Seven Decades,
Women's Bureau Bulletin #218, U.S. Department of Labor (Washington, D.C.:
Government Printing Office, 1951), p. 139.

An obvious conclusion to draw from this discussion
is that domestic service simply did not warrant serious
consideration. Table 1.1 definitely reveals a decline in
the relative importance of service for all women gainfully
employed over the seven decades of this study. Despite
this decline, Table 1.2 reveals that service retained its
position as one of the leading female occupations for these
same decades.

Contemporaries were sometimes puzzled by this lack
of serious scholarly analysis.[6] A few even offered insights into this perplexing question. Piecing these insights together along with the observations of recent inves-
tigators, we can arrive at some conclusions. For example,
scholarship is beginning to come to terms with the fact
that women, as a whole, have never been adequately included in the majority of American labor histories. Then,
and now, it was known that women were not new to the
work force,[7] but their role as workers was generally
neglected. Commenting on this and the two major female
occupations, one writer said that "with regard to the number of women entering two of the five occupational groups,
agriculture . . . and domestic service, public opinion has
little concern."[8]

Closely related to the general neglect of women workers is the fact that domestic service was regarded primarily as a woman's issue. It was a woman's issue, rather
than a labor question, because it was predominately a female occupation. Some did not even accord it the status
of an occupation, but regarded it as a normal feminine
function. Or, as one author sarcastically wrote, it was
"a form of healthy exercise."

Of course women workers have concentrated in those
occupations which could be construed as carryovers from
their female roles in the family: service occupations, including teaching, nursing, office work, and domestic service.[9] However, the assignment of such jobs, even within
given industries, has often been arbitrary. Indeed, label
a job a woman's and it receives a lower rating in skill
and status and pay.[10]

The low status of domestic work evolved from the
fact that it has been designated woman's work by nature
and because of the nature of the work. Unskilled menial
labor performed by individuals--female individuals--in isolation was, and is, not likely to be classed among the
major industries of the nation. Nor did service involve

Table 1.2

The Leading Ten Occupations of Women Workers 1870-1950 in Order of Size, and as Reported in Each Census Regardless of Changes in Definition

1870	1880	1890	1900	1910	1920	1930	1940	1950
Domestic Servants	Domestic Servants	Servants	Servants	Other Servants	Other Servants	Other Servants, Other Domestic and Personal Service	Servants (private family)	Stenographers, Typists, and Secretaries
Agricultural Laborers	Agricultural Laborers	Agricultural Laborers	Farm Laborers (members of family)	Farm Laborers (home farm)	Teachers (school)	Teachers (school)	Stenographers Typists and Secretaries	Other Clerical Workers
Tailoresses and Seamstresses	Milliners, Dressmakers and Seamstresses	Dressmakers	Dressmakers	Laundresses (not in laundry)	Farm Laborers (home farm)	Stenographers and Typists	Teachers (not elsewhere classified)	Saleswomen

Table 1.2 (continued)

1870	1880	1890	1900	1910	1920	1930	1940	1950
Milliners, Dress and Mantua Makers	Teachers and Scientific Persons	Teachers	Teachers	Teachers (school)	Stenographers and Typists	Other Clerks (except clerks in stores)	Clerical and Kindred Workers (not elsewhere classified)	Private Household Workers
Teachers (not specified)	Laundresses	Farmers, Planters, and Overseers	Laundry Work (hand)	Dressmakers and Seamstresses (not in factory)	Other Clerks (except clerks in stores)	Saleswomen	Saleswomen (not elsewhere classified)	Teachers (elementary school)

5

Table 1.2 (continued)

1870	1880	1890	1900	1910	1920	1930	1940	1950
Cotton-mill Operatives	Cotton-mill Operatives	Laundresses	Farmers and Planters	Farm Laborers (working out)	Laundresses (not in laundry)	Farm Laborers (unpaid family workers)	Operatives and Kindred Workers, Apparel and Accessories	Waitresses
Laundresses	Farmers and Planters	Seamstresses	Farm and Plantation Laborers	Cooks	Saleswomen (stores)	Bookkeepers and Cashiers	Bookkeepers, Accountants and Cashiers	Bookkeepers
Woolen-mill Operatives	Tailoresses	Cotton-mill Operatives	Saleswomen	Stenographers and Typewriters	Bookkeepers and Cashiers	Laundresses (not in laundry)	Waitresses (except private family)	Sewers and Stitchers, Manufacturing

Table 1.2 (continued)

1870	1880	1890	1900	1910	1920	1930	1940	1950
Farmers and Planters	Woolen-mill Operatives	Housekeepers and Stewards	Housekeepers and Stewards	Farmers	Cooks	Trained Nurses	Housekeepers (private family)	Nurses, Registered
Nurses	Employees of Hotels and Restaurants (not clerks)	Clerks and Copyists	Seamstresses	Saleswomen (stores)	Farmers (general farms)	Other Cooks	Trained Nurses and Student Nurses	Telephone Operators

Sources: Janet M. Hooks, Women's Occupations Through Seven Decades, Women's Bureau Bulletin #218, U.S. Department of Labor (Washington, D.C.: Government Printing Office, 1951); and Rosalyn Baxandall, Linda Gordon, and Susan Reverby, eds., America's Working Women: A Documentary History--1600 to the Present (New York: Vintage Books, 1976), pp. 406-407.

the investment of large amounts of capital for either the employer or employee. The "products" of domestic work remain extremely transient in nature. Since domestic work involved highly personal relations between employer and employee, often in private homes, many viewed investigation of service an invasion of privacy. Since there were few recorded combinations by either mistresses or maids, domestic work tended to be removed from questions involving trusts, monopolies, and trade unions. In fact, when trade unions were the focus of labor histories, authors pointedly excluded domestics from consideration.[11]

Neglect of domestic service as a significant part of the American labor movement serves as a classic example of the general thrust of labor history in the United States. For more than half of this century, extending far beyond World War II, the labor history of the United States has reflected the conceptual framework of its founding fathers: John R. Commons and his most gifted followers, Selig Perlman and Philip Taft.[12]

In its time this school of thought—the so-called Wisconsin school of labor history—represented a revolt against late nineteenth-century classical economics. Steeped as they were in German historical scholarship, pioneering labor economists viewed historical research as a major experimental tool to use against the abstractions of laissez faire economics. At the center of this intellectual revolt was John R. Commons and his works entitled A Documentary History of American Industrial Society (1910-1911) and A History of Labor in the United States (1918; 1935).[13]

The views espoused by Commons and associates can be found in virtually every American history textbook, in every survey lecture, and in primer courses for both workers and trade unionists. Institutional economics contained important source materials, asked broad questions, and revealed impressive ideas.[14] Since the Wisconsin school often involved field work in the world of industry, service in labor arbitration and in government, it retained much of its vitality over the years. Also integral was the output of a vast body of historical literature on labor relations and trade unionism.[15]

The history of the development of trade unions as institutions and their place in the changing marketplace has an expected scenario. Its major tenets go something like the following: workers are economic creatures who, either in groups or individually, pursue selfish interests

which are often at the expense of others. Thus organizations are formed in respective crafts or industries to defend
material interests against the opposition--the capitalist.
Consequently the worker is concerned with on-the-job benefits, higher wages, and shorter hours. In short, the
worker is scarcity-conscious and unwilling to risk what
little is possessed for some distant, utopian goal.[16]

In the broadest sense, institutional economics was
nothing more than a reflection of the elitism prevalent in
the academic world at large. History had, more or less,
been the special province of a privileged stratum of American society. Attention was primarily devoted to the study
of diplomacy, war, and politics. Democratization of the
profession came only after World War II with the infusion
of students from ethnic and working-class backgrounds.
Only then did the worker become the topic of study. The
handful of students interested in labor history in the 1950s
first attempted to bring scholarship up to the level of
other fields in U.S. history.[17]

Cracks in the Commons edifice first appeared in the
mid-1950s when Vaughn Davis Bornet published an article
in The Historian in 1955 that called for a new labor history. In 1957 Walter Galenson scolded historians for their
lack of interest in labor history. Almost simultaneously,
a group of scholars in New York City began the publication of a labor history bulletin. They also paved the way
for the publication of a scholarly journal. Daniel Bell,
Richard B. Morris, Maurice Neufield, and Galenson, along
with others, were stimulated by the 1955 AFL-CIO merger.
Encouraged by these signs of vigor in the labor movement,
they began the process that led directly to the birth of
Labor History in 1960. Essentially, these authors shared
the views of traditional labor history and were not calling
for a different approach to the subject matter.[18]

It is not too surprising to discover that the work of
this first generation of new scholarship dealt with very
familiar issues--strikes, leaders, organizations, the Left,
and politics. However, the focus of their investigations
became a history of workers. That focus is abundantly
evident in David Brody's Steelworkers in America: The
Non-Union Era (Cambridge, Mass.: Harvard University
Press, 1960), in Herbert Gutman's Work, Culture & Society
in Industrializing America: Essays in American Working-
Class and Social History (New York: Random House, 1966;
Vintage Books, 1977), in Irving Bernstein's The Lean Years:

A History of the American Worker, 1920-1933 (Baltimore:
Penguin Books, 1960), and in Melvyn Dubofsky's We Shall
Be All: A History of the IWW (Chicago: Quadrangle
Books, 1969). At the same time new forces favorable to
writing the history of the American worker came to the
forefront.[19] Among those favorable forces was the reemer-
gence of radicalism, its interrelated concern with poverty
and racism, together with the growing availability of documentary materials. The cry of the New Left in the 1960s
was for a "history from the bottom up," and a "history of
the inarticulate."[20] Significantly, the desire to write the
history of the American working class has lived on in the
younger generation of labor historians, but retaining their
places on the frontier are older scholars like David Montgomery and the late Herbert Gutman.[21]

The other force driving the new labor history
stemmed directly from the brilliant work of select groups
of English social historians. They included Eric J. Hobs-
bawn, George Rudé, Brian Harrison and, first and foremost, E. P. Thompson. Collectively they suggested elements of working-class existence unheard of in the historiography of American labor history. Single-handedly
Thompson, in his Making of the English Working Class
(New York: Random House, 1964), transmitted key insights
to the American scene. These included the notion of an
industrial morality embedded in evangelical religion; the
attempt to find the meaning of nineteenth-century reform
and politics; and finally, the customs and habits of workers in the transition from a preindustrial to an industrial
world.[22]

The application of these new ideas has forced historians in the United States to branch out in various
directions. Their objective has been to investigate fully
the rich fabric of all of American life. Relating directly
to this study on domestic workers is the work of Virginia
Yans-McLaughlin, whose research illustrates the need for
new definitions of women's work. Her objective was to
define conditions such as demographic, economic, and occupational structures over time. Yans-McLaughlin's findings
revealed that Italian women seldom became domestic servants because of family, ethnic, and social characteristics.
In a similar vein David Brody's Steelworkers in America
illustrated why Slavic immigrants were a source of antiunion stability in the nonunion era of the American steel
industry.[23]

Another important application was provided by Daniel T. Rodgers in Work Ethic in Industrial America 1850-1920 (Chicago: University of Chicago Press, 1974). Rodgers examined the transformation of the world of work as the United States industrialized. He then analyzed the meaning of that evolution with respect to the Protestant work ethic as it impacted the worker. This factor has direct bearing on the study of domestic workers. Although such people were not factory workers in any sense, some reformers did advocate a new discipline as a solution to the "servant problem." Furthermore, it has been amply shown that the household was not immune to the changes brought by the Industrial Revolution.[24]

Gutman's path-breaking work in community studies has also developed into another fruitful avenue for labor history. This stems from the strong interest in local history that is so characteristic of much new labor research. It is also rooted in the belief that here lie the cultural beginnings of the working class. An interesting application of community study was used by James R. Green. Two totally different early twentieth-century community settings—the company town and the urban ghetto—were examined. From this perspective Green probed the workers' day-to-day lives, a very necessary component for a meaningful study of domestic service.

Many authors who do not consider themselves labor historians have, nevertheless, provided insights into the world of the worker. Susan Kleinberg has demonstrated the relationship between industrialization and urbanization on the one hand, and women's cultural, social, political, and economic activities on the other hand. Elizabeth Pleck has consistently argued against the arbitrary and unnatural separation of family and labor history. A similar concern can be found in a recent work by Tamara Hareven. Leslie Tentler's study revealed a great deal about adolescent girls' adjustment to factory life, an experience that has an impact on their development as women and mothers. Family history, women's history, and black history formed an essential core in David M. Katzman's study on domestic service. All of these works illustrate how the various strains of the new social history fuse together and provide us with insights on the "concern for the everyday experiences of ordinary people."[25]

Two final areas relative to domestic service are those of social mobility and quantification. Steven Thernstrom's work is the obvious place to begin, especially with Poverty and Progress: Social Mobility in a Nineteenth Century City (Cambridge, Mass.: Harvard University Press, 1964; repr. ed., New York: Atheneum, 1969). Through innovative use of census data, Thernstrom discovered that upward mobility was virtually nonexistent, that wages remained chronically low, that high seasonal unemployment prevailed, and that workers suffered from deprivation and self-sacrifice. Also drawing heavily on quantitative methods is the equally exciting Philadelphia Social History Project, which examined occupational levels over time, working conditions, wage levels, and relative opportunities for advancement. Although not relying upon statistical data to the same degree, David Katzman's Seven Days a Week did illustrate the degree of social and economic mobility available to white (native and ethnic) domestic servants. He also demonstrated the role that southern black migration had on the nature of service by changing a predominately white, live-in occupation to a predominately black, live-out occupation. The issues of mobility are crucial in an understanding of domestic service and various attempts by domestic workers to unionize. Speaking on this issue in a much broader sense, historian Paul Faler wrote:

> [T]he importance of mobility cannot be established without greater attention to the social context in which it occurs; it may either encourage or discourage working-class resistance to capitalism; depending on its relationship to other values by which people judged a social system.[26]

The following investigation on household workers and their efforts to form unions is an attempt to further the understanding of these often forgotten and neglected women. Much like E. P. Thompson, I, too,

> am seeking to rescue . . . [them] from the enormous condescension of posterity. [Even though] their insurrectionary conspiracies may have been foolhardy . . . they lived through these times of acute social disturbance, and we did not. Their aspirations were valid in terms of their own experience; and if they were casualties of

history, they remain, condemned in their
own lives, as casualties.[27]

Chapter 2 presents a historical overview of domestic
service in the United States. In preparing this overview,
I have steeped myself in labor histories, including those
few that dealt with women. I have attempted to use and
summarize the best available periodical literature. I have
sorted through appropriate government reports and have
attempted to incorporate the best of the new research on
women, family, community, and labor history. Finally, I
have relied heavily on Lucy Maynard Salmon's Domestic
Service and David M. Katzman's Seven Days a Week.
Chapter 3 also draws on a wide variety of materials.
One major source of information was nineteenth- and twentieth-century periodical literature. Here, I found rich and
vivid descriptions of the psychology of housework from both
perspectives--the mistresses' and the maids'. Invaluable
were various household and etiquette guidebooks beginning
as far back as Catherine E. Beecher's classic, A Treatise
on Domestic Economy.[28] My model for establishing the
psychology of the household stems from David Brody's
Steelworkers in America and his belief that the diversity
of the new labor and social history necessitates a focus in
order to make the ubiquity of its findings meaningful. He
suggested this could be found by focusing on the meaning
of the work itself.[29] I am also indebted to my friend
Marian J. Morton of John Carroll University for her suggestion that the household could be placed in such a
framework.
Chapter 4 attempts to examine the various worlds of
the women who labored in the homes of others. Part of my
framework was borrowed from E. P. Thompson, particularly
the notion of class as a worldview. I have endeavored to
show how these women of diverse ethnic, racial, and geographic backgrounds possessed a collective "peasant" mentality antithetical to collective action. In this chapter I
have used David Brody's notions of segments of society as
antiunion forces. He labeled them sources of stability,
whereas I have regarded them as preservers of the status
quo. My sources included periodical literature written by
domestics, interviews of domestics by various women reformers and social settlement workers, contemporary ethnic
and secondary ethnic histories, and sociological accounts.
Various sources also deal with black migrants from the

South and white migrants from the country. I also relied
on the autobiography and papers of Jane Edna Hunter.[30]
A southern black migrant herself, Hunter established a
home for black migrants in Cleveland. Knowing firsthand
what it meant to be a migrant and a sometime domestic,
Hunter founded the Phillis Wheatly Association. Training
classes for domestics were provided by the Phillis Wheatly
Association. These papers were a final source for Chapter 4.

Chapter 5 relates the point of view of the mistresses: how they regarded the servants, the problems of
domestic service, and their proposed solutions to those
problems. My main sources were the words and opinions
of mistresses. Colorful, vivid articles written by the employers filled the popular magazines, journals, and newspapers. Proposing every conceivable solution to the "servant problem" except unionization, they, in fact, were
early forerunners of welfare capitalism in the home. This
was a household version of a similar system used by many
corporations in their labor management relations of the
1920s. I am grateful to my friend Lois Scharf of Case
Western Reserve University for her suggestion that I apply
the concept of welfare capitalism to the home.

Chapter 6 continues the theme of preservers of the
status quo by examining the attitudes of organized labor
toward domestic workers. Despite the more or less tolerant
view of the unskilled, the ethnic, the black, and the female laborer by the Knights of Labor and the IWW, the
main union of the period was the AFL. Using labor periodicals and labor leaders' autobiographies, whenever possible,
I attempted to examine these unions with respect to domestic workers. I relied heavily on labor histories, both old
and new; on the American Federationist; the International
Worker; and Solidarity. These last two labor periodicals
were researched at the Walter Reuther Archives of Labor
History at Wayne State University in Detroit, Michigan.

Chapter 7 discusses various attempts by domestics
either to join existing unions or to establish their own.
Again, I used labor histories and the various official union
publications that existed over the seven decades of this
study. Newspapers were also an important source of information. Although I was able to find numerous examples
of collective action, all remained highly ephemeral in nature. Whenever possible, I followed them through from beginning to end. In the most important examples, the fate

of the organized domestics rested in the hands of the union
to which they were affiliated.   These tended to be industrial unions and the two most significant ones, the Knights
of Labor and the IWW, ceased to exist or came to exist
only on paper.

Chapter 8 deals exclusively with the 1930s, although
my intention was not to deal directly with either the Great
Depression or the New Deal.   Rather, I wished to discover
what impact these events had on domestic work and domestic
workers.   Significant labor legislation and the attitude of
the Roosevelt family, particularly Eleanor's attitude, were
favorable to unions.   In Eleanor's case this even included
domestic workers.   The YWCA and government offices became very active in their push for training schools, the
establishment of standards, and the incorporation of domestics in government legislation such as the Social Security Act.   My major objective was to see the extent to which
any or all of this activity benefited the servants.   My
chief sources were periodical literature, government reports,
newspapers, and labor histories.   In addition, I used the
papers of the Cleveland branch of the YWCA, located at
the Western Reserve Historical Society.   Select materials
related to my topic were generously made available to me
by the national YWCA, located in New York City.   Once
again, I am indebted to my friend Lois Scharf, whose wise
suggestion it was that I extend this study through the
1930s.

The Great Depression and the New Deal served as a
kind of litmus test to the hypothesis that--given different
circumstances, given an environment in which the status
quo was changed--domestics, like other workers, would be
able to form successful unions.   This was not to be, for
one of the more remarkable things about service occupations was how very little did change over the course of
decades this study covers.   Thus Chapter 9 attempts to
conclude in the conceptual framework of change within
continuity.

NOTES

1.   Alta, The Shameless Hussy: Selected Stories,
Essays, and Poetry (Trumansburg, N.Y.:   Crossing Press,
1980), p. 8.

2. Salmon's work had a second edition in 1901, which included a supplementary chapter dealing with European domestic service; discussions of U.S. service were not altered. See Lucy Maynard Salmon, Domestic Service (New York: Macmillan, 1897; repr. ed., New York: Arno Press, 1972). Other important works dealing with service since Katzman's study are Daniel E. Sutherland, Americans and Their Servants: Domestic Service in the United States from 1800-1920 (Baton Rouge, La.: Louisiana University Press, 1981); and Faye E. Dudden, Serving Women: Household Service in Nineteenth-Century America (Middletown, Conn.: Wesleyan University Press, 1983).

3. Rheta Childe Dorr, What Eight Million Women Want (Boston: Small, Maynard, 1910; repr. ed., New York: Kraus Reprint, 1971), pp. 253-54; B. Eleanor Johnson, "A Study of Household Employment in Chicago," Journal of Home Economics 25 (February 1933):115; Mary Anderson, "Domestic Service in the United States," Journal of Home Economics 20 (January 1928):7; and Salmon, Domestic Service, pp. 1-2.

4. I. M. Rubinow, "The Problem of Domestic Service," Journal of Political Economy 14 (October 1906):502.

5. Salmon, Domestic Service, p. 102.

6. For example, I. M. Rubinow of the Departments of Agriculture and Commerce and Labor tried to deal with domestic service from a supply and demand perspective in "Household Service as a Labor Problem," Journal of Home Economics 3 (April 1911):131-40.

7. Consult Edith Abbott and Sophonisba P. Breckinridge in "Employment of Women in Industries--Twelfth Census Statistics," Journal of Political Economy 14 (January 1906):14-15.

8. Philip S. Foner, Women and the American Labor Movement: From Colonial Times to the Eve of World War I (New York: Free Press, 1979), p. ix; and Edith Abbott, Women in Industry: A Study in American Economic History (New York: D. Appleton, 1910), p. 2.

9. Another point of view is provided by Patricia Branca in "A New Perspective on Women's Work: A Comparative Typology," Journal of Social History 9 (Winter 1975):141.

10. Jane Seymour Klink, "Put Yourself in Her Place," Atlantic Monthly, February 1905, p. 169; Rheta Childe Dorr, "The Prodigal Daughter," Hampton's Magazine, April 1910, pp. 681-82; and Edith H. Altbach, Women in America (Lexington, Mass.: D. C. Heath, 1974), p. 67.

11. Dorr, "The Prodigal Daughter," pp. 681–82; Salmon, Domestic Service, pp. 2–5; and Herbert R. Northrup, Organized Labor and the Negro (New York: Harper & Brothers, 1944), p. xv. See Theresa M. McBride, The Domestic Revolution: The Modernization of Household Service in England and France (New York: Holmes & Meier, 1976), pp. 9–10.

12. David Brody, "Labor History in the 1970s: Toward a History of the American Worker," in The Past Before Us: Contemporary Historical Writing in the United States, Michael Kammen, ed. (Ithaca, N.Y.: Cornell University Press, 1980), p. 253; Herbert G. Gutman, Work, Culture and Society in Industrializing America (New York: Random House, 1966; Vintage Books, 1977), pp. 9–10; and Paul Faler, "Working Class Historiography," Radical America 3 (March–April 1969):56.

13. Brody, "Labor History in the 1970s," p. 253.

14. See James R. Green, The World of the Worker: Labor in Twentieth-Century America (New York: Hill & Wang, 1980), p. xi, for an analysis of the Wisconsin school.

15. Faler, "Working Class Historiography," p. 56; Gutman, Work, Culture and Society, pp. 9–10; and Brody, "Labor History in the 1970s," p. 253.

16. John R. Commons et al., History of Labour in the United States, vol. 1 (New York: Macmillan, 1918), p. 10.

17. Brody, "Labor History in the 1970s," p. 254.

18. Robert H. Zieger, "Workers and Scholars: Recent Trends in American Labor Historiography," Labor History 13 (Spring 1972):247–48.

19. Brody, "Labor History in the 1970s," p. 255.

20. See Jesse Lemisch, "The American Revolution Seen from the Bottom Up," in Towards a New Past: Dissenting Essays in American History, Barton J. Bernstein, ed. (New York: Random House, 1967; Vintage Books, 1969), pp. 3–45.

21. For a general critic of New Left historiography, consult Irwin Unger, "The New Left and American History: Some Recent Trends in United States Historiography," American Historical Review 72 (July 1967):1237–63. Also see George Rawick, "Working Class Self-Activity," Radical America 3 (March–April 1969):23–31.

22. Brody, "Labor History in the 1970s," pp. 256–57.

23. See Virginia Yans-McLaughlin, "Italian Women and Work: Experience and Perception," in Class, Sex, and the Woman Worker, Milton Cantor and Bruce Laurie, eds. (Westport, Conn.: Greenwood Press, 1977), pp. 101–19, and Brody, Steelworkers in America, Chapter 5. For a discussion of older ethnic literature and its relation to work, consult John Evanshon et al., "Literature on the American Working Class," Radical America 3 (March–April 1969): 32–33; 36–55.

24. A small sampling of this dialog can be found in American Kitchen Magazine, November 1901–February 1902. Also consult Ruth Schwartz Cowan, "The Industrial Revolution in the Home: Household Technology and Social Change in the Twentieth Century," Technology and Culture 17 (January 1976):1–23.

25. Brody, "Labor History in the 1970s," pp. 259–60; Susan Kleinberg, "The Systematic Study of Urban Women," Historical Methods Newsletter 9 (December 1975):14–25; Elizabeth H. Pleck, "A Mother's Wages: Income Earning among Married Italian and Black Women, 1896–1911," in A Heritage of Her Own: Towards a New Social History of American Women, Nancy F. Cott and Elizabeth H. Pleck, eds. (New York: Simon & Schuster, 1979), pp. 367–92; Tamara Hareven and Randolph Langenbach, Amoskeag: Life and Work in an American City (New York: Random House, 1978); Leslie Tentler, Wage Earning Women, Industrial Work and Family Life in the United States, 1900–1930 (New York: Oxford University Press, 1979); Gutman, Work, Culture & Society, pp. xii–xiii; and Peter N. Stearns, "Toward a Wider Vision: Trends in Social History," in The Past Before Us, p. 224.

26. Brody, "Labor History in the 1970s," pp. 260–61; "The Philadelphia Social History Project: A Special Issue," Historical Methods Newsletter 9 (March–June 1976): 43–181; Katzman, Seven Days a Week, Chapter 2; and Faler, "Working Class Historiography," pp. 67–68. Further insights to these questions may be found in The Past Before Us, Chapters 8, 10, 11, and 13.

27. Thompson, The Making of the English Working Class, pp. 12–13.

28. Catherine E. Beecher, A Treatise on Domestic Economy (New York: Marsh, Capen, Lynn, and Webb, 1841; repr. ed., New York: Schocken Books, 1977).

29. Brody, Steelworkers in America, Chapter 1; and Brody, "Labor History in the 1970s," pp. 268–69.

30. Jane Edna Hunter, A Nickel and a Prayer (Cleveland: Elli Kani, 1940).

2

An Overview: A Summary of the History of Domestic Work in the United States

"From the Beginning: Housework"[1]

The history of domestic service in the United States can be best understood by discussing each of the four distinct phases it has passed through. The first period lasted from early colonization to the American Revolution. The second phase extended from the Revolution until about 1850. The third period lasted from the 1850s to about the turn of the twentieth century. The final stage began with the twentieth century and continued until the 1930s.[2]

As with many types of work, these time periods have much less to do with internal occupational changes than with external changes acting upon society at large. For example, along with the physical, philosophical, commercial, and philanthropical changes affecting domestic service were various inventions of the latter part of the eighteenth century. The discovery and application of steam and electric power saw the rapid transference of woolen and cotton manufacture from the home to the factory. The facts associated with the development of the modern factory system are familiar enough. Much less known are the effects in the household. The shift from individual to collective enterprise, from a domestic to a factory system, released a vast amount of labor previously performed by women in the home. This division of labor imposed by the factory system demanded a readjustment of work. An immediate result was a decrease in the number of women partially occupied in household duties to an increase in demand for those fully occupied in domestic work.[3]

No less significant in rendering a change in household employment were certain political, economic, and social

forces.   Significant among these was the discovery of the
New World.   Colonization afforded the opportunity for the
transplantation, and eventual employment, of a significant
number of individuals belonging to the lower classes of
society.   In the colonial period, all types of service were
performed by blacks, Indians, and three additional classes--
convicts, redemptioners, and free willers.[4] Convicts, free
willers, and bond servants tended to be of English origin.
The earliest redemptioners came from either Germany or
Switzerland.   Many of these people who were destined to
become the servants of the New World had been beggars,
vagrants, political prisoners, or even criminals in the Old
World.   In fact, so desirous was the Old World to rid itself of these low-placed creatures on the social scale that
between 1661 and 1680 various plans were proposed to the
King and Council for the creation of an office whose sole
function was to be transporting them out of the country.
Although not unknown in any colony, the great majority of
these people ended up in Maryland and Virginia.[5]

Of these classes of Christian or white servants (so
named to distinguish them from blacks and Indians), the
free willers were the most unfortunate.   Found only in
Maryland, they were granted a stipulated number of days
to dispose of themselves under as advantageous terms as
possible.   If they failed to achieve this objective in the
allotted time, they were sold for the return passage.   Of
course, most failed in their efforts.   Servants could be
had for such a trifling that few people were even remotely
interested in considering those who wished to establish
their own terms of service.   Colonists saw little, if any,
difference between political prisoners and felons.   However,
the colonists preferred either of them to redemptioners.   A
felon's period of service was fixed at seven years, while
that of a redemptioner was only five.   Of the various
groups, redemptioners had a particularly interesting history.[6]

Whatever the origin or fate of redemptioners, they
never came to replace the older system of bonded or inden-
tured servitude.   The great majority of these individuals
sold themselves into service.   During most of the seventeenth century, this was the chief method by which the
poor could come to the colonies.   Indenture appears to
have varied little from colony to colony.   Stripped of its
cumbersome legal terminology, its form was simple.   The
major ingredients consisted of the three following points:

(1) the length of time in service; (2) the nature of service to be supplied; and (3) the compensation for service rendered.[7]

For the most part indenture for colonial women seems to have been a binding out to service. This may well have involved learning to spin, knit, or sew, and possibly acquiring a trade. Some fortunate few even learned to read. But unlike male servants, females were not taught to write or cypher. Women's wages were already less than men's. On the average, female servants earned half the amount of their male counterparts. Early records indicate women servants earned about £3 to £6 a year. These sums appear rather constant from 1639 to 1680 in both northern and southern colonies. By the middle of the eighteenth century, wages had increased to around £8 to £10 for women servants and £16 to £20 for male servants. Since these later figures represent wages paid in Philadelphia, they may be higher than those paid in rural areas.[8]

Whatever the wages, whatever the terms of contract, service in colonial times, North or South, was harsh. It was said by some that European servants groaned under a burden worse than that of Egyptian bondage. In the South drudge work was the lot of both servant and slave. Only the most intelligent workers were reserved for labor in the home. The gulf that separated servant and employer was wide, if not impossible to span. Service was difficult to secure and once obtained was often unsatisfactory. Servants bemoaned their existence composed, as it was, of hard work and ill treatment. Master and mistress complained of inefficient service and ungrateful workers. Both sides were justified in their complaints.[9] In sum, the colonial period was not the Arcadian time that many writers longingly depicted.[10]

If Arcadia ever existed in the history of domestic service, it was probably in the so-called log-cabin period.[11] The first significant event that ushered in change occurred at the time of the Revolution. Excepting the African slave trade, previous systems of labor supply were cut off. Gradually unfree labor was replaced by free labor in the North. In the South black slaves supplanted all other systems, and the slave now inherited the reproach previously attached to unfree white labor.[12] In New England and small towns free laborers employed as domestics were the social equals of their employers. This spirit of equality was further abetted by the notions embodied in the Declara-

tion of Independence and the concepts of liberty, equality,
and fraternity of the great French upheaval of 1789. Workers and employers belonged, by birth, to the same section
of the nation, were probably from the same community, frequently shared the same religious beliefs, were members of
the same church, and shared the same associates. The relation of master and servant had been superseded by that
of mistress and maid.[13]

This condition of democracy in service in the North
and slavery in the South remained intact until about the
middle of the nineteenth century. Nevertheless, undercur-
rents were at work eroding the foundations of "the golden
era of domestic service."[14] The increasing tempo of the
Industrial Revolution gave rise to a larger pool of mobile
workers in new occupations that competed for servants.
Those who disliked service could now find alternative employment in a mill or factory. Domestic service that previously stood almost alone now had numerous competitors.
Improved methods of transportation added to the possibili-
ties by making vast areas of the nation accessible. These
combined forces tended to drive native-born women out of
domestic work. On the other hand, industrialization and
urbanization brought increased wealth and leisure time to
middle-class women. This situation created greater demand
for servants and so-called idle time for women of the middle
class.[15]

Middle-class women found new outlets for their energy and time by enlisting their services in various ante-
bellum reform movements, by engaging in philanthropic and
charitable activities, and by taking classes and forming
literary clubs. These same women were somewhat unhappy
with their independent and democratic-minded help. Indicative of this unhappiness was their stated desire for
European servants. Coupled with ever increasing wealth
and more luxurious life-styles, the caste line in the home
was beginning to reappear by mid-nineteenth century. The
U.S. mistresses of middle-class homes wished for servants
rather than employees.[16] This preference forced more
native-born women to avoid domestic service lest they, too,
fall under the social ban associated with this occupation.
Such was the situation when important events in Europe
and Asia altered the face of household service in the United
States again.[17]

The first of these developments was the Irish famine
of the 1840s. The Irish presence in America was not new,

but never had their numbers been so many as following the potato famine, which began in 1845. In the preceding decade Irish arrivals had averaged about 35,000 annually. By 1846 the number had risen to 51,752, but in the following year their numbers had swelled to 105,536. By 1851 Irish immigrants to the United States numbered 221,253. Thereafter, their numbers fluctuated from year to year, but averaged between 50,000 to 75,000 persons until the last eight years of the nineteenth century.

Furthermore, almost half of these immigrants—49 percent, in the 1800s—were women classified as unskilled workers. Essentially two occupations were available to them. The first was in the modern factories, where manufacturing techniques were simplified enough to fully utilize unskilled labor. The second option was in domestic service. Here their physical strength helped compensate for ignorance of American ways and lack of skill. In no time at all, the Irish were an important group heavily engaged in household work. Speaking to this point with reference to Boston, historian Oscar Handlin claimed that "Irish help" was gladly accepted as a replacement for native-born Americans. "Bridget" became a familiar fixture in hotels and homes because she was loyal, charged cheap wages, and maintained her good spirits.[18]

Second only in importance to the Irish economic dislocations were those in Germany and Scandinavia. Freeholders in Norway and Sweden as well as in Württenberg, Baden, Bavaria, and the Rhineland saw their land holdings shrink continuously through centuries of division. Finally, they could shrink no more. Decreasing mortality rates with concurrent population increases further circumscribed opportunities. Many people sought new futures in America. Similar problems were even more acute in southwestern Germany. Small-scale farming became relatively unprofitable and further stimulated the movement toward large-scale agriculture. On top of all these economic difficulties came the political revolutions of 1848. Although many of the Scandinavian and German immigrants moved to farmlands in the North and Midwest, many others assumed household employment previously performed by native-born Americans.[19]

The final foreign influence on the history of domestic service from the Revolution to 1850 was the establishment of treaty relations between China and the United States in 1844. When gold was discovered in California in

1848 and when the railway network reached the Far West in the late 1860s, the way was paved for a great influx of Chinese on the Pacific Coast. Many of these oriental immigrants found their way into domestic service. They became formidable competitors to other nationalities employed in household service in the West.[20]

The transformation of the second phase of domestic service was all but complete. The Irish were in the East; the Germans in the Midwest; the Scandinavians in the North and Midwest, and the Chinese on the Pacific Coast. Everywhere north of the Mason–Dixon line a new social and economic element existed in domestic service. The all-present foreign elements caused native-born Americans to reject household employments for fear of losing social position by competing directly with foreign labor. The result was a change in the relationship of employer and employee. Faintly sketched economic lines, barely visible in the earlier part of the century, had become boldly drawn caste barriers. Only the southern black was missing from the ranks of the Irish, the Germans, the Scandinavians, and the Chinese. But southern blacks, too, joined forces in the South, following Emancipation.[21] Not that they came to do anything significantly different than they ever had during their centuries of enslavement. But while they continued in these same household tasks, they received remuneration in money for their labor. This payment, as effectively as had slavery, prevented most native-born white women of the South from entering domestic service.[22]

Thus, the second period in the history of domestic service ended much like the first--a high preponderance of foreign-born and black women in service and a definite barrier existing between mistress and maid. Furthermore, the 1850s were a time when women workers, whatever their origin of birth, were experiencing depressed economic conditions. They were locked into employments categorized as "women's occupations." These occupations included cigar making, upholstering, and bookbinding; the various serving trades, including dressmaking, tailoring, cap and vest making, artificial flower making, seamstress work, and millinery work; and finally, domestic and personal service, including housekeeping, cooking, and working in hotels as maids, waitresses, laundresses, and personal servants. Virtually all of these occupations were already overcrowded before the immigrant arrivals. Based on data collected and compiled by Philip S. Foner, mid-nineteenth-century

conditions in these occupations reveal that: (1) women's
wages rose little during the 1850s and in some areas actively declined[23]; and (2) women were invariably paid half
the wages men received for comparable work. Real or not,
the assumption for these remunerations was the belief that
women's wages were part of a family wage. In this same
period the cost of living soared and real wages declined.
The New York Tribune, for example, claimed that provisions
in the city increased 50 percent between 1843 and 1850.
All workers' incomes fell far below suggested minimums
when combined with seasonal and irregular employment patterns. Added to these facts were the depression years of
1853 to 1854 and 1857. As expected, women fared the worst.
The position of female domestics was significant, in light
of these conditions, for as Carl Degler has pointed out,
throughout the nineteenth century service remained the
single largest occupation for women. In 1850 alone, more
women were engaged in domestic service than all other
major female occupations combined.[24]

A clear indication of the end of one period in the
history of domestic service and the beginning of another
was the reintroduction of the word "servant" when referring
to white employees. Partly because she had witnessed the
significance of "help" while growing up in Fulton, New
York, Lucy Maynard Salmon was the first to treat this
occupational transformation. Salmon was also the first to
discuss the significance of "help" as an early form of service. The daughter of neighbors had helped and eaten
with young Lucy's family. According to Salmon, the term
"servant" came from Europe and implied one who performed
menial labor. In this sense menial labor was applied to
those engaged in domestic work.[25]

This theme has recently been given a full treatment
in a new study on nineteenth-century domestic service.
Recast in modes of the "hired girls" to the "domestics,"
Faye E. Dudden has reconstructed the old Salmon thesis
and incorporated some of the new social history. In so
doing, Dudden demonstrates how, beginning in the 1820s,
but even more so in the 1830s, Americans began to employ
more servants to work in a clearly domestic sphere. Furthermore, they did so at a time when urbanization was
accelerating. Urbanization facilitated the establishment of
private domestic realms within the confines of middle-class
families. Here the popular theories of domesticity were
played out because they required the necessary physical

space for a separate women's sphere—an area of intimacy
and spiritual comfort.[26]

Living in a world romanticized by writers like
Catherine Beecher, these women from comfortable economic
backgrounds were able to enjoy changes made possible by
new educational and employment opportunities.[27] Often
their homes were too large to run alone. Much household
labor—baking, laundering, and ironing—still occurred in
the home. Most basic chores associated with house cleaning were still done by hand. Ideally a family would employ two servants, but often it managed with one. Typically the servant woman was a black or immigrant "girl"
who acted as chambermaid, cook, baker, cleaning woman,
silver polisher, washerwoman, and ironer, and if unlucky,
general household worker. Understandably the general
worker was particularly hard to come by.[28]

Washing and ironing were sometimes sent out or
done by a woman who came in one or two days a week.
Except in the South, hired servants were seldom found in
less than middle-class homes. But in some instances small
shopkeepers and skilled craftsmen might take in a hired
"girl" from the country. She would exchange household
labor for room and board. In short, during much of the
nineteenth century it was difficult for a woman to manage
a respectable home alone.[29]

These changes were not so beneficial for the woman
who came from the poorer strata of society. The demarcation between these two groups of women is perhaps best
illustrated by Gerda Lerner's phrase, "the lady and the
mill girl." New mass production methods made it increasingly difficult for men to support their families and they
sometimes found their trade or craft downgraded by new
production techniques. Workers' families and poorer families underwent an additional hardship because they were
cut off from economic makeshifts available in the country.
For example, the urban environment was seldom conducive
to gardening, gathering fuel, or hunting and fishing.
Confronted by these conditions, such families felt a real
need to push their children into the labor market. Thus
some of their daughters went into domestic service either
to contribute to the families' sustenance or to relieve the
families of their maintenance. Perhaps more than the mill
girl, the lady's opposite in the 1830s was the domestic.[30]

But more than the strenuous demands of household
labor impelled the middle-class family to hire servants.

Medical authorities of the late nineteenth century cautioned women against excess physical labor. Medical guidebooks advocated that middle-class adolescent girls be excused from physically strenuous household responsibilities. Mature women were warned against undertaking physical activity during menstruation. A widespread belief of the time held regular work schedules injurious to a woman's health.[31] One can better comprehend the chasm that separated mistress and maid during the late nineteenth century because this advice was not applied to domestic servants.[32] In time, employing servants served to prove the establishment of middle-class standing in the community for the woman and man of the house. To the women, servants represented the attainment of a leisurely life-style; to the men, it indicated just how successful they were as family providers. In the South it was widely held that middle-class white women did not undertake household duties alone. These same southerners believed such duties were the responsibility of blacks. Because the Pacific Coast and Midwest lacked the constant influx of either blacks or immigrants, servants were scarcer. However, this only served to increase the differences in standing between families with or without domestics. Thus everywhere in the United States a middle-class life-style demanded servants, sometimes for the comforts they could provide, at other times as indicators of family status in the community.[33]

Increasing wealth, luxury, and economic distinctions were particularly evident and part and parcel of urban growth. It was primarily in U.S. cities that servants were both wanted and employed. For example, between 1830 and 1870 the urban population of the United States increased at a rate of nearly 19 percent a year. Serious housing shortages were created. Homes were scarce and rents were high. More and more people began residing in hotel apartments and boarding houses. In public facilities like these, all domestic responsibilities were assumed by the establishment. Wealth contributed to their development and increased the demands for domestic servants. Commenting on these American trends was the Viennese-born Francis Joseph Grund. Referring to fashionable American women in New York City, Grund said, "One-half of them . . . live in boarding-houses, and the other half in houses kept by their servants."[34] Catering to the urban milieu for status, these rich women placed great emphasis on both the number and qualities of their servants. Desiring to differentiate themselves from one another and the urban masses, families of wealth surrendered more and more of the household responsibilities to nurses, tutors, and servants. Not surprisingly, in great metropolitan areas such as New York City close to one quarter of all immigrant residents were employed as household help.[35]

By 1870 the cry that the servant girl was disappearing began to be heard. Only the West appeared to be an exception, for there female servants tripled in number between 1880 and 1890. The ratio of servants to families and the population also increased. Distance from ports of entry for Europeans and from sources supplying southern blacks created great demands in the West. For a time in 1880, Chinese men servants were a majority in Washington and California. When the western states began to industrialize and urbanize, Chinese migration slowed and female servants began to fill the void. Reflecting the demands were the highest servant wages in the nation. (Table 2.1 illustrates the wages paid by geographic section.) Industrialization occurred more slowly in the West than in midwestern states like Michigan and Ohio. Consequently opportunities outside of household labor for working women expanded less proportionately. For example, in 1880 a larger proportion of women from either Ohio or Michigan had worked outside of domestic service. However, the situations were reversed in 1900.[36]

Elsewhere in the nation, by 1870 the number of servants in relation to families peaked. Estimates varied from one servant for each 6.6 families to one servant girl for every eight families. In the thirty years from 1870 to 1900 the demand for help doubled, but the supply increased by only half, and from 1900 to 1910 by only 5 percent. In the same thirty-year period the number of self-supporting women in the labor market more than tripled. One self-supporting woman out of two selected housework in 1870, but by 1900 only one woman in every four did so. Generally these positions were filled by poor white girls, immigrants, and blacks. Of these, only blacks were significantly represented in the paid labor force after marriage. The shortage in household work was held responsible for numerous American social ills. One such change was "the rapid growth in apartment-houses with restaurants, family hotels, and the like. . . ." Consequently, "Homes are destroyed because servants cannot be secured. . . ." In turn, the intelligence office, the employment bureau of

Table 2.1

Domestic Workers' Wages by Geographic Section (Weekly)

	Average Weekly Wage	
Geographic Section	Men	Women
Pacific coast	$7.57	$4.57
Eastern section	8.68	3.60
Middle section	7.62	3.21
Western section	6.69	3.00
Border section	4.86	2.55
Southern section	3.95	2.22
United States	$7.18	$3.23

Source: Lucy Maynard Salmon, Domestic Service (New York: The Macmillan Company, 1897, reprint ed., New York: Arno Press, 1972), p. 88.

domestics, was charged with leading young women astray and contributing to the servant shortage.[37] (Table 2.2 presents a concise summary of changes in domestic service from 1870 to 1900.)

Domestic girl shortages were partially related to two changes in the amount and sources of European immigration to the United States. Industrialization moved southward and eastward in Europe as the nineteenth century progressed. People uprooted their lives as they abandoned their small villages and farms to move into cities and towns. They traversed national boundaries and crossed oceans. Their movement was worldwide, but the United States with a high standard of living and a reputation as the land of golden opportunity attracted the bulk of migrants. Between 1880 and 1930 the United States embraced 27 million immigrants from southern and eastern European nations. This flood did not stop newcomers from western and northern European countries, but after 1890 they ceased to have the same impact as their eastern and southern counterparts. For example, the peak year for nineteenth-century immigration was 1882. Of a total 788,992

Table 2.2

Statistics on Domestic Service, 1870–1900

Supply and Demand. From 1870 to 1900, the demand for servants doubled while the supply increased only by half.

Within that period:
The total population increased 95 percent - from 38,558,371 to 75,994,575.

The number of families increased 114 percent - from 7,579,363 to 16,239,797.

The working population increased 132.15 percent - from 12,505,923 to 29,073,233.

The number of servants increased only 49 percent - from 975,734 to 1,453,677.

The percentage in four successive decades fell from 47.58 to 36.64 to 30.37 to 24.13.

This can be stated in another form: In the decade from 1870 to 1880, the number of working-women increased 44.2 percent, but the number of servants increased by only 11 percent.

Ostracism of Domestic Service. From 1870 to 1900, the number of working women trebled, but the percentage entering domestic service fell steadily.

In 1870 there were 1,836,288 working-women, of whom 873,738 were servant girls - or 47.58 percent.

In 1880 there were 2,647,157 working-women, of whom 969,975 were servants - or 36.64 percent.

In 1890 there were 4,005,532 working-women, of whom 1,216,639 were servants - or 30.37 percent.

In 1900 there were 5,319,397 working-women, of whom 1,283,763 were servants - or 24.13 percent.

In the decade 1880 to 1890, the number of working-women increased 51.3 percent, but of servants, only 25.4 percent.

In the decade of 1890 to 1900, the number of working-women increased 32.8 percent, but of servants, only 5.5 percent.

Source: I. M. Rubinow and Daniel Durant, "The Depth and Breadth of the Servant Problem," McClure's Magazine, March 1910, p. 586.

immigrants in that year, 250,630 were from Germany, but only 16,918 came from Russia and the Baltic countries, 32,159 were from Italy, and 27,935 from the Austro-Hungarian Empire. The peak year for twentieth-century immigration was 1907. Of the 1,285,349 recorded arrivals, only 37,807 came from Germany, but 258,943 came from Russia and the Baltic States, 285,731 from Italy, and 338,452 from the Austro-Hungarian Empire. Many believed the "new" immigrant possessed less capacity and willingness for Americanization. In addition, these immigrants from southern and eastern Europe were less inclined to enter domestic service. The overall competence of those who did was considered inferior. More and more writers and housewives harkened back to more ideal times.[38]

The reduction in immigrants, and particularly in immigrants entering domestic service, was revealed in an overall analysis of the 1880 and 1900 census data. Table 2.3 summarizes these data.

Table 2.3

Servant Population by Race and
Nativity, 1890 and 1900

	1890		1900	
	Number	Percent	Number	Percent
Native White	541,575	44.5	604,135	47.1
Foreign White	374,253	30.8	332,863	25.9
Negro	299,473	24.6	345,373	26.9
Other	1,238	0.1		
TOTAL	1,216,639	100.0	1,283,763	100.0

Source: I. M. Rubinow, "The Problem of Domestic Service,"

Journal of Political Economy 14 (October 1906):506.

Surprisingly, native-born women constituted about one half of all servants and had increased in percentage from the previous years (44.5 percent to 47.1 percent). Obviously they were filling the void left by foreign whites in this same period. These changes did not indicate preferential demand, for it was a well-known fact that American middle-class women preferred foreign-born servants. The general assumption behind this preference was the belief that foreign help was easier to manage. The translation of this expression "easier to manage" was understood by employers to mean extracting more favorable service including longer hours, more work, and lower wages. Table 2.3 indicates another more important trend, one that became increasingly significant in the twentieth century--an increase in the black servant population.39

Table 2.4

Nationality of Domestic Servants, 1900

Nationality	Number of Women Employed	Number of Servants	Percentage of Servants in Total Number of Women Employed
Sweden	81,148	45,794	56.4
Norway	47,934	22,519	47.0
Denmark	15,580	6,867	44.1
Hungary	14,631	6,087	41.6
Austria	25,590	8,909	34.8
Ireland	634,201	195,000	30.8
Switzerland	15,125	4,646	30.7
Germany	538,192	160,939	29.9
Canada, English	102,181	27,521	26.9
Bohemia	25,719	6,316	24.6
Poland	40,816	8,815	22.9
France	21,164	4,719	22.3
Scotland	46,173	9,516	20.6
England and Wales	158,912	28,708	18.1
Russia	40,816	5,853	14.3
Canada, French	78,979	8,092	10.3
Italy	26,093	2,382	9.2
All other nationalities	149,828	24,028	16.0
United States of native parentage native-born	1,927,811	350,287	18.2

Source: I. M. Rubinow, "The Problem of Domestic Service," Journal of Political Economy 14 (October 1906):508.

In a detailed analysis of servant nationality, as shown in Table 2.4, I. M. Rubinow of the U.S. Departments of Agriculture and Commerce and Labor revealed that the largest numbers of foreign-born entering domestic service in 1900 were still from northern and western European nations--Sweden, Norway, and Germany. These nationalities had never been accused of lacking in self-respect and pride. Their entry into service occupations must, therefore, have reflected a lack of availability in other more desirable occupations. Concurrently it would follow that these same groups would leave household labor when options occurred.[40]

More favorable occupational options appear to have been available for members of these ethnic groups by the second generation. Furthermore, departure from domestic service was not a phenomenon confined to those nationalities alone. As revealed in Table 2.5, virtually every second-generation ethnic group managed to leave household occupations. In his discussion of this tendency, David Katzman has pointed out that in 1900, 60.5 percent of all Irish-born female wage earners in the United States were employed as either laundresses or servants. Only 18.9 percent of the next generation continued to work in these professions. In Massachusetts in 1900, 53 percent of all Irish-born women worked as domestic servants. (This figure excluded laundresses.) But only 11.2 percent Irish second-generation women continued in service work. There was a 43 percent difference between first- and second-generation Irish domestics in New York--from a high of 60 percent to a low of 17 percent. For the Irish service had been the vehicle for entry and upward mobility in the United States. The same proved true for Scandinavian women (although less so for Norwegians). Clearly, no foreign-born woman formed a permanent servant class in the United States.[41]

Adding to these declining populations after 1900 was a reduction in young women in the work force. Compulsory education, increased family prosperity, and child-labor legislation enabled more teenaged girls to remain at home. For example, in 1880 almost 10 percent (93,000) of all female servants were between the ages of ten and fifteen. They comprised 9.4 percent of all female domestics in the country. Thereafter, their numbers declined. In 1920 only 31,000 young white women were servants. By then the black migration northward was under way, filling the void--a void altering not only the racial composition of

Table 2.5

Propensity of Second-Generation Women for
Household Labor, 1900

Birthplace of one or both parents	SERVANTS		LAUNDRESSES		
	Number	Percent of group's wage earners	Number	Percent of group's wage earners	Percent in domestic service
Sweden	10,728	44.5	430	1.8	46.3
Ireland	62,159	16.0	11,338	2.9	18.9
Norway	12,088	48.2	413	1.6	49.8
Denmark	2,889	42.4	84	1.2	43.6˙
Hungary	247	12.2	14	.7	12.9
Germany	102,109	27.1	10,091	2.7	29.8
Austria	1,041	20.0	72	1.4	21.4
Poland	2,521	20.4	509	4.1	24.5
England and Wales	14,931	15.5	1,810	1.9	17.4
Russia	1,001	17.3	41	.7	18.0
Italy	536	9.3	93	1.6	10.9

Source: U.S. Senate, 61st Congress, 2nd Session, Document No. 282, Reports of the Immigration Commission, Occupations of the First and Second Generations of Immigrants in the United States (Washington, D.C.: Government Printing Office), 1911, pp. 71-79.

domestic service but its character as well.[42] In a popular weekly periodical a young domestic addressed herself to the issues which contributed to this transformation by saying:

> I am sorry, but under present conditions it is impossible for me to write anything on the subject. This may seem incredible, but it will not when I tell you that from six a.m. to eight p.m. I don't get time to write so much as a postal card. After the day is over I am too tired, confused and nervous to do anything except look over the paper and go to bed. Including the basement, this house has four stories, and

I have to go from bottom to top, or from
top to bottom, about forty times a day.

As to the article in The Independent, the young
woman had no experience worth mentioning.

I cannot see why anyone of pride and
spirit would choose that kind of work, as
she says she would unless compelled to
earn her living. The negroes in the South
have as much chance of social recognition
as have those who do domestic service in
the North. Between them and society there
is a great gulf fixed. . . . The very
name servant girl carries along with it a
degrading sense of servility and serfdom
that is resented by the most ignorant of
them.[43]

Despite the almost continuous expansion of employment opportunities for women, the nineteenth century scarcely indicated the changes that would come to female workers,
particularly domestics, during the twentieth. As late as
1890 the typical female worker was easily identifiable. She
was single and young with little education or training.
Often the offspring of immigrants or native-born farm parents, she occupied her time between school and marriage
in one of the various unskilled urban jobs available.
Equally identifiable are the significant variants to this
female wage earner: married immigrant women in northern
cotton mills; unconventional women who worked even though
those of similar circumstances did not; widows; wives of
husbands who did not support them; and southern black
women in farm or domestic work. Also excluded were middle-
and upper-class women. They and their families' prejudice
against paid employment was reinforced by the sparsity of
appropriate jobs for the daughters of those making their
way up the economic and social ladder of the American
class system. Once such ascent had begun, no family
could permit their daughters to suffer the dirt, noise,
drudgery, and especially dangers of unskilled factory
labor. Certainly they could not be allowed to mingle with
the uncouth immigrants who continued to toil there. Equally if not more out of the question was domestic service.[44]

By the turn of the century, women were still primarily employed in manufacturing, agriculture, and domestic service. In New York City alone more than 350,000
women were gainfully employed, and of these almost 150,000
were domestic workers or personal servants.[45] Up through
1910 the number of females working in public and private
housekeeping continued to increase. The decline that occurred between 1910 and 1920 was partially a reflection of
the increasingly unpopular status of such work by women
noted earlier and partially a result of child labor legislation and changes in immigration. In addition, significant
new demands created by World War I that continued into
the 1920s caused a shift in industrial needs. On top of
this, more and more women entered professions (nursing
and teaching), clerical work, and sales positions. Particularly appealing to the young woman who might otherwise
have gone into the factory or service was the department
store. All of these elements combined and constituted compelling reasons for the declining share of females in household employment.[46]

The total number of women employed in domestic
work recovered to around 2 million between 1920 and 1930.
This increase was partially attributable to accelerated immigration from countries that had traditionally supplied
servants to America. From 1930 to 1940 approximately a
quarter of a million women entered the ranks as domestic
service workers. This brought their total to 2,187,983 by
1940. Table 2.6 shows the percentage of changes from
1930 to 1940. The increase of 13.5 percent did not reflect
women workers' preference for service occupations. In
fact, just the opposite continued to be true: women tended,
if possible, to undertake other occupations in preference
to household employment. Undoubtedly the depressed economic conditions from 1930 to 1940 afforded most women
seeking gainful employment little choice of opportunity.
And even though such conditions forced women into these
occupations, servants declined in importance among all
women workers from 17.9 percent in 1930 to 16.8 percent in
1940. Other changes, relative to domestic servants in the
ten-year period from 1930 to 1940 are indicated in Table
2.7. Table 2.8 illustrates the changes in percentages for
women employed in service occupations for each decade of
the twentieth century up to 1940, after which domestic service ceased to be a significant employer of women in the
United States.[47]

Table 2.6

Female Workers Percentage Change, 1930 to 1940

	Number		Percent Change
	1930	1940	
Women domestic service workers	2,187,983	1,927,527	+ 13.5
Housekeepers and servants, private family	1,993,200	1,584,589	+ 25.8
Laundresses, private family	194,783	342,938	- 43.2

Source: Janet M. Hooks, Women's Occupations Through Seven Decades, Women's Bureau Bulletin #218, U.S. Department of Labor (Washington, D.C.: Government Printing Office, 1951), p. 142.

Whatever other changes the decades of the twentieth century might bring, the true watershed for domestic service proved to be those ushered in by World War I. In general, the impact of the war on women's employment was in residual jobs that resulted from the expansion in large bureaucratic corporations and from the continual growth of huge retail outlets. However, it was in manufacturing occupations that the most readily available alternatives to household work lay.[48]

Women bound for domestic service lacked adequate knowledge of English, social status, education, and the commercial skills required in offices and shops. In the years between 1910 and 1920, the number of manufacturing openings for women stabilized, but factory employment opportunities continued to expand. Manufacturing and mechanical plants in 1910 confined women to nonfactory handwork such as millinery or dressmaking. In that year only 28 percent of all women in the clothing industry decreased; factory work increased. By 1920, 44.4 percent of all women in industry labored in factories. In 1930 that number had

Table 2.7

General Trends in Service Occupations,
1930 to 1940

	1940	1930
Number of persons in population for each		
woman domestic service worker	60.2	63.7
Number of families for each woman		
domestic service worker	16.0	15.5
Women domestic service worker as		
percent of all women in the		
labor force or gainfully employed	16.8	17.9
Women as percent of all domestic		
service workers	93.1	94.1

Source: Janet M. Hooks, Women's Occupations Through Seven Decades,
Women's Bureau Bulletin #218, U.S. Department of Labor (Washington, D.C.:
Government Printing Office, 1951), p. 143.

increased to 61.7 percent. And despite the fact that the
overall number of female manufacturing employees remained
stable, the number of women in the factory continued to
grow. The greatest increase occurred between 1910 and
1920. Fifty-two percent of women in manufacturing worked
in factories in 1910; by 1920 they had increased to 66
percent.[49]

Thus expansion took place in chemical, food-process-
ing, automotive, and electrical factory employments. Generated by new technology induced by the war and spurred
on by the consumerism of the 1920s, these industries compensated for the decline in more traditional female manufacturing jobs. However, this was not true for married
and immigrant women. Factory labor posed serious language barriers and was not compatible with raising a
family. Since live-out work had come to domestic service
by the 1920s, it offered opportunities once found in occupations like the sewing trades. Therefore, changes in
manufacturing and shifts in immigration helped create an
increase in the pool of servants during the 1920s.[50]

Table 2.8

Percent Changes of Women in Service
Occupations, 1900 to 1940

	Women service workers in private or public housekeeping [1]	
	Number	Percent change from preceding census
1940	2,831,874	+ 32.0
1930	2,146,360	+ 58.2
1920	1,356,531	- 14.9
1910	1,593,586	+ 11.4
1900	1,430,656	- 9.8

[1] Includes charwomen and cleaners, and the following workers,
whether or not in private families: cooks, housekeepers, stewards, and
hostesses, servants, and waitresses.

Source: Janet M. Hooks, Women's Occupations Through Seven Decades,
Women's Bureau Bulletin #218. U.S. Department of Labor (Washington, D.C.:
Government Printing Office, 1951), p. 139.

But by this time race, more than any other factor,
was the primary force behind the changes in household
work. The nature of this change made domestic service an
occupation much like every other: the employee lived independent of the employer. With the end of World War I,
the number of white females in domestic work decreased
significantly. Concurrently black women—heretofore concentrated in household and laundry work in the South—began migrating in great numbers to northern cities. These
same migrants took the domestic positions abandoned by
whites who found more desirable jobs available. The expansion in women's work in shops and offices had little
impact on black women at this time. While there is little
doubt that discrimination barred their entry, there is also
some reason to believe black females favored service occupations, for live-out work was most compatible with marriage.[51] The changing racial composition in service occupations is illustrated in Table 2.9.

Table 2.9

Percentage Distribution of Female Servants and
Laundresses by Nativity and Race,
1890–1920 (16 years and over)

	1890*	1900	1910	1920
SERVANTS				
Native-born white	44	45	41	39
Foreign-born white	32	28	27	21
Negro	24	27	32	40
LAUNDRESSES				
Native-born white	15	21	20	18
Foreign-born white	15	13	10	9
Negro	70	65	69	73
SERVANTS AND LAUNDRESSES				
Native-born white	40	40	35	33
Foreign-born white	29	24	22	18
Negro	31	35	43	49

*1890: 15 years and over.

Sources: U.S. Bureau of the Census, Statistics of Women at Work
(Washington, D.C.: Government Printing Office), 1907, pp. 159-185; Joseph H.
Hill, Women in Gainful Occupations 1870 to 1920, Census Monograph IX
(Washington, D.C.: Government Printing Office), 1929, pp. 38; 90; 96; 105; 117.

Numerous factors combined during the war years and
the 1920s to push and pull blacks northward in the Great
Migration. Contributing significantly was black aversion
to southern white racial prejudice, which had shown itself
in various forms, including discrimination in schools, housing, court systems, and most blatantly in the violence of
the lynch mob. But more than dissatisfaction with southern
race relations lay behind this massive movement of black
humanity. Trouble inherent in the tenancy system of the
South intensified as a result of the ravages of the boll
weevil. This creature first appeared in the southwest
corner of the southern states just prior to World War I.
From there it spread insidiously, moving both east and
north. The economic demoralization wrought by the boll
weevil was compounded by a series of heavy rainfalls and
floods occurring in 1916. Alone they did great damage.

But the rains and floods made combating the boll weevil
more difficult since it thrived in wet weather.   Southern
landowners began replacing cotton and tenants.   New
crops and farming methods required fewer laborers.   Many
black farm hands were displaced.   Since most of their
agricultural experience had been confined to raising cotton,
their ability to learn and adapt to new methods was limited.[52]

At the same time as these developments were impact-
ing southern blacks, conditions in the North were combining to create an economic situation into which they could
move.   World War I had generated an increased need for
labor and had all but stopped the flow of European workers to the United States.   Furthermore, many immigrants
had returned to their native lands in response to the call
to arms.   Workmen who had remained were given the opportunity to advance into more skilled and higher paying occupations.   This particularly urgent demand for unskilled
labor pulled huge waves of southern blacks into northern
industries.   (Table 2.10 illustrates the flow of European
immigrants prior to and during World War I.)   Part of this
irresistible pull to northern industry was due to the fact
that wages were considerably better than in the South.[53]

Table 2.10

Volume of European Immigration, 1913-1918

Year	Volume of Immigration	Year	Volume of Immigration
1913	1,197,892	1916	298,826
1914	1,218,480	1917	295,403
1915	326,700	1918	110,618

Source: Louise Venable Kennedy, The Negro Peasant Turns Cityward: Effects
of Recent Migration to Northern Centers (New York: Columbia University Press,
1930), p. 43.

Tied closely to all the "pull" elements of the Great
Migration was the meaning it had for those of the younger
generation who in some instances were better educated.
Black southerners born after 1890 tended to view their
situation as one of overall stagnation. Charles S. Johnson
commented on this in his classic study of rural black life
in the South. He found that older members of the Macon
County, Alabama, communities he examined seemed to find
ample satisfaction in the old culture. However, they were
aware of differences in the attitudes of younger people,
especially those who had been away. Caleb Humphries
typified the life expectations of the older generation while
visiting the Red Cross Office in Montgomery. When a white
man entered, Humphries immediately assumed he was the
governor of the state. "He was tall as a tree, and I said
'Good-morning Master'--so uster slavery I still say hit.
They [other Negroes] stopped me from hit 'cause dey say
you don't hafta treat white folks like dat dese days."[54]
Likewise, Arthur F. Raper found poorly educated adult
blacks remained in Greene County, Georgia, while those
with a high school education or better tended to leave.
And in his study on the blacks of St. Helena, Clyde Vernon
Kiser discovered that young blacks were basically discontent with island life--its routine and monotony. As one
young woman said, "Got tired living on Island. Too lone-
some. Go to bed at six o'clock. Everything dead. No
dances, no moving picture show, nothing to go to. . . ."[55]
Although southern and northern cities shared the
results of the Great Migration, it was to the North that
the greatest numbers traveled. The Middle Atlantic states
had a 43 percent increase in their black population, while
the blacks of the East North Central states grew by 71
percent. A high preponderance of those migrants concentrated in urban centers, the largest urban centers. For
example, 60 percent of Illinois's black population resided
in Chicago; 66 percent of all Negroes in Michigan lived in
Detroit; and more than 75 percent of all New York blacks
were concentrated in New York City. Eight cities, Pittsburgh, Philadelphia, Cincinnati, Columbus, Detroit, New
York, and Chicago, contained 38 percent of the entire black
population of the North. By contrast, they comprised only
20 percent of the total northern population. Any consideration of black motives for such relocations inevitably brings
about the realization that the motives were not unique.
In fact, the desire to share in the advantages offered by

urban industrial life in northern American cities was
shared by whites, both native and foreign-born.[56]
 A sharp increase in black migrant populations to
northern cities meant a concurrent increase in the supply
of black servants. This was especially the case since
black women had the highest propensity to work as domestics. Migrants from foreign nations and rural regions
have always supplied urban homes with large, if not the
major, sources of household workers. With World War I
virtually ending immigration, the flow of blacks northward
increased. Since more and more white women found positions outside of domestic work, they constituted an ever
smaller number of servants. But the great majority of
black women entering northern cities found housework their
only available opportunity. Thus their increase was not
relative because while the total number of servants was
declining, the number of black servants in northern cities
was increasing. By 1920 black female domestics were no
longer confined to the South (see Table 2.11). Between
1910 and 1920 the proportion of blacks among servants
doubled. Nationwide they constituted more than 39 percent
of all domestics in cities with populations of one hundred
thousand or more. The following northern cities had a
majority of female black servants by 1920: Indianapolis;
Camden, New Jersey; Kansas City, Missouri; Kansas City,
Kansas; and Philadelphia. Also black women came to dominate the hand-laundry business in the North and West as
they already did in the South. Most important, black
women in urban America formed a servant and laundress
class, as no white group had ever done before.[57]
 The degree to which more black than white women
held paid jobs indicated how many more black women were
available for domestic service. Even though the proportion
of female wage earners increased between 1890 and 1920,
the difference between white and black women did not significantly decrease. In either decade black women were
at least twice as likely to be employed as white women.
Some of the difference was due to the fact that black urban
women outnumbered black urban men much more than their
white counterparts. The simple reason for this difference
was the fact that Negro women could find jobs as servants
more easily than men. But more than any other factor,
black women continued to work after marriage, whereas
most white women did not. The high proportions of working and married black women indicated an essential differ-

Table 2.11

Distribution of Female Servants in Regions:
By Nativity and Race, 1900 and 1920
(16 years and over)

	1900			1920		
	Native-born White	Foreign-born White	Negro	Native-born White	Foreign-born White	Negro
United States	45	28	27	39	21	40
THE NORTH	54	37	9	50	31	19
New England	36	59	5	41	51	8
Mid-Atlantic	44	43	12	39	37	24
Eastern North Central	69	25	6	63	21	16
Western North Central*	68	23	10	69	14	17
THE SOUTH	20	3	77	15	3	82
South Atlantic	19	3	78	13	2	85
Eastern South Central	21	1	78	14	1	85
Western South Central	24	5	70	19	6	75
THE WEST	60	35	3	58	30	9
Mountain Basin and Plateau	61	32	6	67	22	9
Pacific	59	37	3	53	24	9

*Distribution does not equal 100 percent due to rounding off, or in the West
because of small percentage of Asians.

Sources: 1900: U.S. Bureau of the Census, Statistics of Women at Work
(Washington, D.C.: Government Printing Office, 1907), p. 42; 1920: Joseph H.
Hill, Women in Gainful Occupations 1870 to 1920 Census Monograph IX
(Washington, D.C.: Government Printing Office, 1929), p. 89.

ence in black and white life cycles. This difference
greatly affected the domestic servant population for, unlike
the case for whites, household employment did not serve as
a temporary stage in the lives of black women.[58]
     What role the southern slave system played in bring-
ing married black females into the work force remains un-
clear. However, there is no question that well into the
twentieth century significant numbers of married black
women worked just as they had throughout the nineteenth--
whether slave or free. In 1920 nearly one third of all
married Negro women living with their husbands worked as
compared to 6.5 percent of all married white women. Four
fifths of married Negro women worked as either farm laborers,

domestic servants, or laundresses. In 1920 they constituted more than one quarter of all married women in the work force. Married women tended to work out of economic necessity, but this was particularly true of blacks. Mary White Ovington confirmed this in her study of Negro life in New York City. Ovington found much the same as had W. E. B. DuBois in his 1897 investigation of Philadelphia's Seventh Ward. Speaking directly to this point was a 1920 Department of Labor, Women's Bureau report that said, "It is a well-known fact that most Negro women must continue as breadwinners practically all their lives, marriage rarely meaning a withdrawal from the wage earning ranks."[59]

Live-out domestics had dominated in the South since the days of slavery, but the system did not become popular in the North until World War I. This tied in closely with the preponderance of more married women, particularly black and older, finding employment as servants in northern cities. Live-out jobs allowed married black women to work and thus help supplement their husbands' inadequate wages, while still raising a family. Emancipation had firmly locked live-out service to southern black women. They now transported it northward. By the 1920s race and domestic service as a live-out labor system had become closely associated with one another.[60]

Although the high point for household work as a major female employer in the United States had peaked prior to our entry into World War II, the characteristics of that occupation continued throughout the 1930s. Generally speaking, "servant occupations" relied on less favored segments of the work force. This was especially true for those who worked in private homes--47.4 percent were nonwhite in 1940. In contrast, only 14.4 percent of all other gainfully employed were nonwhite. The Great Depression and New Deal years did little to alter the image of the twentieth-century black "cleaning woman."[61]

NOTES

     1.   Dave Berry, "From the Beginning: Housework," Cincinnati Enquirer, 1 March 1982, sec. B, B1.
     2.   Earlier research on domestic service divided the history into three periods. Based on my own research and that of David M. Katzman, I concluded that the final period, 1850 to the present, needed further division. For the

earlier time periods see Lucy Maynard Salmon, Domestic
Service (New York: Macmillan, 1897; repr. ed., New York:
Arno Press, 1972), p. 16; ibid., "Some Historical Aspects
of Domestic Service," New England Magazine, April 1893,
p. 178; Mary Roberts Smith, "Domestic Service: the Responsibility of Employers," Forum, August 1899, p. 678;
and Katzman, Seven Days a Week: Women and Domestic
Service in Industrializing America (New York: Oxford University Press, 1978), Chapter 2.

3. This transformation created a servant group in
the true sense of the word. See Theresa M. McBride, The
Domestic Revolution: The Modernisation of Household Service in England and France 1820-1920 (New York: Holmes
& Meier, 1976), p. 11; and Salmon, "Some Historical Aspects
of Domestic Service," pp. 175-76.

4. Blacks were employed as domestics--North and
South--as far back as the colonial days. See Katzman,
Seven Days a Week, pp. 203-4.

5. Compare Salmon, "Some Historical Aspects of
Domestic Service," p. 179 and ibid., Domestic Service, pp.
17-18, 20, to Abbot Emerson Smith, Colonists in Bondage:
White Servitude and Convict Labor in America 1607-1776
(Chapel Hill, N.C.: University of North Carolina Press,
1947; repr. ed., New York: W. W. Norton, 1971), pp.
20-21 on the origins of redemptioners.

6. A very thorough discussion of redemptioners can
be found in ibid., pp. 20-25.

7. Salmon, Domestic Service, pp. 19, 21-22; ibid.,
"Some Historical Aspects of Domestic Service," p. 179.

8. Edith Abbott, Women in Industry: A Study in
American Economic History (New York: D. Appleton, 1910),
pp. 30-31, 263-66.

9. Salmon, Domestic Service, pp. 26-27, 31, 52-53;
Julia Cherry Spruill, Women's Life and Work in the Southern
Colonies (Chapel Hill, N.C.: University of North Carolina
Press, 1938; repr. ed., New York: W. W. Norton, 1972),
pp. 76-77. Also see Smith, Colonists in Bondage, Chapter
12 and James D. Butler, "British Convicts Shipped to American Colonies," American Historical Review 2 (October 1896):
12-33.

10. See, for example, "A Vanishing Relation," Independent, August 23, 1906, p. 466; Alice Henry, Women and
the Labor Movement (New York: George H. Doran Company,
1923), p. 34; and Eleanor Roosevelt, "Servants," Forum and
Century, January 1930, p. 24. Also consult Rebecca Harling

Davis, "The Recovery of Family Life," Independent, September 21, 1905, p. 675; and Bertha M. Terrill, Household Management (Chicago: American School of Home Economics, 1914), p. 77.

11. Frances M. Abbott, "How to Solve the Housekeeping Problem," Forum and Century, February 1893, pp. 781–82.

12. Considerable question remains as to whether or not the status of black labor was ever the same as that of white. Two important articles dealing with this question are Oscar and Mary Handlin, "Origins of the Southern Labor System," William and Mary Quarterly 3rd Series 7 (April 1950):199–222 and Carl N. Degler, "Slavery and the Genesis of American Race Prejudice," Comparative Studies in Society and History 2 (October 1959):49–66. The definitive study remains that of Winthrop D. Jordan, White Over Black: American Attitudes Toward the Negro 1550–1812 (Chapel Hill, N.C.: University of North Carolina Press, 1968; repr. ed., Baltimore: Penguin Books, 1969).

13. Salmon, "Some Historical Aspects of Domestic Service," p. 179; Smith, "Domestic Service," pp. 678–79; Elizabeth Faulkner Baker, Technology and Woman's Work (New York: Columbia University Press, 1964), p. 54.

14. Smith, "Domestic Service," p. 679.

15. Salmon, "Some Historical Aspects of Domestic Service," pp. 177, 180; ibid., Domestic Service, pp. 66–68; Nancy F. Cott, The Bonds of Womanhood: "Woman's Sphere" in New England, 1780–1835 (New Haven: Yale University Press, 1977), pp. 48–49. These changes also meant that women's economic function in the family differed. See Susan J. Kleinberg, "The Systematic Study of Urban Women," Historical Methods Newsletter 9 (December 1975):15.

16. Consult Salmon, Domestic Service, pp. 70–71. An excellent discussion of the black/white, servant/mistress caste line is provided by Katzman, Seven Days a Week, Chapter 5.

17. Salmon, "Some Historical Aspects of Domestic Service," p. 177; and Smith, "Domestic Service," p. 679. Also see Barbara Welter, "The Cult of True Womanhood," American Quarterly 18 (Summer 1966):151–74; Mary Beth Norton, "The Paradox of Women's Sphere," in Women in America: A History, pp. 139–49; Kathryn Kish Sklar, Catherine Beecher: A Study in American Domesticity (New Haven: Yale University Press; repr. ed., New York: W. W. Norton, 1976).

18. Salmon, "Some Historical Aspects of Domestic Service," p. 180; U.S. Department of Commerce, Bureau of the Census, The Statistical History of the United States: From Colonial Times to the Present, with an Introduction and User's Guide by Ben J. Wattenberg (New York: Basic Books, 1976), pp. 105–6; and Oscar Handlin, Boston's Immigrants: A Study in Acculturation, rev. ed. (Cambridge, Mass.: Harvard University Press, 1941; repr. ed., New York: Atheneum, 1969), p. 61.

19. Domestic service did more than provide employment opportunities for ethnic women. See Lawrence A. Glasco, "The Life Cycles and Household Structure of American Ethnic Groups: Irish, Germans, and Native-born Whites in Buffalo, New York, 1855," in A Heritage of Her Own: Towards a New Social History of American Women, Nancy F. Cott and Elizabeth H. Pleck, eds. (New York: Simon & Schuster, 1979; Touchstone Book), pp. 268–89. Figures for German immigration into the United States can be found in U.S. Department of Commerce, Bureau of the Census, The Statistical History of the United States, pp. 105–6. Also see Robert Ernst, Immigrant Life in New York City 1825–1863 (New York: King's Crown Press, Columbia University, 1949).

20. Salmon, Domestic Service, p. 64; U.S. Department of Commerce, Bureau of the Census, The Statistical History of the United States, pp. 107–8. Also see Lucie Cheng Hirata, "Chinese Immigrant Women in Nineteenth Century California," in Women of America: A History, Carol Ruth Berlin and Mary Beth Norton, eds. (Boston: Houghton Mifflin, 1979), pp. 223–44. It should also be noted that the competition for service jobs in the Far West involved men. Many Chinese and later Japanese men entered domestic service. By 1880 both California and Washington had more male than female servants. Consult Katzman, Seven Days a Week, pp. 45, 55–56.

21. Philip S. Foner, Women and the American Labor Movement: From Colonial Times to the Eve of World War I (New York: Free Press, 1979), Chapter 6; and ibid., Organized Labor and the Black Worker: 1619–1973 (New York: International Publishers, 1976), pp. 5–6.

22. Salmon, "Some Historical Aspects of Domestic Service," p. 181; and Katzman, Seven Days a Week, pp. 149, 198.

23. Domestic service is believed to be one of those occupations in which wages declined from $1.25 a week in

1832 to about $1.08 a week in 1850. Consult Stanley Lebergott, Manpower in Economic Growth: The American Record Since 1800 (New York: McGraw-Hill, 1964), p. 284.

24. Foner, Women and the American Labor Movement, p. 85; New York Tribune, 15 November 1850; and Carl N. Degler, At Odds: Women and the Family in America from the Revolution to the Present (New York: Oxford University Press, 1980), p. 372. An excellent series of articles describing female working conditions, including those of domestics, in New York City is the series entitled "Labor in New York: Its Circumstances, Conditions, and Rewards." See the New York Tribune, pp. 18, 22, 25-26, 28-29 August; 3, 5, 9, 11, 13, 15-17 September, 4 October, and 8, 11, 18 November 1845. Consult Lebergott, Manpower in Economic Growth, p. 520, for the breakdown of female occupations in 1850.

25. Louise Fargo Brown, Apostle of Democracy: The Life of Lucy Maynard Salmon (New York: Harper & Brothers, 1943), p. 5; Salmon, Domestic Service, pp. 71-72.

26. Faye E. Dudden, Serving Women: Household Service in Nineteenth-Century America (Middletown, Conn.: Wesleyan University Press, 1983), pp. 44-47. Other but more brief accounts of this transformation can be found in Paul E. Johnson, A Shopkeeper's Millennium: Society and Revivals in Rochester, New York, 1815-1837 (New York: Hill & Wang, 1978); Mary P. Ryan, Cradle of the Middle Class: The Family in Oneida County, New York, 1790-1865 (Cambridge: Cambridge University Press, 1981), p. xiii and Chapter 4; and Sam Bass Warner, Jr., The Private City: Philadelphia in Three Periods of Its Growth (Philadelphia: University of Pennsylvania Press, 1968), pp. 65-67.

27. See Catherine Beecher, A Treatise on Domestic Economy (New York: Marsh, Capen, Lynn, and Webb, 1841; repr. ed., New York: Schocken Books, 1977; Studies in the Life of Women). For educational and employment opportunities, consult Thomas Woody, A History of Women's Education in the United States, 2 vols. (New York: Octagon Books, 1966); and Richard M. Bernard and Marie A. Vinovskis, "The Female School Teacher in Antebellum Massachusetts," Journal of Social History 10 (March 1977): 332-45.

28. U.S. Industrial Commission Report, 18 vols., "Domestic Service" by Gail Laughlin, vol. 14 (Washington, D.C.: Government Printing Office, 1900-1902), pp. 748-49, 751-52.

29. Katzman, Seven Days a Week, pp. 149–50.

30. Gerda Lerner, "The Lady and the Mill Girl: Changes in the Status of Women in the Age of Jackson," Midcontinent American Studies Journal 10 (1969):5–15; Joseph Kett, Rites of Passage: Adolescence in America, 1790 to the Present (New York: Basic Books, 1977), pp. 30, 151–52; Dudden, Serving Women, pp. 45–46.

31. For samples of such material, consult Catherine Beecher, Letters to the People on Health and Happiness (New York: Harper & Brothers, 1855); William A. Alcott, The Young Woman's Book of Health (New York: Miller, Orton, and Mulligan, 1855). A modern survey is found in Janice Delaney, Mary Jane Lupton, and Emily Toth, The Curse: A Cultural History of Menstruation (New York: E. P. Dutton, 1976; repr. ed., New York: New American Library, 1977; Mentor Book).

32. A classic example of the complexities involved in the relationship between industrialization and the Cult of True Womanhood was reflected in the Women's Trade Union League. See Robin Miller Jacoby, "Women's Trade Union League and American Feminism," in Class, Sex, and the Woman Worker, Milton Cantor and Bruce Laurie, eds. (Westport, Conn.: Greenwood Press, 1977; Contributions in Labor History, Number 1), pp. 203–4.

33. Katzman, Seven Days a Week, p. 149.

34. Francis Joseph Grund, Aristocracy in America: From a Sketch-Book of a German Nobleman (London: Richard Bentley, 1839; repr. ed., with a Foreword by George E. Probst; New York and Evanston, Ill.: Harper & Row; Harper Torchbooks, 1959), p. 59.

35. Degler, At Odds, pp. 373–74; Barbara J. Berg, The Remembered Gate: Origins of American Feminism: The Woman and the City, 1800–1860 (Oxford University Press; Urban Life in America Series, 1980), pp. 77–98; and Ernst, Immigrant Life in New York City, pp. 65–67.

36. Katzman, Seven Days a Week, pp. 55–56.

37. Degler, At Odds, p. 155; "An Unsettled Question," Outlook: A Family Paper, July 7, 1894, p. 59; Lady Grove, "Hotels as Homes?" Critic: An Illustrated Monthly Review of Literature, Art and Life, October 1902, pp. 353–54; Kellor, Out of Work; ibid., "Intelligence Offices," Atlantic Monthly, 1904, pp. 458–64 and "The Servant Question Plus the Employment Bureau," Harper's Bazaar, January 1905, pp. 15–19; I. M. Rubinow and Daniel Durant, "The Depth and Breadth of the Servant Problem," McClure's

Magazine, March 1910, p. 576. Only Sheila M. Rothman disagreed about the shortage of servants. See *Woman's Proper Place: A History of Changing Ideals and Practices, 1870 to the Present* (New York: Basic Books, 1978), pp. 16–17.

38. Leonard Dinnerstein and David M. Reimers, *Ethnic Americans: A History of Immigration and Assimilation* (New York: Dodd, Mead, 1975), pp. 36–37; U.S. Department of Labor, Bureau of Labor Statistics, *Women in Domestic Work: Yesterday and Today* by Allyson Sherman Grossman, Special Labor Force Report, p. 242 (Washington, D.C.: Government Printing Office, 1981), p. 19; Grover G. Huebner, "Americanization of the Immigrant," *Annals of the American Academy of Political and Social Science* 27 (May 1906):193; Smith, "Domestic Service," pp. 679–80; Carroll D. Wright, "Why We Have Trouble with Our Servants," *Ladies Home Journal*, March 1904, p. 22; Peter Gabriel Filene, *Him/Her/Self Sex Roles in Modern America* (New York: Harcourt, Brace, Jovanovich, 1974; Mentor Books, 1976), p. 8. A classic example of a group of "new" immigrant women who did not enter domestic service is Virginia Yans-McLaughlin, "Italian Women and Work: Experience and Perception," in *Class, Sex and the Woman Worker*, pp. 101–19.

39. I. M. Rubinow, "The Problem of Domestic Service," *Journal of Political Economy* 14 (October 1906):506–7; Isaac A. Hourwich, *Immigration and Labor: The Economic Aspects of European Immigration to the United States* (New York: G. P. Putnam's Sons, 1912; repr. ed., New York: Arno Press and the *New York Times*, 1969), pp. 67, 165. Two fine studies reflecting black trends in northern cities are Mary White Ovington, *Half a Man: The Status of the Negro in New York* (New York: Longmans, Green, 1911), p. 79; and Isabel Eaton, "Special Report on Negro Domestic Service in the Seventh Ward, Philadelphia," in W. E. B. DuBois, *The Philadelphia Negro: A Social Study* (Philadelphia: University of Pennsylvania, 1899; repr. ed., with an Introduction by E. Digby Baltzell, New York: Schocken Books, 1967), pp. 427–89.

40. Rubinow, "The Problem of Domestic Service," p. 509.

41. Katzman, *Seven Days a Week*, pp. 70–71.

42. Ibid., pp. 71–76.

43. "A Servant Girl's Letter," *Independent*, January 2, 1902, p. 36.

44. Degler, At Odds, p. 373; Robert W. Smuts, Women and Work in America (New York: Columbia University Press, 1959; repr. ed., New York: Schocken Books, 1971), pp. 38, 48–49.

45. As late as 1906 the U.S. Department of Commerce and Labor, in its report on women workers, considered domestic service beneath the dignity of economic study. See Izola Forrester, "The Girl Problem," Good Housekeeping, September 1912, p. 376.

46. James R. Green, The World of the Worker: Labor in Twentieth-Century America (New York: Hill & Wang: American Century Series, 1980), p. 105; U.S. Department of Labor, Bureau of Labor Statistics, Women in Domestic Work, p. 17; Janet M. Hooks, Women's Occupations Through Seven Decades, Women's Bureau Bulletin No. 218, U.S. Department of Labor (Washington, D.C.: Government Printing Office, 1951), pp. 139–40; Rothman, Woman's Proper Place, pp. 52–53; Foner, Women and the American Labor Movement, pp. 258–59; Katzman, Seven Days a Week, p. 48. See Lorenzo J. Greene and Carter G. Woodson, The Negro Wage Earner (Washington, D.C.: Association for the Study of Negro Life and History, 1930; repr. ed., New York: Russell & Russell, 1969), Chapter 12 for a discussion of the black domestic.

47. Hooks, Women's Occupations through Seven Decades, p. 142; U.S. Department of Labor, Bureau of Labor Statistics, Women in Domestic Work, p. 18; and Katzman, Seven Days a Week, p. 48.

48. Ibid.

49. Ibid.

50. Ibid., pp. 51–52. A very different view is offered by William H. Chafe in The American Woman: Her Changing Social, Economic, and Political Roles, 1920–1970 (New York: Oxford University Press, 1972), pp. 51, 53–58, 60–61, 89–90, 195.

51. U.S. Department of Labor, Bureau of Labor Statistics, Women in Domestic Work, p. 18; Katzman, Seven Days a Week, pp. 72–73.

52. Kenneth L. Kusmer, A Ghetto Takes Shape: Black Cleveland, 1870–1930 (Urbana, Ill.: University of Illinois Press, 1976), pp. 157–58; Louise Venable Kennedy, The Negro Peasant Turns Cityward: Effects of Recent Migration to Northern Centers (New York: Columbia University Press, 1930), pp. 44, 46–48.

53.   Ibid., pp. 43–44, 48; Sterling D. Spero and Abram L. Harris, The Black Worker: The Negro and the Labor Movement (New York: Columbia University Press, 1931; repr. ed., with a Preface by Herbert Gutman; New York: Atheneum, 1968; Studies in American Negro Life), pp. 149–50.

54.   Charles S. Johnson, Shadow of the Plantation (Chicago: University of Chicago Press, 1934; Phoenix Books, 1966), p. 28.

55.   Arthur F. Raper, Preface to Peasantry: A Tale of Two Black Belt Counties (Chapel Hill, N.C.: University of North Carolina Press, 1936; repr. ed., with a Preface by Gilbert Osofsky; New York: Atheneum, 1968; Studies in American Negro Life), pp. 193–94; Kiser, Sea Island to City: A Study of St. Helena Islanders in Harlem and Other Urban Centers (New York: Columbia University Press, 1932; repr. ed., with a Preface by Joseph S. Himes; New York: Atheneum, 1968; Studies in American Negro Life), p. 133.

56.   Spero and Harris, The Black Worker, pp. 150–51; Kennedy, The Negro Peasant, pp. 26, 32, 56–57.

57.   Katzman, Seven Days a Week, pp. 72–73, 75–76, 79–80.

58.   Ibid., pp. 72, 79–83.

59.   Degler, At Odds, p. 391; Katzman, Seven Days a Week, pp. 82–83; Ovington, Half a Man, p. 77; W. E. B. DuBois, The Philadelphia Negro, pp. 193–94; and U.S. Department of Labor, Women's Bureau, Family Status of Breadwinning Women in Four Selected Cities (Washington, D.C.: Government Printing Office, 1926), p. 14.

60.   U.S. Department of Labor, Bureau of Labor Statistics, Women in Domestic Work, p. 18; Katzman, Seven Days a Week, pp. 60, 62, 72, 198–99.

61.   Hooks, Women's Occupations through Seven Decades, pp. 143–44. Katzman argues persuasively that the forerunner of this twentieth-century cleaning lady was the southern black washerwoman. See Seven Days a Week, pp. 72, 85; and Carter G. Woodson, "The Negro Washer Woman, a Vanishing Figure," Journal of Negro History 15 (July 1930):269–77.

3

The Psychology and Nature of Housework

"Domestic labor = 0"[1]

In his pioneering study of the American steelworker, historian David Brody began by establishing the ingredients which constituted the method and psychology of steel making. Brody returned to this emphasis in an important review essay on labor historiography in the 1970s.[2] In culling the diverse directions of the new social and labor history, argued Brody, historians have repeatedly "rediscovered the need to see the workers they are studying in the context of the job and industry and often indeed to define their analyses in terms of collective activity and labor organization." This essential framework, with its emphasis on the method and psychology of work, is equally meaningful for an understanding of domestic service. Steel technology created psychological results which defined the industry's treatment of its work force. Treatment based on an economizing drive in steel meant low wages, long hours, bleak working conditions, and antiunionism. Lack of uniform standards in domestic service made for long hours, lack of personal freedom, poor living and working conditions, unsatisfactory hiring and firing, and eventually salary disagreements. Lack of uniformity in working standards stemmed in large part from the fact that service was based on a highly personal foundation; workers were expected to be servile and dependent on the whims of their employers. Most servants tended to work and live in relative isolation, making organization of any type difficult.[3] In an increasingly industrial nation domestic service remained essentially nonindustrial. Thus it was task- rather than time-oriented. It was labor-intensive, and even when successfully completed, no product was produced. All such factors contributed to the workers' loss of caste or social status. As many writers said, the "crux of the problem . . . [was] the medievalism of the home."[4]

For domestic servants the conditions under which they would labor were well forecast at the time they were hired. There were essentially three methods of finding work as a household worker. None of them was based on standard requirements or uniformity. Whether a woman answered a newspaper ad, was placed on the basis of a personal reference, or went through an intelligence office (the term applied to agencies that supplied servants), it was the worker and not her labor that was hired. In each and every case the hiring process and procedure were highly personal. Personalization was further compounded because unorganized domestics faced hundreds of separate employers who seldom hired more than one worker at a time.[5]

With virtually no exception, the lack of standards, the lack of uniformity, and the personalization worked to the disadvantage of the servant. In one such instance the plight of a young Swedish woman was involved. Treated badly by the man of the house, she feared to appeal to her mistress. Because she worked alone, there were no witnesses to her alleged abuse. Consequently she feared to speak out, certain it would mean instant dismissal. Such dismissal would probably prohibit her finding another, not to mention, a good position. But to leave without any explanation meant she would be denied a reference. In another case a young woman answered a newspaper ad and applied for work at the home of her potential employer. Questioning the prospective employee profusely about her experience and residential history, the lady of the house moved on to a more personal examination. "You look hardly strong enough to do all my work, washing and ironing too. . . . You are a nice <u>looking</u> girl; yes, a <u>very</u> nice looking girl." Little wonder the servant felt like she "were a prize cow up for sale."[6]

Intelligence offices were seldom more humane, discriminating, or systematic in their methods. Undertaking the most thorough investigation of these agencies was the reformer and social worker, Frances Kellor. In her four-city study Kellor found 834 licensed agencies. Of these, 522 were in New York City, 115 in Chicago, 110 in Philadelphia, and 87 in Boston. She found that three fifths of these offices supplied household workers and that over half

were exclusively for this purpose. In most places where
intelligence offices existed, Kellor found them unregulated
by law and using methods that included "the most un-
dreamed of frauds and immoralities." Whenever possible,
the agencies made the "girls" over to suit whatever position was available. Often employees were forced into jobs
where they were not qualified or where they had no interest in working.[7]

All types of intelligence offices existed. In New
York City alone Kellor found some that depended on immigrant women, black women, native-born women, and even
"green girls"--so-called because they were new arrivals in
the country and knew little, if any, English. The managers and proprietors of these agencies varied, but few were
young. Typically this was not an enterprise undertaken
by people possessing great integrity or ability; it was a
makeshift endeavor. Little ambition was shown other than
the desire to collect fees. One author concluded that, like
domestic service, this enterprise was identified with people
who had failed elsewhere. Nor was there much about the
offices themselves conducive to self-pride and dignity.
One office, for example, had a waiting room for employers
that was handsomely furnished with pictures on the walls,
easy chairs, and rugs. No employee seeking housework
was allowed to enter there until or unless she was summoned for an interview. No similar facilities awaited the
servants, who had a separate waiting room. The employer's facility was invariably labeled "Ladies" or "Ladies
Entrance." Occasionally, it was known as "Employers."
The other facility was labeled "Servants" or "Girls." At
places where employees might find a decent, comfortable
waiting room, employer reaction would be less than positive. One woman refused to patronize a decent office because she claimed it was an attempt "to put ladies and
servants on an equality by giving them [the servants]
such waiting rooms." However, this very same woman
wanted to hire a servant who was "neat, clean, temperate,
and moral." Another woman also objected to such an office
because it afforded courteous treatment to the employees.
She went on to say, "Treat them like cattle--that's my
kind of an office."[8]

Although it would be an overstatement to say that
the intelligence offices treated all domestics like cattle, it
would not be inaccurate to conclude that the treatment they
afforded tended to be inconsiderate and rude. Once inside,

employees were constantly harassed about paying their
fees. If their response was negative, they were told to
pay or leave. Women who were strong enough and persistent enough to remain were ignored, passed over for employment, or sneered at with nasty remarks until they
could no longer endure such disagreeable treatment. And
like those who had responded to newspaper ads, the domestics were pored over and peered at much as if they were
animal entrants in a stock show. Their clothes, foot size,
and the condition of their hands were commented upon.
Such behavior occurred in both the inferior and the best
offices. There were the additional humiliating comments
and questions. Many women would return from an interview and burst into tears over the indignities inflicted
upon them. As Frances Kellor wrote, "There is but little
about most offices to make girls feel the dignity or worth
of household work, and nothing which indicates that it
may prove attractive."9

Since virtually nothing was done to correct this
situation, most servants relied on the personal-referral
system, a system that became increasingly ineffective as
migration, immigration, and urbanization increased in tempo.
Black domestics seldom had much of a choice. In Philadelphia, for example, blacks made little use of intelligence
offices. Often their business was not appreciated. In
other cases they were charged exorbitant fees. The only
such offices patronized by Philadelphian blacks were those
run by trusted members of their own race. Generally
blacks offered their services by way of recommendations
from former employers. Some traveled door to door and
were hired because of their general bearing or personal
appearance.10

Whatever the place or method of hiring--newspaper
ad, intelligence bureau, or personal reference--domestics
constantly complained because they were fired with insufficient notice and then cheated out of their pay. Such problems stemmed not only from the informal and personalized
nature of the hiring process but also from the fact that
most agreements were based on an oral understanding.
For example, it was generally understood that agricultural
servants were hired on a yearly basis, and their employment was directly affected by seasonal needs. This custom
was modified when applied to domestic servants whose terms
were understood to run from month to month. Payment was
also to follow in kind. Although these agreements were

invariably made by mistress and maid, the law presumed
the wife was acting as the agent of her husband. It was
he who was bound to the contract by law. The exception
to this rule applied if the mistress intended payment to
come from her own separate estate. In most cases, then,
a servant was hired by the wife acting as an "agent" for
her husband to employ service for an understood, but not
stipulated, period of time, and solely on an oral agreement.[11]

    Termination of service could occur under a variety
of circumstances and for a variety of reasons. First and
most obviously, employment ended by mutual consent. When
the length of service was not stipulated, but payment occurred on a monthly basis, the presumption was that the
contract ran from month to month. If the servant was dis-
missed at month's end, the employer would be liable for
an entire month's salary. If the understanding covered a
longer length of time and the servant was forced to leave
early through no fault of her own, she was due all wages
up to the time of dismissal. However, there were a variety
of reasons for a justifiable preemptive discharge. Discharged under these circumstances, a servant could collect
only what was due unless her contract stipulated otherwise.[12]

    The cause for discharge put the onus on the servant,
not the mistress. For example, a servant could be fired
at once for willful disobedience of a lawful order. If the
disobedience was so minor that the employer suffered little
by its consequence, and it was a first offense, the servant
need not be let go. But consider how difficult willful disobedience could be to determine. Furthermore, how could
previous infractions be established? In essence, it was
the employer's word against the employee's. There was
little doubt as to which would prevail if such a case was
tested![13]

    Other grounds for dismissal were equally dubious--
robbery, petty thievery, immorality, wanton negligence,
and inefficiency. Inefficiency was defined as just grounds
if it prevented "carrying out to the master's reasonable
satisfaction the purpose for which the servant was hired."[14]
But without a written contract how could such a concept be
mutually understood? Petty thievery might also be difficult
to establish, especially if a servant had the misfortune of
working for an individual who constantly schemed to tempt
her. This was often done by willfully leaving money

around. Lillian Pettengill, a housemaid in Philadelphia
in the 1890s, was tested in this fashion. Inefficiency
could also be tested. This was achieved by placing items
where they did not belong. Pettengill's counterpart, the
house cook, related such an incident:

> Oh, she try me, too, MIT pins. . . . She
> take eight pins 'nd stick ZWEI in every
> corner; UND I take out, sweep, and put
> back. 'Ah Frieda,' she say to me, 'you
> no sweep in corners like I tell you.' 'See,
> I find these eight pins, ZWEI in every
> corner.' Wise to such tricks, the wiley
> Frieda responded by saying, Yes, I do
> sweep in corners . . . UND I find pins; I
> take out pins, I sweep carpet, I put back
> pins. You put pins in corner yourself,
> you can take out.[15]

Whatever the nature of service rendered or the reasons for dismissal, no employer was required by law to
provide a servant with a recommendation or character reference. If references were provided, they were considered
privileged communications. But this, too, worked to the
employees' disadvantage because it meant they were exempt
from liability, or libel suit, unless it was established
there was a willful attempt to malign.[16] One consequence
of these conditions was an exceptionally high turnover rate
in domestic service. Servants either left, as did Lillian
Pettengill, or they were let go. One study of domestics in
Baltimore, Maryland, revealed that the largest group let
go was released because there was "no further need of services." A reason as vague as this had virtually no bearing on a servant's ability. Nor was it a reason over
which the servant could exercise much control.[17]

Once hired (and in some instances prior to it), the
"girl" underwent the ceremony of visiting her room. Often
included in the contract of the live-in servant, but not
expressly arranged, was room and board. Nor was the
employer bound to furnish other necessities like medical
care or medicine. As for accommodations, the wise mistress
carefully cleared and put in order the servant's quarters
the day prior to her visit. Often this room was situated
on the third floor in the back of the house. It was furnished with items long since discarded by the family. But
this was the lucky servant indeed![18]

Since work and home were one, accommodations were a major concern for the live-in servant. However good or bad these living conditions might be, they were always inferior to those of the family. What is more, the servant was powerless over the living environment. Thus it was not uncommon to find domestics living in unventilated closets or rooms opening off from only the kitchen--small and windowless. When planning her new three-story house, one mistress purposely put in attic windows so high up that they were virtually useless. Questioned by the architect she replied, "Oh, those are for the maids; I don't expect them to spend their time looking out."[19]

Legend were servant complaints about small, hot and/or cold rooms. It was quite common to find that the only unheated room in the house or apartment was occupied by the domestic. Unable to keep help through five winter seasons, one mistress refused to see her unheated servants' quarters as the source of the problem. In another otherwise splendid home servants' quarters were hot in summer and cold in winter. The one room contained four beds for five adults. All lived together. In addition, the room contained two bureaus, one tiny closet, and one waterstand. One family had their maid sleep on the ironing board that had been placed over the bathtub. Another maid slept her nights away on a mattress laid over basement washtubs. A thin mattress on the dining-room table served as a bed for two servants in yet another home. Overcrowding was common, and many times men and women were forced to live together. Yet the employers were shocked when they found their women servants had gone astray.[20]

Crowded, close conditions did little to facilitate sanitary living accommodations. A cook reported she was obliged to supply her own mattress because the one she was given was filthy beyond description. In small basement rooms housing two to six people, no systems of sanitation or regulations for linen changing existed. One employer vehemently complained that her last "girl" was unclean and untidy. The investigator was then shown the room where the accused had lived--it was a room partitioned off from the coal bin. Yet the employer maintained this fact was unrelated to the difficulty.[21]

Bathing facilities were yet another problem. Often they were restricted or so hard to use that servants were totally discouraged from even trying. One servant girl wrote, "Don't you think a girl should have use of the bathtub? The lady I live with regards me as one of the family, but she never thinks of letting me use the bathtub." Another wrote, "Will you not call the attention of housewives to the impossibility of their expecting a neat girl to spend her spare time in a room where everything is out of repair and ragged?"[22] Authors sometimes warned householders against such conditions for fear the ramifications might impact the family. How often, Charles F. Wingate wrote, could a serious outbreak of disease be traced back to the family's failure to care properly for their servants? Since they lived under the same roof, one could not escape their influence. Thus:

> when one finds damask and solid silver in
> the dining room with cheap furniture and
> uncarpeted floor in the attic, it [was] not
> surprising to learn that in such a house-
> hold a beloved child [had] died from a
> disease contracted from a nurse . . . or
> that others were poisoned by food kept in
> a refrigerator connected with the sewer.

Furthermore, Wingate admonished the mistress and master to:

> take care that the kitchen is not dark,
> damp, and dingy. Don't expect domestics
> to bathe in a cellar nor leave them without
> any resources for cleanliness except the
> laundry wash tubs; neither require a ser-
> vant to toil up three flights of stairs with
> a pitcher of water every day when a set
> basin can be placed to her room. Again,
> don't fail to supply hot as well as cold
> water for servants' baths as the average
> domestic does not appreciate the virtues of
> cold water bathing.[23]

Another important issue relative to living-in for the domestic was the sense of isolation and ensuing lack of privileges. Here, as everywhere else, the variations were limited only by the number of mistresses who employed maids. Very often the employer imposed a minute number of regulations and admonitions which originated back in the days of feudal obligation. They might apply to one's liberty to go out, to dress as one pleased, or to one's right to receive visitors. The meaning of the latter was intensified by the unwillingness of associations to accept domestics as members and by the lack of enthusiasm for servants to join organizations of any kind. One writer, therefore, surmised that the social opportunities for domestics were limited to the dance hall, park bench, summer excursion boat, or cheap theater. In addition, few employers would allow their servants permission to play a musical instrument. Fewer still granted their help access to the family library; others stated they could use the family library, but were restricted in their selection of reading material.[24] Seldom were servants encouraged to have or allowed to have visitors. If they were, their visiting places were greatly restricted. This was especially true if the visitors were men. Thus most male company was confined to the kitchen or laundry room. Even then, the right was scarcely respected, for as one servant said, "The attitude of the members of the family when they come into the kitchen where a girl is having company is often humiliating. . . . Some of them rattle the door good and hard . . . or come in with a broad grin or snicker which is disgusting or amusing, according to the people involved."[25]

In virtually every case, when women were asked if they preferred factory or shop work to service, they chose either of the former. The preference was not based on a dislike of housework as such, but rather on the fact that shop or factory work was viewed as according the worker greater freedom and societal respect. For to become a servant one almost had to take vows of obedience, celibacy, and poverty.[26] The consequence of this was the belief, shared by many, that only the leftovers went into service-- the inefficient, the servile, or the penurious. Working women weighed their options and chose that which offered them more of a personal life. As one servant so poignantly said, "Home is the place where loved ones live--a place of freedom, with the companionship of equals on equal terms. Home is not the kitchen and back bedroom of a house belonging to another."[27]

As with accommodations, privileges, and freedom, the servants' diet depended upon the generosity, wisdom, and eating habits of the employer. The general rule here was the help ate less expensively than those for whom she worked. Inez Godman discovered this while posing as a domestic, when she happened into the kitchen and came

upon another servant eating as though famished. Further
investigation revealed the woman had previously been employed as a chambermaid in a home where several maids
worked. Separate cooking had been done for them. One
domestic found that mistresses sometimes fed their pet cats
and dogs meat in the dining room, while servants in the
kitchen went without adequate food. Others resented being
fed whatever happened to be left over. Many regarded
their food as both insufficient and cheap. In some instances, if there was not enough to eat or unexpected
guests arrived, the servant went without. Frances Kellor
discovered girl after girl warning against accepting certain positions because of the food. Food preference was
often determined by the employer's personal likes or dis-
likes. Consequently a frequently heard comment was, "We
do not get enough of the food we need."[28]

Conditions under which the servant labored were no
more regulated or standardized than any other facet of her
life. Often the only thing mutually understood was that
the first week of employment was a trial period for both
parties. But even this was unwritten, giving rise to a
complex of problems. Aware of this fact, reformers constantly advocated the use of written contracts. Only then,
they claimed, would mutual responsibilities be clearly
spelled out. But in reality neither employer or employee
seems to have favored the widespread use of such a device. Both probably believed the complex interpersonal
relations involved in hiring a person, rather than her
labor, were unamenable to precise definition. Neither
woman possessed great knowledge of the commercial world.
For either party to legally enforce a contract, she would
have to rely heavily on the legal system. Litigation was
an expensive proposition, especially in light of the small
sums involved. Furthermore, use of the legal system
might have served to strengthen the servants' rights--
something employers preferred to regard as their granted
privilege. Precision in the form of a written contract
might well have curtailed this potential exercise of power
and control.[29] In justifying such a position, one contemporary wrote:

> The workers cannot be watched, and the
> limit of authority cannot be defined, no
> definition of mutual service and obligation
> can be made; no fixed contract can be

> drawn up. For the home is a place where
> things cannot be regulated by rule and
> schedule. It is a place of adjustment,
> like the joint in a suspension bridge.
> Weather, health, railroad schedules, busi-
> ness appointments, and social engagements,
> must be taken as fixed; the home must
> vary to meet them, and must be always
> ready.[30]

Securing employment through whatever service, the servant began work almost immediately. Virtually no time was allowed for adjustment to the new surroundings, to the new work schedules, new tasks, or work equipment. If the servant did not make this adjustment quickly, she was considered "slow" or "stupid." An important premise for these inauspicious beginnings was the widely held assumption that housekeeping came naturally to women, that somehow they knew what to do as by inspiration. Another was the notion stemming from this that the mistress was a competent instructor. Both notions, of course, were faulty.[31]

Writers often warned against beginning the mistress-servant relationship in such a fashion for they were fully cognizant of the problems that were bound to develop. To prevent such difficulties, they stipulated how important it was to begin properly. It was, therefore, the employer's responsibility to clearly state what was expected from the employee. Innovation afterward would be resisted as the servant was bound to feel imposed upon. Presenting the domestic with a weekly agenda and accompanying her on the first day was one author's recommendation for making sure the terms and standards were properly understood. A commonly recommended work order was something like the following: Monday--washing; Tuesday--ironing; Wednesday--mending; Thursday--cleaning silver, preserving; Friday--sweeping and window cleaning; Saturday--thorough cleaning of kitchen closets, cellar, baking. A schedule such as this one, experts believed, made for a well-ordered household. A home run in such fashion would make for content and responsible servants for they would know exactly what had to be done. Even though work might actually be more arduous in such a home, the servant would be more successful than in a home with no system and a capricious mistress. At all costs, wrote one expert, avoid "ALL UNNECESSARY INTERFERENCE WITH A SERVANT'S MODE

OF WORK. . . . ALWAYS GIVE HER AN OPPORTUNITY FOR
USING WHAT KNOWLEDGE SHE HAS."[32]

How many employers were willing or able to carry
out such prescriptions is impossible to determine. But
some domestics concluded the problem was that mistresses
simply were ignorant of service work. "Don't I know the
way the hussies'll do, comin' out of a bog maybe, an'
not knowing the names even, let alone the use, of half
the things in the kitchen."[33] Another claimed there was
no limit to the variety and amount of work. And would
not the patience of a saint be tried by the unreasonable-
ness and selfishness of the mistress? One servant, recalling her many positions as a domestic, believed them all
similar in nature, because during her twelve years in
service, she had yet to work for a mistress who was not
selfish, arrogant, and wise in her own conceits. Another
servant, who worked all day in the basement or laundry,
was told at 4:30 P.M. to prepare an impossible evening
meal. Groceries had not even been ordered from the market. Using what was available in the house, the servant
prepared an altogether different meal. That evening she
was reprimanded for not obeying orders. One mistress,
applying for help at an intelligence office said, "Well, I
want a girl not afraid of work, one who can bring in coal
and wash skylights and tend the furnace and chop wood.
She doesn't have to do it in my house, but I want her to
know how—that's my principle. I am allright to live with
if a girl will work, but I am the devil to get along with
if she won't." Little wonder domestics were hesitant to
believe in work schedules or employers' intentions to follow them.[34]

Other thinkers questioned the application of systematic principles, schedules, and the like to household labor.
Most did not question these as ultimate goals, but rather
questioned them with respect to housework in an industrial
world. Jane Addams, for example, considered housework a
"belated industry." In her mind the industrial isolation
of the home resulted in an isolation of the worker which
always yielded a lack of progress in the products and
methods of that trade. It also caused a lack of aspira-
tion and education in the worker. Household labor had
simply not kept up with other industries! For Addams,
this was largely attributable to the absence of esprit de
corps among the employees. Collectively they were best
kept from fresh achievements much as the absence of edu-

cation deprived them of the ability to improve their work
tools. Thus one set of utensils had to serve diverse purposes, lessening both the volume and quality of work.
This meant that the amount of capital invested in these
implements was disproportionate to the yield when compared to the accomplishments of other industry.[35]

Even more devastating was the workers' social isolation. Addams thought this especially important since
domestics were drawn largely from the ranks of the poor
who were "nothing if not gregarious." For Addams, this
meant that the young woman would be removed from family,
friends, and associates. But she would also be placed
with strangers in strange situations and expected to work
by their standards. Under normal circumstances this was
difficult enough to accomplish. One writer said of this,
"The easiest thing in the world to say, and about the
most difficult to do, is work by method. Even when one
has arranged a plan sheer willpower is needed to carry it
out. To train another person to work by one's own plan
is even more irksome. This is particularly true . . . with
housework, where one labors more or less alone. . . ."[36]

But method was difficult to achieve in housework
for other equally complex reasons. Women's work at home
was visibly distinguished from men's, especially when the
latter moved from the household/farm/craft shop to separate
facilities. Then the rhythms of the adult male and female
work patterns diverged. In an agricultural society this
had not been true; both were seasonal and discontinuous.
Many things determined this pattern in addition to economic
incentive. These included legal obligation, family position,
and tradition. The dominant characteristic of an artisanal/
agricultural society was, as E. P. Thompson has labeled
it, "task-oriented" rather than disciplined by time. "Time
discipline" was demanded by industrial capitalism. Task
orientation implied that the worker's own sense of need
and order dictated work performance. Perceived necessity
determined both delay or intensification in the work process. The result was irregular work patterns. Male occupations in America moved toward time discipline, but
housework, largely the dominion of adult women, did not.
It above all other occupations retained the irregularity
and responsiveness to natural and immediate demands as
well as the intermixture typical of preindustrial work.
Even when domestic chores decreased in scope or modernized
with the advent of new technology, they remained task-

oriented. Human need, not the clock, regulated the sewing
of garments, the preparation of meals, and especially the
tending of children. It would also prove particularly difficult to adapt women's work patterns to time discipline,
especially since employment outside the home was intermit-
tent and sporadic.37

Granted the use of a schedule or regimen in housework did not make it the idyllic occupation that advocates
believed it would. For one thing a regimen or schedule
did nothing to alter the personal nature of service. Nor
did the schedule put housework on a time or business basis.
The domestic was often caught in the middle, wanting the
existence of a schedule, but then lamenting the absence of
the personal element. In any case few could have argued
that the schedule imposed on Inez Godman, at the turn of
the twentieth century, made her existence as a servant any
easier. Despite the fact that Thursdays were set aside
for cleaning the sitting room, Godman was first required
to straighten her own room. It took two hours to finish
the sitting room because she had to move everything out,
including much china, bric-a-brac, and a new, heavy
carpet. The room was shaded by inside blinds. Her mistress ordered her to dust each slat. Within these two
hours she was called away five times to answer the door-
bell and twice to tend the bread she was baking. But the
day was not finished when the sitting room was done shortly after noon. Lunch had to be hurriedly prepared; this
she served at one. At two-thirty Godman thought all was
in order and began to return to her room. The mistress
appeared and informed her that the kitchen floor needed
wiping. Since the floor was large and covered with oil-
cloth, this task took half an hour to complete. Then at
three o'clock she was able to return to her room, where
she did some mending, rested, and freshened up. But four
o'clock arrived all too quickly, for that meant that she
had to begin preparing dinner. This proved to be a complex and further exhausting chore which required three
hours. Thus came the end to one day in a so-called regulated home! Small wonder domestics claimed their weari-
ness at week's end was extreme.

> I have heard people tell of being too tired
> physically to rest, without believing the
> condition literally possible. I know better
> now. That first Saturday night I could

have diagramed most of the muscles in
relative position by their respective aches;
and the different joints also.[38]

Neither did advances in technology do much by way
of improving conditions, although many reformers and experts had high expectations.[39] Although primarily concerned with technology's impact on the middle-class housewife, Ruth Schwartz Cowan has clearly demonstrated that
while less burdensome physically, the new skills and jobs
created by household technology did not necessarily provide increased leisure time. Her work reveals that household technology came to have its first widespread ramifications in the 1920s, the same decade that the number of
women employed in service dropped from 1,851,000 in 1910
to 1,411,000. Ignoring entirely the question as to what
role, if any, technology played in this decrease, Cowan's
work leaves little doubt that both expectations and time
spent in housework remained the same or increased. Given
this fact, is it not possible to conclude that women with
servants would expect higher standards from their help?
Certainly these changes brought in by technology appear
to have made neither mistress nor maid any happier with
each other. Commenting on technology's early impact, one
writer said, "Recent investigations [reveal that] labor
saving utensils, have greatly facilitated housework, yet
housekeeping is still accompanied with much dissatisfaction
on the part of the employer and employee."[40] Furthermore,
many kitchens in the nation resisted change. Prior to and
by the end of World War II, the basic complaints about
service work remained much as they always had been.
These included long hours, poor working conditions, and
now low pay.[41]

Intimately bound up with questions relating to working conditions, standardization, and technology was the
matter of hours. Servants worked both longer days and
weeks compared to other working women. Often when legislation limited the workday and week for women, it specifically excluded domestic servants. This was true, for example, of LaFollette's Eight Hour Law for Women in the
District of Columbia. When state legislatures began to restrict the working hours of women, domestics were once
again excluded. Thus Josephine C. Goldmark reported in
1906 that the states of Massachusetts, New York, Indiana,
and Nebraska prohibited women from working at night. In

New York and Nebraska the ban covered only industrial
and commercial occupations, while in Massachusetts and
Indiana it applied only to women in manufacturing. Nineteen other states limited the working day and week for
women, but most of the legislation was only applicable to
manufacturing. Two other states, Pennsylvania and California, had more general legislation, but both excluded
domestics.[42]

Their exclusion from legislation meant that domestics
were still working a seven-day week when other working
women had their week limited to five and one half days.
Throughout the nineteenth century most servants continued
to work at least a ten-hour day; the full working day
averaged between ten to twelve hours. Only gradually, as
the length of the working day for other working women decreased, did it do likewise for domestics. Yet the gap
always remained. In fact, one of the most frequently
cited reasons for the preference to factory versus home was
the number of required hours. One domestic said, "I don't
know as you are treated any better in the factory, but at
least your time is your own. In housework I used to be
on duty from 6:30 [A.M.] to 9:30 at night, and could not
sit down to read or sew without danger of being inter-
rupted."[43] And even when live-in work was no longer
predominant, long hours remained an important grievance
"Throughout the country, more than two million women are
engaged in domestic work, the largest occupational group
for women. About half are Negro . . . many . . . work
for as little as two dollars a week and as long as 80
hours a week. . . ."[44]

Onerous and burdensome as long weeks filled with
long days were, they constituted only part of the problem
of hours for the domestic servant. Unlike other working
women, servants had no free time except that granted by
their mistresses. As one writer said, this was because
housework covered a larger area of life. And as long as
the servant lived in, there was virtually no separation
between the hours of relaxation and the hours of work.
When one employer was questioned as to her expectations
for servants' hours, she replied, "24." Domestics verified
such women by their testimony:

> Mistresses are sometimes of opinion [sic]
> that every waking hour of the servant be-
> longs to them, with the expectation of a few

> hours stipulated for at the time of engage-
> ment, consequently the servants have no
> time for themselves--even for needlework--
> except it be stolen.[45]

Nor were domestics often compensated for these overtime
hours, except occasionally with a cast-off article of clothing.[46]

Unlike the issue of overtime, the wages of servants
were a matter covered by law. In fact, wages were considered an issue of first-class obligation on the part of
the master. Payment was based upon prior specific agreement, but in lieu of that, what was considered just and
reasonable. The servants' wages were never due in advance, and were thus paid only for work actually completed. Any servant, no matter how inefficient, was owed
payment as long as her services were retained. In this
case the amount was determined on the basis of worth--the
worth of those services. Because the law held servants'
wages as very sacred, numerous states had special statu-
tory provision to protect their right to secure payment.
For example, even the family Bible or the employers' wed-
ding ring, articles ordinarily exempt from execution on a
judgment for debt, could be taken to pay servant wages.
Should such judgment not satisfy the servant, arrest could
follow.[47]

Such was the theory and letter of the law. Application was sometimes another matter. On occasion, wages
were withheld and without good cause. The assistant at-
torney for the New York City Legal Aid Society reported
that two thousand domestics in 1900 had gone to the society
for aid in the collection of wages due them. Although
these two thousand women were a small percentage of New
York City's 146,722 domestics, their claims do indicate a
certain degree of legal impropriety. Fully 75 percent of
those who applied were found to have meritorious claims.
It was also discovered that in approximately half of these
cases, the wages had been deliberately withheld. In the
other 50 percent a misunderstanding of the rights of those
concerned was involved, the mistake having been committed
by the employer. The 25 percent not judged meritorious
involved employees who had erred in their understanding
of the employer's duties and rights in the employee-
employer relationship.[48]

In any case actual wage schedules were seldom as much a concern in service as in other occupations, for it was generally conceded that domestics made as much or more than women in comparable unskilled occupations.[49] In this sense service was unique, for it was discussed in strictly noneconomic terms. When servants were concerned about wages, it was not as much with the actual amounts as it was with allocation. As on other issues, this crucial matter was determined by the mistress, for a good percentage of the wage could be in kind. Freedom was the bottom line because servants could seldom order their incomes to reflect personal priorities. Once again, their situation was unique when compared to women employed in factories, offices, and shops.[50]

The nature of housework--its virtual lack of standards--in the various facets examined so far leads almost invariably full circle, back to the personal nature of service. As one contemporary historian has written, "Master and servant: for millenniums this has been an intense human relationship, sometimes short-lived, sometimes lifelong, but rarely casual, indifferent, or uncharged with emotion." Few have been gifted or graced enough to play either role well; most found the first uneasy and the second irritating and unpleasant. In any case there was exploitation for even if servants "be fed well and used kindly . . . they were always used."[51] That degree of use might well have depended upon the historical position of women, their economic options, and the economic function and importance accorded to those options. This supposition appears to have validity for the "household problem is, in fact, an industrial problem; it is an economic problem, a social problem and a psychological problem. . . ."[52]

Using the concept of the specialization of functions developed by Donald J. Treiman in his work on a standard occupational prestige scale, we can examine the historical evolution of domestic service over time in line with these criteria. In his attempt to develop a scale for occupations across cultures and through time and space, Treiman discovered that all occupations possess a specialization of functions. These include skill, authority, and economic control. They are the basic resources which characterize the various occupations because they are the essential aspects of power. In other words they supply the crucial means to achieve desired goals. Thus if the desired goal is to be a clerk, one must possess the skill of literacy.

The more powerful the desired goal--occupation--is, the more essential it becomes to have competent individuals in those positions. For example, it is far more crucial to have surgery done well than it is to have garbage collected well. Since the importance of well-performed surgery is significant, it is equally necessary to attract competent persons into it. And one of the major ways of attracting more capable individuals into certain occupations is by rewarding them well. Consequently those occupations which necessitate the most skill will be more powerful and likewise be the most lucratively rewarded.[53]

Skill, authority, and economic control yield privilege, but this relationship may change over time. The relationship may change depending upon the needs of any given society at any point in time. For instance, in a farming society a certain set of skills will be in greater demand because they are of greater importance. In a farming society the greater power and privileges will be granted to a farmer rather than to a hunter. Greater privilege reflects greater prestige and prestige reflects moral worth. The moral worth of occupations reveals their control over socially valued rewards and resources which, in turn, indicate their power and privilege.[54]

On an individual level it would follow logically that part of the notion of self-concept, what E. H. Erikson has brilliantly called "ego-identity," would represent a sense of being unique--a unique individual in one's own right within a social setting. This sense of identity is strengthened by the continual mastery of useful actions. The individual has cognitive knowledge of these accomplished actions and has them affirmed by consistent recognition on the part of others. In fact, there is little doubt that self-esteem is greatly affected by an income of esteem received from others. The income of esteem is directly related to what the individual has actually accomplished. Thus the experience of efficacy, based on our effectiveness in dealing with the world around us, is an essential aspect of self-esteem. One of the simplest ways of achieving this is by pitting mind and/or muscles against inanimate obstacles as in work.[55]

The converse--the so-called inferiority complex--often develops when obstacles, external or internal, block the development of a personal pattern of achievement which is capable of supporting self-esteem. This, for example, is likely to occur if one's particular skills are not greatly

valued in society. As Gordon Allport has stated, "Mental
health and happiness . . . depends upon the person finding some area of success somewhere. . . ."[56] Success
might well come from an individual's position or status in
society, especially through group memberships.

Groups play a particularly significant part in the
formation and maintenance of an individual's sense of his
or her value. This is especially true for adults as they
come to be identified with their occupation and occupational
group. Each and every individual is a part of many
groups and subgroups of groups. No matter how active the
person may be in choosing those memberships, they "react
upon him, shape him in the direction of their norms and
expectations, and strongly affect his conception of what he
is and what he is doing in the world."[57]

The relevance of these concepts for domestic service,
the servant, and the mistress is trenchant. This becomes
particularly evident in light of the seminal study, Working
Life of Women in the Seventeenth Century by Alice Clark.
Her work illustrates how seventeenth-century Englishwomen
once belonged to craft guilds, acted with the power of at-
torney in the absence of their husbands, performed their
late husbands' jobs, and had professional standing as
teachers and midwives. This, wrote Clark, was "the greatest productive capacity which women possessed when society
was organized on the basis of Family and Domestic Industry." But by the end of the seventeenth century women
had lost these positions, and "capitalism was the means by
which the revolution in women's economic position was ef-
fected in the industrial world." For Clark three developments were intimately bound up in this revolution as it
impacted women. In the first place, the family wage was
substituted by an individual wage. This freed men to organize themselves in the competitive world, and it was this
world which came to dominate the labor market. Second,
wage earners withdrew from their home life and worked on
the premises of the master. This prevented the wage earner's wife from entering her husband's occupation. And
finally, a very rapid increase in wealth took place, which
permitted upper-class women to withdraw entirely from the
business world. With the strong force of economic necessity removed, Clark concluded, "There has been a marked
tendency in English life for the withdrawal of married
women from all productive activity and their consequent
devotion to the cultivation of idle graces. . . ."[58]

Clark's time frame is inappropriate as far as the
New World is concerned. A similar transformation would
have to wait until later. Colonial society was underdeveloped, labor was scarce, and without sufficient numbers of
women. The wife's function as the manager of the household was essential to the preservation of colonial society.
Although women had occupational options, most remained
primarily involved in crucial domestic responsibilities.[59]
More important, this work was regarded as demanding and
important, thus according those who performed it both self-
esteem and high status. In the preindustrial colonial
economy there was little, if any, room for an ornamental
woman.[60]

Colonial society seems to have encouraged women to
work lest they become recipients of tax relief. Women artisans as well as businesswomen and professionals did exist in colonial times (of course, they were few in number).
The greatest variety of options were available to young
single women who tended to live in urban areas. The largest numbers of those employed outside the home gravitated
into the various aspects of the clothing trades, which had
originated in the home. Poor white women and free black
women were generally washerwomen or domestics. Considerable numbers of the latter were bound out to service in
various contractual relationships.[61]

Basically the preindustrial colonial period in American history was relatively favorable to free, white, middle-
class women. Despite the fact that the norm for adult females remained within the various household occupations,
implying a degree of dependence on men, both men and
women were bound by an interlocking web of dependence.
When the subsistence farm was supplemented by the commercial farm, when journeymen were bossed by master
craftsmen and subsumed custom work for work in the market, and when earning a wage and desire for profit became the typical mode of providing, the economic role of
women became strikingly singular and prominently dependent.[62] Until that time--generally believed to be sometime
in the 1830s--the:

> efficient administration of . . . [the] home
> . . . required these duties in every Ameri-
> can housewife. In the time when steam
> was merely something that came out of a
> tea kettle and electricity only a menacing

adjunct of thunderstorms, before the factory
system or public utilities had been dreamed
of, the burden of manufacture was on the
housekeeper, and if she shifted it at all it
was to the shoulders of another woman.
The servant was her one labor saving device.[63]

Possessing the resources of skill, authority, and
economic control within the perimeters of their existence,
middle-class women made use of servants. Servants completed the less rewarding aspects of household duties, the
so-called drudge-work which one might argue exists in all
occupations. Servants could and were sometimes treated
poorly, but less because of the work they performed than
because of who they were.[64]

A clearer explanation of such treatment is provided
by the discipline of sociology, specifically, one of its
subdivisions—social problems. In the broadest sense,
human beings have not always possessed the ability to see,
let alone understand, the plight of those less fortunate
than themselves. Two historical currents, secular rationalism and humanitarianism, helped make such understanding
possible. By secular rationalism is meant the conceptual
conversion of issues from the ancient theological contexts
of good and evil to the rational context of analytical com-
prehension and control. This development came full force
in western Europe during the Age of Reason or the En-
lightenment. The second historical current, humanitarianism, may be properly defined as the gradual widening and
institutionalization of compassion. Of course, compassion
is a very individual sentiment, but its inclination is fundamentally determined by socially dictated boundaries and
channels. Because compassion is also timeless and universal, its intensity and objects differ from time to time. Of
concern here is early nineteenth-century compassion, often
interpreted in histories of modern Europe as a consequence
of the humanization of the upper class.

The pithy insights of the French political commentator Alexis de Tocqueville reveal how vividly this occurred
in the wake of the American and French revolutions. He
characterized this as a tendency of equalization in social
ranks.[65] Tocqueville made reference to the following passage written by a French gentlewoman, Madame de Sévigné,
in 1675 after the brutal civil repression of an abortive tax

revolt in Brittany. It is prudent to remember that Sévigné
was not a brutish or sadistic woman. In fact, she was
reported to have been a doting mother, a good friend, and
even indulgent with her servants:

> You talk very pleasantly about our miseries,
> but we are no longer so jaded with capital
> punishments; only one a week now, just to
> keep up appearances. It is true that a
> hanging now seems to me quite a cooling
> entertainment. I have got a wholly new
> idea of justice since I have been in this
> region. Your galley slaves seem to me a
> society of good people who have retired
> from the world to lead a quiet life.[66]

Madame de Sévigné did not lack the ability to feel
compassion per se; it was her social limit of compassion,
and this she was incapable of transcending. As Tocqueville explained, she was able to understand suffering only
in persons of quality. Was the class elevation of character necessary to bring about change? No, believed Tocqueville, instead, there would be a basic alteration in the
relation of societal ranks to one another. The achievement
was in the making as the waves of civil and political
democracy were swallowing up social insensitivities and
parochialisms. When completed, when the widening of
political democracy had run its course, the effect would be
the widening of the operative social field in the recognition of human suffering. The eloquence of Tocqueville's
following words expressed the change best:

> When all the ranks of a community are
> nearly equal, as all men then think and
> feel in nearly the same manner, each of
> them may judge in a moment the sensations
> of all the others; he casts a rapid glance
> upon himself, and that is enough. There
> is no wretchedness into which he cannot
> readily enter, and a secret instinct reveals
> to him its extent. It signifies that not
> strangers or foes are the sufferers; imagi-
> nation puts him in their place; something
> like a personal feeling is mingled with the
> pity and makes himself suffer while the
> body of his fellow creature is in torture.[67]

Only the second period in the history of domestic
service saw the coalescing of two essential elements with
respect to women.[68]   First, they retained a relatively wide
variety of occupational options.   These, along with the
majority of domestic activities, accorded them authority
and economic control.   Second, a widening of the effective
field in the recognition of humanity brought mistress and
maid together to form a unique sense of mutual respect and
cooperation.   Domestic work was a function of the age
serving both as a kind of "apprenticeship" to female
duties.[69]

During the later years of this period, the merchant
capitalism of the 1830s was giving rise to industrial capitalism.   The basic modes of production in the nation
changed, altering women's economic function.   The impact
was all but totally wrenching, particularly with respect to
the role middle-class women played in the American economy.
Simultaneously the tremendous growth of industry served as
a powerful magnet for immigration.   Immigrants pouring
into the country filled the ranks as the new industrial
work force, or labored as domestics in the homes of middle-
class women.   In the home--that most personal and inti-
mate of institutions, where the most personal of relations,
that between mistress and maid prevailed--occurred the
separation of race, religion, education, tradition, and social prejudices.   The result, many believed, was a lowering in the quality of those employed in the home as servants.   Lower-quality workers lowered the status of the
work, which thus served to attract fewer quality workers.
"Because there is this indefinable social stigma attaching
to service, intelligent, self-respecting women shun it; because self-respecting women shun it, the stigma increases.
Cause and effect are reciprocal."[70]   Furthermore, as one
former servant concluded:

> [I]t is human nature to desire to be appre-
> ciated and no girl of any refinement or
> education would willingly place herself in
> such a position, where every effort to
> please, no matter how great is met with
> indifference, and unkindness. . . . I
> would rather remain what I am now--a
> clerk with a small salary, and receive
> kind and respectful treatment, than to be a
> servant-girl and receive sneers and insults,
> both direct and indirect of my mistress.[71]

Degradation of housework with respect to those who performed it and societal value of it thus changed worker and employer relationships.[72] The societal value of domestic occupations changed because it came to represent everything industrial occupations were not, for at the same time "inferiors" were entering homes, middle-class women were absolved of their previous functions and responsibilities. The reason was simple: the increasing impact of industrialization made distinctions—clear distinctions—between male and female work. In other words it is fair to say that the Industrial Revolution "was the soil in which feminism grew."[73] Freed to pursue ways of making use of their increased leisure time, more and more middle-class women undertook reform activities and self-education. In this sense their horizons were broadened. But on the other hand, new thoughts were generated about middle-class women and work, eventuating in the creation of the respective "spheres" for the sexes. In short, by the time of Jacksonian America women were essentially confined to the home. Their female duties were to be patient, submissive, and active in the cultivation and spread of virtue.[74] The domestic sphere was to be the umbrella, sheltering women from the harsh realities of the world at large. Home was the soil where the gentle energy for a soothing, taming character were nurtured into the blossoms of harmony and social order.

The "Cult of True Womanhood" with its assertion that women were mysteriously but certainly different from men had arrived.[75] Womanliness could be found in the uniquely feminine role of bearing and nurturing children.[76]

Domestic work, now done by the poor, the immigrant, and the black woman, represented all that was no longer desirable for women of comfortable means. Performed by "inferiors," it was solitary in nature, nonindustrial or task-oriented, unskilled, nonproductive, personal and servile in nature. Little wonder that women workers sought to avoid service work whenever possible![77] Little wonder that mistresses held views of housework like the following: "Now, I am one of the kind who have no talent for such things! The kitchen and housework and sewing are absolutely hateful to me—utterly uncongenial to my turn of mind. The height of my earthly ambition is to have nothing to do but paint on velvet all day." Domestic labor truly had come to equal zero.[78]

Viewed from such a perspective, household labor could possess no dignity. Nor could the woman who performed this work--work devoid of skill, authority, and economic control--be worthy of considerate treatment. Tocqueville's effective field of recognition had virtually vanished because "to know the workman one must have been a workman himself, and above all, REMEMBER it." In addition, "the housekeeper must know the household affairs and RESPECT them if she would have others do the same."[79]

There is scant evidence to indicate that mistresses remembered this advice. In fact, just the opposite was the case; the prevailing attitude was intent on "keeping her in her place." But this was really meant to say, "Let no one suppose that this person has anything in common with me!"[80] Indicative of this was the prevalent practice of calling servants by their first names. Some women did not mind terribly if their mistress took this liberty, but it was deeply resented when all family members did likewise. On numerous occasions the practice was adopted by occasional visitors at the house, by the grocers' and butchers' boys, and even by the iceman. Said one servant, "I am Mary to every guest in the house and every stranger who appears at the kitchen door; in fact, how can I respect myself when no one else shows me any!" Bad as this was, some employers who had women in their employment for years had no notion as to their surnames. "Why, really, I don't believe I know; you see, she is just Katie to us."[81] But worst of all was the degree of this indignity inflicted upon black servants:

> No white person, not even the little chil-
> dren just learning to talk, no white person
> at the South ever thinks of addressing the
> negro manor woman as Mr., [sic] or Mrs.,
> or Miss. The women are called "Cook," or
> "Nurse," or "Mammy," or "Mary Jane" . . .
> as the case might be, and the men are
> called "Bob," or "Boy," or "Old Man," or
> "Uncle Bill," or "Pete." In many cases
> our white employers refer to us, and in
> our presence, too, as their 'niggers.' No
> matter what they call us--no matter what
> they teach their children to call us--we
> must tamely submit, and answer when

called; we must enter no protest; if we did
object, we should be driven out . . . and,
in applying for work at other places, we
should find it very hard to procure another
situation. . . . When our intending employers would be looking up our record, the
information would be given . . . that we
were 'impudent,' 'saucy,' 'dishonest,' and
'generally unreliable.'[82]

Although there were always people who advocated
considerate and humane treatment for servants, even such
persons sometimes possessed a condescending attitude toward
their servants, which some might characterize as paternalism. This paternalism could be benevolent, indifferent, or
even hostile, but the basic premise was often a superior/
inferior attitude. Although not necessarily typical, in one
family of five daughters the mother was pressured into
hiring a domestic because the girls claimed they would not
be considered anybody socially without a servant. Of
course, another argued, servants should be well treated
because in this fashion you would be assured of getting
the best work from your "machine." They should be well
treated because the mistress in the best "Christlike spirit"
would help those who came from poverty, ignorance, lack
of training, and bad upbringing. This justified showing
servants how to properly use their money and what kind
of clothes to buy "instead of the showy things they were
having."[83] It also justified visiting the servant's surroundings "and to use the old Yankee term, to 'poke
around' a little occasionally in [their] . . . bedrooms."[84]
The ultimate experession of paternalistic control was
displayed in the all too frequent sexual exploitation of
servants. Often cut off from normal social contact by a
mistress who regulated hours, days out, and visitors, servants led a singularly solitary existence. Speaking of
her practices in this regard, one mistress said, "I have
required of all that they retire at nine o'clock . . . I
have been very particular about their company. . . ."
She went on to report, "I require my maid to introduce me
to every person she brings on my premises, and if I find
him or her objectionable I say so. . . ."[85] Imposed isolation created by employers such as this one made servants
feel not only singularly lonely but particularly powerless.
Little wonder they were especially vulnerable to sexual
exploitation by male members of the household.[86]

Sexual harassment in whatever form-- innuendos, suggestive comments, leering gestures, pinching, touching, or actual rape--is but one type of violence perpetrated on women workers. As in other forms of violence, sexual harassment is an assertion of power, dominance, and control. In this respect the mere threat is often as significant as any actual act. However, such violence occurring in the workplace is especially coercive, for the woman's economic survival may be involved. In other words, sexual harassment served to remind women of how powerless they actually were. Furthermore, consider how potent such an exercise of power was when workplace and home were one and the same! Seen in this perspective, such behavior by those in power was not so much a deviant act as it was a socially condoned one. Thus it may well have acted to keep women in their place, especially if their participation in the work force increased along with a pattern of employment segregation. One source believed the weight of evidence showed that women in working-class positions (i.e., domestic service), those on the bottom of the employment and social hierarchy, were the most common victims.[87]

Sexual exploitation in the home frequently occurred between master and maid or the master's sons and maid for another important reason.[88] The nineteenth-century Cult of True Womanhood expected women of the "better sort" to be the guardians of purity. In fulfillment of this role, middle-class and upper-class mothers were often lacking in warmth and incapable or unwilling to provide physical affection. Servant women not bound by the same expectations since they were from the lower classes (working-class English nannies and black nursemaids, for example) often provided homes with the only genuine expressions of love and affection. Such expressions achieved legitimacy and then extended on into adult behavior patterns.[89]

Interpersonal relations, especially in the context of a highly private and emotion-laden institution like the home, are seldom one-dimensional. And although one might argue persuasively that the servant was a used worker, she was but a lower-echelon victim of an otherwise victimized sex--not victimized in the sense of physical abuse, such as the servant subject to sexual exploitation but to psychological abuse in the sense of having become all but absolutely dependent. The economic shift from home to factory denied middle-class women a sense of their own worth, which their previous economic function in a home-based economy had provided. Charlotte Perkins Gilman, herself a victim of this transformation, said, "She [the wife] is supported by him on account of her sex. It is a low position in this mighty world so complex and stirring, so full of noble activities, to earn no higher place than was open to the slave of countless centuries ago, but it is a far lower position to be fed and clothed as a sex-dependent, a creature without economic usefulness. . . ."[90]

In her thoughtful study on Catherine Beecher, Kathryn Kish Sklar pointed out that while men, too, lost at the expense of this transformation from home to factory, the displacement of women was more thorough and complete. Sklar also argued that the ideology of self-sacrifice, epitomized by the Cult of True Womanhood, did not compensate fully for women's status loss, and it was virtually useless in restoring self-esteem. Her premise that Beecher's ideology of domesticity was her attempt to overcome this deterioration in female status still rings true. Yet this emphasis on status loss is perhaps overdrawn—overdrawn in the sense that, bereft of economic and relative political status, Catherine Beecher was still Catherine Beecher, a woman prominent, well-known, and from a relatively powerful family. This, and this fact alone, enabled Beecher—as it did other women of similar background—to have far more options than a lowly servant woman. The truly significant loss for middle-class women came not so much in the form of societal status as from an internal sense of self.[91]

As W. V. Silverberg has pointed out:

> Throughout life self-esteem has these two sources: an inner source, the degree of effectiveness of one's own activity; an external source, the opinions of others about oneself. Both are important but the former is the steadier and more dependable one. Unhappy and insecure is the man who, lacking an adequate inner source for self-esteem, must depend for this almost wholly upon external sources. It is the condition seen by the psychotherapist almost universally among his patients.[92]

Manifestations of middle-class female loss of self-esteem have expressed themselves in various ways throughout history. Both mistress and maid, bound together as they were by the uniqueness of their situation, became victims. The relatively powerless, selfless mistress vented her anger on her maid, a person more helpless than herself. What better form of expression, what better target than an economically, socially, ethnically, or racially different woman who performed so-called drudge work? Commenting directly on this point, one servant said, "Women lost many of their finer attributes in dealing with paid servants; how to get the most possible out of them is the thought of most. . . ." And if these same servants were young and/or inexperienced, all the better. "Most ladies don't want girls that know their work and that is why the unskilled get the work, for they get them to do anything, where girls that know their work won't do it." Or as one schoolteacher said, "Mistresses are glad to get young girls whom they can train to their liking, as the experienced ones are independent and want too many privileges."[93]

Another manifestation of lack of self-esteem, and typically a nineteenth-century phenomenon, was hysteria, a kind of selflessness turned inward and outward. Alan Krohn characterized this as "the myth of passivity," for through hysteria--expressed in a rather wide variety of behavior patterns--"the Victorian woman could feel as if she were fragile and meek, while, in her behavior, the meaning of which her ego was able to shield from awareness, she betrayed her passion for power, erotic pleasure, and moral control."[94] Even the more sociologically bound interpretation of Carroll Smith-Rosenberg does not discount the hysterics' desire to escape the powerless state at tremendous personal cost. Certainly Sklar's treatment of Catherine Beecher leaves little doubt as to those personal costs. And even more telling was the tragic life of Alice James, in fact of the entire James family. Alice James, the sister of William and Henry James, like many of her generation never gained what she so passionately wanted-- recognition of herself on her own merits. This singular lack of self, or ego strength may have caused terror for all those who resided in the home--family, servants, and self. For as one perceptive late nineteenth-century author wrote, a deep cause for clinging to feudal servility in the home "was the liking of human nature to command its inferiors. Women especially do not want intelligent equals to serve them: they want an inferior, a subordinate--a servant, not an employee. . . ."[95]

Thus for the servant treatment retained its basic characteristics. It remained menial, personal, and servile in nature. The increasing propensity of blacks to enter this occupation did nothing except perhaps intensify these characteristics. Nor did the value of housework ever return to its preindustrial status. In fact, as Rose Schwartz Cowan has aptly demonstrated, the work became highly emotionalized, far out of proportion to its inherent value. Now rather than hysteria the pervasive illness was the malady so well characterized by Betty Friedan as "the problem that has no name." In the end, lacking in skill, authority, and economic control, domestic labor still equaled zero.[96]

NOTES

1. Flora McDonald Thompson, "The Servant Question," Cosmopolitan: A Monthly Illustrated Magazine, March 1900, p. 526.

2. David Brody, "Labor History in the 1970's: Toward a History of the American Worker," in The Past Before Us: Contemporary Historical Writing in the United States, Michael Kammen, ed. (Ithaca, N.Y.: Cornell University Press, 1980), p. 168.

3. In an early twentieth-century study domestic isolation was considered prohibitive to a social life and organizations of any type. For specific statistical details, consult U.S. Industrial Commission Report, 18 vols., "Domestic Service" by Gail Laughlin, vol. 14 (Washington, D.C.: Government Printing Office, 1900-1902), p. 758.

4. David Brody, Steelworkers in America: The Non-Union Era (Cambridge, Mass.: Harvard University Press, 1960), p. 2; I. M. Rubinow and Daniel Durant, "The Depth and Breadth of the Servant Problem," McClure's Magazine, March 1910, pp. 519, 581.

5. Rubinow and Durant, "The Depth and Breadth," p. 580; Frances A. Kellor, Out of Work: A Study of Employment Agencies: Their Treatment of the Unemployed, and Their Influence Upon Homes and Business (New York: G. P. Putnam's Sons, 1905), p. 17; and David M. Katzman, Seven Days a Week: Women and Domestic Service in Industrializing America (New York: Oxford University Press, 1978), pp. 35-36, 40, 150.

6. Grace Abbott, The Immigrant and the Community (New York: Century Company, 1921), p. 51; and Lillian Pettengill, Toilers of the Home: A Record of a College Woman's Experience as a Domestic Servant (New York: Doubleday, Page, 1903), p. 5.

7. Kellor, Out of Work, pp. 1, 9; ibid., "The Servant Question plus the Employment Bureau," Harper's Bazaar, January 1905, p. 15. Also, Abbott, The Immigrant and the Community, p. 51.

8. Frances Kellor, "Immigration and Household Labor: A Study of Sinister Social Conditions," Charities: A Weekly Review of Local and General Philanthropy, February 6, 1904, p. 151; and ibid., Out of Work, pp. 25, 35, 108.

9. Ibid., pp. 11-14, 121-22. Also see Catherine Webb, "An Unpopular Industry: The Results of an Inquiry Instituted by the Women's Industrial Council into the Cause of the Unpopularity of Domestic Service," Nineteenth Century and After, June 1903, p. 991.

10. Frances Kellor, "The Servant Question plus the Employment Bureau," p. 15; ibid., Out of Work, p. 70; and Isabel Eaton, "Special Report on Negro Domestic Service in the Seventh Ward, Philadelphia," in W. E. B. DuBois, The Philadelphia Negro: A Social Study (Philadelphia: University of Pennsylvania, 1899; repr. ed., with an Introduction by E. Digby Baltzell, New York: Schocken Books, 1967), p. 436.

11. L. H. Baright, "Women and Law," Harper's Bazaar, January 1901, pp. 394-95.

12. Ibid., p. 395.

13. Ibid.

14. Ibid.

15. Pettengill, Toilers of the Home, pp. 215-16.

16. L. H. Baright, "Women and Law," Harper's Bazaar, September 1901, p. 493.

17. Pettengill, Toilers of the Home, pp. 363-64; and "Domestic Workers in Baltimore," Monthly Labor Review 20 (February 1925):236-37.

18. Miriam Allen de Ford, "The Hired Girl," New Republic, March 4, 1931, p. 69; Baright, "Women and Law," September 1901, p. 492.

19. Katzman, Seven Days a Week, pp. 107, 109-10; and Rheta Childe Dorr, What Eight Million Women Want (Boston: Small, Maynard, 1910; repr. ed., New York: Kraus Reprint, 1971), p. 263.

20. Kellor, Out of Work, pp. 136–38; Helen Campbell, Prisoners of Poverty: Women Wage-Workers, Their Trades and Their Lives (Boston: Roberts Brothers, 1887; repr. ed., Westport, Conn.: Greenwood Press, 1970), pp. 230–31; Dorr, What Eight Million Women Want, pp. 262–63.

21. Kellor, Out of Work, pp. 136–38.

22. Ibid., "The Housewife and Her Helper," Ladies Home Journal, April 1906, p. 36; April 1907, p. 42.

23. "Servants and Sanitation," Country Life in America, January 1909, p. 285. In no law was the employer bound to provide for the servant's medical needs. If this was done, the sum could be deducted from the servant's wages unless the domestic had stipulated that payment was to be made in such manner. See Baright, "Women and Law," September 1901, p. 492.

24. Lillian Pettengill also discovered that public libraries were hesitant to grant domestics borrowing privileges without a written voucher from employers. See Toilers of the Home, p. 381.

25. Mary Roberts Smith, "Domestic Service: The Responsibility of Employers," Forum, August 1899, pp. 682–93; Webb, "An Unpopular Industry," p. 994; Rheta Childe Dorr, "The Prodigal Daughter," Hampton's Magazine, May 1910, pp. 683–84; "Privileges of Servants," Outlook, March 17, 1900, pp. 614–15; and Kellor, "The Housewife and Her Helper," February 1907, p. 32.

26. This complaint about wages seems not only unusual for the time (1898), but also inaccurate. See Bolton Hall, "The Servant Class on the Farm and in the Slums," Arena, September 1898, p. 375 for this view and the corrective analysis in Lucy Maynard Salmon, Domestic Service (New York: Macmillan, 1897; repr. ed., New York: Arno Press, 1972), pp. 93–99.

27. "The Servant Class on the Farm and in the Slums," p. 375; Ida Jackson, "The Factory Girl and Domestic Service," Harper's Bazaar, October 1903, p. 955; Mary E. Trueblood, "Housework versus Shop and Factories," Independent, November 13, 1902, p. 2693; and Rubinow and Durant, "The Depth and Breadth," pp. 578, 580.

28. Katzman, Seven Days a Week, p. 110; Inez A. Godman, "Ten Weeks in a Kitchen," Independent, October 17, 1901, p. 2463; "The Experiences of a 'Hired Girl,'" Outlook, April 6, 1912, p. 779; Jackson, "The Factory Girl and Domestic Service," p. 957; Webb, "An Unpopular Industry," p. 991; Kellor, "The Housewife and Her Helper,"

Ladies Home Journal, November 1905, p. 24; and ibid., Out of Work, p. 135.

29. Katzman, Seven Days a Week, pp. 106-7. However true the above was, in practice there were laws which provided for the specifics of the master-servant relationship. For example, consult Baright, "Women and Law," January 1901, pp. 394-95; September 1901, pp. 492-93.

30. Annie Winsor Allen, "Both Sides of the Servant Question," Atlantic Monthly, April 1913, p. 499. By 1935 little had changed. See, for example, Mary Anderson, "Domestic Apprenticeship--Different Forms of Realizing in the United States," Journal of Home Economics 27 (January 1935):7.

31. Katzman, Seven Days a Week, p. 106; Ethel Peyser, "That Servant Problem," North American Review 233 (January 1932):82; Izola Forrester, "The Girl Problem," Good Housekeeping, September 1912, p. 379; Catherine Owen, Progressive Housekeeping: Keeping House without Knowing How, and Knowing How to Keep House Well (Boston: Houghton Mifflin, 1889), p. 13; and Charlotte Perkins Gilman, The Home: Its Work and Influence (New York: McClure, Phillips, 1903), pp. 111-12.

32. Owen, Progressive Housekeeping, pp. 14, 17-18, 118; and Bertha M. Terrill, Household Management (Chicago: American School of Home Economics, 1914), pp. 183-84.

33. Campbell, Prisoners of Poverty, pp. 226-27.

34. Florence Morse Kingsley, "The Maid and the Mistress," New Outlook, October 1, 1904, p. 296; A. O. C., "A Letter and a Reply on the Servant Question," Colliers: The National Weekly, April 22, 1911, p. 36; "The Experiences of a Hired Girl," p. 779; and Kellor, Out of Work, pp. 142-43.

35. "A Belated Industry," pp. 538-39. Agreeing strongly with this position was I. M. Rubinow in "Household Service as a Labor Problem," Journal of Home Economics 3 (April 1911):131-32. Also see C. Helené Barker, Wanted, a Young Woman to Do Housework: Business Principles Applied to Housework (New York: Moffat, Yard, 1915), pp. 1, 19.

36. Addams, "A Belated Industry," pp. 543-44; "The Visiting Housekeeper," Good Housekeeping, January 1912, p. 60. Also see Alice Henry, Trade Union Women (New York: George H. Doran, 1923), pp. 166, 236.

37. Nancy F. Cott, The Bonds of Womanhood: "Women's Sphere" in New England, 1780-1845 (New Haven: Yale University Press, 1977), pp. 58-61. A host of other

seminal articles on this question should be consulted. For example, see E. P. Thompson, "Time, Work-Discipline and Industrial Capitalism," Past and Present 37 (December 1967): 55-97; Arthur Cole, "The Tempo of Mercantile Life in Colonial America," Business History Review 33 (Autumn 1959): 277-99; Keith Thomas, "Work and Leisure in Pre-Industrial Society," Past and Present 29 (December 1964):50-66; Richard D. Brown, "Modernization and the Modern Personality in Early America, 1600-1865: A Sketch of a Synthesis," Journal of Interdisciplinary History 2 (Winter 1972):1220-28. Also consult ibid., Modernization: The Transformation of American Life, 1600-1865 (New York: Hill & Wang, 1976); and Herbert G. Gutman, Work, Culture and Society in Industrializing America: Essays in American Working-Class and Social History (New York: Random House, 1966; Vintage Books, 1977), pp. 3-78.

38. Godman, "Ten Weeks in a Kitchen," p. 2460; Pettengill, Toilers of the Home, p. 9; and Kellor, "The Housewife and Her Helper," p. 36. And see Webb, "An Unpopular Industry," pp. 991, 993 for more domestics' observations.

39. Interesting reform and utopian views may be found in Edward Bellamy, "A Vital Domestic Problem," Good Housekeeping, December 21, p. 1889; W. D. Howells, A Selected Edition of W. D. Howells, Edwin H. Cady, ed., vol. 20: The Alturian Romances (Bloomington, Ind.: Indiana University Press, 1968), pp. 8-9, 12, 15, 166-67; H. G. Wells, "Will There Be Servants in 2000 A.D.?" Current Literature 32 (April 1902):426-27.

40. Barker, Wanted, a Young Woman to Do Housework, p. 2.

41. Ruth Schwartz Cowan, "The Industrial Revolution in the Home: Household Technology and Social Change in the 20th Century," Technology and Culture 17 (January 1976):9, 13-16. Also see ibid., "Two Washes in the Morning and a Bridge Party at Night: The American Housewife between the Wars," Women's Studies 3 (1976):147-72; and "A Case of Technological and Social Change: The Washing Machine and the Working Wife," in Clio's Consciousness Raised: New Perspectives on the History of Women, Mary Hartman and Lois Banner, eds. (New York: Harper & Row; Harper Torchbooks, 1974), pp. 245-53; Hooks, Women's Occupations through Seven Decades, p. 132; and Katzman, Seven Days a Week, pp. 95, 134.

42. Barker, Wanted, a Young Woman to Do House-
Work, p. 63; Josephine C. Goldmark, "Working Women and
the Laws: A Record of Neglect," Annals of the American
Academy of Political and Social Science 28 (September 1906):
70-71; and Lucille Eaves, A History of California Labor
Legislation, University of California Publications in Economics II (Berkeley, Calif.: University of California,
1910), pp. 204-5.

43. Jackson, "The Factory Girl and Domestic Service," p. 957.

44. Louise Mitchell, "Slave Markets Typify Exploitation of Domestics," Daily Worker, 5 May 1940, cited in
Gerda Lerner, ed., Black Women in White America: A Documentary History (New York: Random House, 1972; Vintage
Books, 1973), p. 230. Tremendous variation exists as to
the actual number of hours domestics worked. See Katzman,
Seven Days a Week, p. 112 for the best compilation of
these variations.

45. Webb, "An Unpopular Industry," pp. 993-94.

46. Katzman, Seven Days a Week, pp. 112-13, 143,
174-75; "Employers of the Household," p. 858; Allen, "Both
Sides of the Servant Question," p. 497; Jackson, "The Factory Girl and Domestic Service," p. 954; U.S. Industrial
Commission Report, "Domestic Service" by Gail Laughlin, pp.
756-58; and Kellor, Out of Work, p. 140. Compared to
other workers, domestics had no fixed customs with regard
to vacations. See Trueblood, "Housework versus Shop and
Factories," p. 2692.

47. Baright, "Women and Law," September 1901,
p. 492.

48. U.S. Industrial Commission Report, "Domestic
Service" by Gail Laughlin, pp. 757-58.

49. The most thorough and exhaustive analysis of
domestic wages can be found in Stanley Lebergott, Manpower in Economic Growth: The American Record Since
1800 (New York: McGraw-Hill, 1964), pp. 278-85, 382-83,
476-78, 502-6, 526, 542, 547. Late nineteenth-century
analysis is located in Salmon, Domestic Service, Chapter 5;
and ibid., Progress in the Household (Boston: Houghton
Mifflin, 1906), pp. 115-16; U.S. Industrial Commission Report, "Domestic Service" by Gail Laughlin, pp. 747-48, 751;
Trueblood, "Housework versus Shop and Factories," p. 2691;
Jackson, "The Factory Girl and Domestic Service," pp. 955-
56; and Kellor, Out of Work, p. 138.

50.   Katzman, Seven Days a Week, pp. 141, 147.
One economic facet which did disturb domestics was their
unlikely chance of achieving promotion.   See Pettengill,
Toilers of the Home, p. 367; Barker, Wanted, a Young
Woman to Do Housework, p. 21; Trueblood, "Housework
versus Shop and Factories," p. 2693; and Terrill, Household Management, pp. 81, 89.

51.   J. H. Plumb, "The Vanishing Servant," Horizon
15 (Summer 1973):10–11.

52.   Ethel M. Smith, "America's Domestic Servant
Shortage," Current History 26 (May 1927):218.

53.   "A Standard Occupational Prestige Scale for
Use with Historical Data," Journal of Interdisciplinary
History 7 (Autumn 1976):287–88.

54.   Ibid., p. 289.

55.   Robert W. White, The Abnormal Personality,
3rd ed. (New York: Ronald Press Company, 1964), pp.
149–51; and E. H. Erickson, Childhood and Society (New
York: W. W. Norton, 1950), pp. 207–18; 237–43.

56.   White, The Abnormal Personality, pp. 159–61,
163; Gordon W. Allport, "The Ego in Contemporary Psychology," Psychological Review 50 (September 1943):451–78.
The notion of inferiority complex originates with the work
of Alfred Adler.   For example, consult his work, The Practice and Theory of Individual Psychology (New York: Harcourt, Brace & World, 1929).

57.   White, The Abnormal Personality, p. 166.   Lest
it be thought that such notions from an "alien" subject
matter be astray, see Cott, The Bonds of Womanhood, pp.
19–20.

58.   Alice Clark, Working Life of Women in the
Seventeenth Century (London: Frank Cass and Company,
1919; repr. ed., New York: Augustus M. Kelly, 1968), pp.
290, 295–96.

59.   Nancy Cott was far more cautious with respect
to the economic options available to colonial women.   See
The Bonds of Womanhood, pp. 20–22.

60.   Philip S. Foner, Women and the American Labor
Movement: From Colonial Times to the Eve of World War I
(New York: Free Press, 1979), pp. 7–8.

61.   Ibid., pp. 8–11.   See Chapter 2 for a more
complete discussion of bound domestics.

62.   Cott, The Bonds of Womanhood, pp. 21–22; Faye
E. Dudden, Serving Women: Household Service in Nineteenth
Century America (Middletown, Conn.:   Wesleyan University

Press, 1983), p. 9, Chapters 1–2; and David Schob, Hired Hands and Plowboys: Farm Labor in the Midwest, 1815–1860 (Urbana, Ill.: Illinois University Press, 1975).

63. Martha Bensley Bruere, "The New Home-Making," Outlook, March 16, 1912, p. 591.

64. "Labor in New York: Its Circumstances, Conditions and Rewards," No. 20, Domestic Service, New York Tribune, 6 November 1845.

65. Robert A. Nisbet, "The Study of Social Problems," in Contemporary Social Problems, Robert K. Merton and Robert A. Nisbet, eds. (New York: Harcourt, Brace & World, 1966), pp. 7–8.

66. Alexis de Tocqueville, Democracy in America, rev. ed., trans. Henry Reeve, vol. 2 (New York: Colonial Press, 1899), p. 175.

67. Ibid.

68. See Chapter 2, especially pp. 29–33.

69. Cott, Bonds of Womanhood, pp. 28–29.

70. Smith, "Domestic Service," p. 686.

71. "The Working-Girl Question," Chicago Daily Tribune, 28 September 1873.

72. Nisbet, "The Study of Social Problems," p. 10. In Seven Days a Week, pp. 188, 200–201, Katzman discusses how the black servant was invisible.

73. Aileen S. Kraditor, ed., Up from the Pedestal: Selected Writings in and History of American Feminism (Chicago: Quadrangle Books, 1968).

74. A fine example of this is classically illustrated in Carroll Smith-Rosenberg's "Beauty, the Beast and the Militant Woman: A Case Study in Sex Roles and Stress in Jacksonian America," American Quarterly 23 (October 1971): 562–84. Also consult Johnny Farragher and Christine Stansell, "Women and Their Families on the Overland Trail to California and Oregon, 1842–1867," Feminist Studies 2 (Winter 1975):150–66. The best early economic discussion of the ornamental middle-class woman is still in Thorstein Veblen, The Theory of the Leisure Class (New York: Random House, 1934).

75. The classic article here is Barbara Welter, "The Cult of True Womanhood," American Quarterly 18 (Summer 1966):151–74. Also see Mary Beth Norton, "The Paradox of Women's 'Sphere,'" in Women in America: A History, Carol Ruth Berkin and Mary Beth Norton, eds. (Boston: Houghton Mifflin, 1979), pp. 139–49.

76. Cott, <u>Bonds of Womanhood</u>, Chapter 1, Kraditor, ed., <u>Up from the Pedestal</u>, pp. 14–15; and Foner, <u>Women and the American Labor Movement</u>, pp. 38–39.

77. Trueblood, "Housework versus Shop and Factories," pp. 2691–93; Jackson, "The Factory Girl and Domestic Service," pp. 953–57; U.S. <u>Industrial Commission Report</u>, "Domestic Service" by Gail Laughlin, pp. 756–59; and Gertrude Barnum, "Fall River Mill Girls in Domestic Service: A Strike Time Experiment," <u>Charities: A Weekly Review of Local and General Philanthropy</u>, February 11, 1905, pp. 550–51.

78. Gilman, <u>The Home</u>, pp. 105–6; Smith, "Domestic Service," pp. 681–83; "A Vanishing Relation," <u>Independent</u>, August 23, 1906, p. 467; and Marion Harland, <u>Common Sense in the Household: A Manual of Practical Housewifery</u> (New York: Charles Scribner's Sons, 1890), p. 3; Ida Tarbell, "Social Standing of Our Houseworkers," <u>Ladies Home Journal</u>, March 1913, p. 26. The reordering of the meaning of work would also make organized labor's recognition of domestics virtually impossible; see Chapter 6. See "The Working-Girl Question," <u>Chicago Daily Tribune</u>, 28 September 1873, for a former domestic's view.

79. Terrill, <u>Household Management</u>, p. 95.

80. Smith, "Domestic Service," p. 687.

81. Kellor, "The Housewife and the Helper," June 1907, p. 30; and ibid., <u>Out of Work</u>, pp. 10–11.

82. A Negro Nurse, "More Slavery at the South," <u>Independent</u>, January 25, 1912, p. 198.

83. It seems domestics did not need this assistance considering the sayings they accumulated. See Salmon, <u>Domestic Service</u>, Chapter 5; Trueblood, "Housework versus Shop and Factories," pp. 2691–93; U.S. <u>Industrial Commission Report</u>, "Domestic Service" by Gail Laughlin; and Katzman, <u>Seven Days a Week</u>, p. 309.

84. "The Home Club--The Servants' Side of the Servant Question," <u>Outlook: A Family Paper</u>, March 16, 1895, p. 440; Terrill, <u>Household Management</u>, pp. 84–85, 181–83; Wingate, "Servants and Sanitation," p. 285; and Harland, <u>Common Sense</u>, p. 361.

85. Godman, "Ten Weeks in a Kitchen," p. 2462; Ellen H. Richards, "The Eight Hour Day in Housekeeping: Conditions of Eight Hours a Day Work in the Trades," <u>American Kitchen Magazine</u>, November 1901, p. 48; Kellor, "The Housewife and Her Helper," October 1905, p. 21; Goodwin, "An Appeal," p. 755.

86. Katzman, Seven Days a Week, p. 216; also see Dorr article, "The Prodigal Daughter," Hampton's Magazine, April-May 1910.

87. Mary Bularzik, "Sexual Harassment at the Workplace," Radical America 12 (July-August 1978):25-26, 30, 39.

88. In the American South this was merely a carry-over from the days of slavery. See Katzman, Seven Days a Week, pp. 216-17.

89. Bularzik, "Sexual Harassment," p. 29; and Plumb, "The Vanishing Servant," p. 11.

90. Charlotte Perkins Gilman, "Economic Basis of the Woman Question," in The Women, Yes!, Marie B. Hecht et al., eds. (New York: Holt, Rinehart & Winston, 1973), p. 87. Also consult Carol Ruth Berkin, "Private Woman, Public Woman: The Contradictions of Charlotte Perkins Gilman," in Women of America: A History, pp. 150-76.

91. Kathryn Kish Sklar, Catherine Beecher: A Study in American Domesticity (New Haven, Conn.: Yale University Press, 1973; repr. ed., New York: W. W. Norton, 1976), pp. 193-95. The implication is not that Sklar neglected the psychological self as an important factor, but rather that a stronger emphasis was placed on status. An interesting view of Harriet Beecher Stowe is provided by Daniel T. Rodgers, The Work Ethic in Industrial America 1850-1920 (Chicago: University of Chicago Press, 1974), p. 188.

92. W. V. Silverberg, Childhood Experience and Personal Destiny (New York: Springer Publishing, 1952), p. 29.

93. Webb, "An Unpopular Industry," p. 996. Katzman argued that loss of control was one of the major reasons mistresses opposed the change from live-in to live-out service. See Seven Days a Week, pp. 159-60.

94. Alan Krohn, Hysteria: The Elusive Neurosis (New York: International Universities Press, 1978), p. 187.

95. Smith, "Domestic Service," p. 686; Sklar, Catherine Beecher, p. 195; Carroll Smith-Rosenberg, "The Hysterical Woman: Sex Roles and Role Conflict in 19th Century America," Social Research 39 (Winter 1972):652-78; Jean Strouse, Alice James: A Biography (Boston: Houghton Mifflin, 1980). Also consult Rosemary Dinnage, review of Alice James: A Biography in New York Review of Books, 22 January 1981, pp. 3-8.

96.   Cowan, "'Industrial Revolution' in the Home,"
p. 23; Betty Friedan, The Feminine Mystique (New York:
Dell Publishing, 1963); Edith Altbach, Women in America
(Lexington, Mass.:   D. C. Heath, 1974), pp. 4-5.   Cowan
argues persuasively that the mystique dates back to the
1920s rather than the 1950s, as Friedan had believed.

4

Preservers of the Status Quo: The Workers

"sister,
your name is not a household word."[1]

That domestic work equaled zero was a fact well-known to servants. Thus when opportunity in other occupations became available, women workers seized it. On some occasions they even returned to former occupations that had not proven all that satisfactory. Over and over again women, native and foreign-born, expressed their dislike of servant life.[2] "Society has no use for us, and we object to being patronized. If I could only make people understand that it is not being a servant that is hard, but being treated as an inferior." Not only were the words "service" and "servant" disliked, they were hateful because the really unpleasant facet about domestic service was how it damaged self-respect. No wonder American women rejected service work and immigrant women "as they became Americanized, also looked down upon it."[3] In fact, settlement workers reported that housework was generally frowned upon by most iimmigrant women. One employer even discovered that when she and her family were away for the summer, the servants hid the fact that they were employed as domestics. The root of the problem was not so much a dislike of housework per se, but the inability of workers to believe that the work itself was important. And this, believed Ida Tarbell, was the fault of the American woman for not "making a democratic trade of housework and a democratic profession of housekeeping." In fact, this failure made the domestic "the pariah among woman workers."[4]

Still all these reasons and preferences aside, women did become domestic workers. The first and most obvious

reason for doing so was that they had no other choice.
A recent arrival to the nation would have few friends or
acquaintances, and would therefore waive social considerations, especially considering the relatively good wages servants were paid. Often members of certain ethnic groups,
Poles for example, would select types of work which would
provide immediate returns--that is, employment which would
ensure quick and certain accumulations of cash.[5] In most
instances, when choices did exist, they were found in urban
areas. Even here the options were between approximate
occupations, never widely diverse ones. For example, the
women might choose between domestic service or unskilled
factory work. They did not have the choice of professional
or even commercial work and domestic labor. As the following evidence reveals, even the ever preponderate presence of the Irish servants was the result of necessity
rather than choice:

> You wanted me to tell you what makes
> girls dissatisfied when the pay is good
> and the work ain't really so hard as in
> factories. Yet factories have no trouble in
> getting help and ladies do, and you wanted
> me to say what makes there be so many
> girls that can't do their work satisfactory
> though housework is easy beside machines.
> You said if I would tell what happened to
> me and what I seen it would show up
> things, since I was a living out girl for
> 15 years, coming to this country when I
> was 15, green as any you would find. . . .
> I was an awful willing little girl and any-
> one with patience could have thought just
> a little bit how they had felt in a strange
> country like me. . . . Nobody never takes
> a green girl who don't have to. You just
> get work in citys, and as soon as they
> find out you don't know nothing they fire
> you. The only places that will keep girls
> like that is places where they want a awful
> strong girl to do rough work and there
> you learn everything all wrong.[6]

So, too, was this true of native-born Americans migrating
from the country village to the city. Musing on this fact,

one writer said, "It has come to be understood, at least
in my part of the world, that the girl in the kitchen is
there from misfortune, never from preference."[7]

Black migrants found this particularly true, regardless of whether they were skilled or unskilled, educated or
uneducated. Thus Jane Hunter, a southern trained black
nurse, found cleaning positions, with the help of her
cousin, her only option for survival after arriving in
Cleveland, Ohio. Establishing herself professionally,
Hunter still needed to fall back on domestic work during
slack times. Similar circumstances prevailed in Philadelphia, even though black women openly expressed their
contempt for domestic work.[8]

Reluctant entry into service occupations was not
conducive to activities that might improve either workers'
occupational preparation or performance. And as long as
workers were ill prepared to provide good service, mistresses would hold less than positive attitudes about them
and their work. If mistresses held negative views of their
servants and housework, servants could only continue to
believe the work was degrading. Rather than desiring to
find ways of improving themselves or their occupation, domestics would seek ways to leave service work as rapidly
as possible. This was especially true when the workers
felt they had no control over their occupation and/or if
they had higher expectations for themselves. The latter
was especially important for many immigrants since they
regarded the United States as a land of golden opportunity.
Servants and parents of servant girls saw little need or
value in training schools for domestic work. Nor did they
see much value in performing the work to the best of their
ability. Consequently it was widely held that "servants
demand as much and give as little as they can; they are
shiftless, spoil pots and pans, use quantities of material
for cooking, waste coal, and throw away good food."[9]

Equally difficult was the servant woman who wished
to be regarded as a lady and then treated accordingly.[10]
Then there were those who were bad-tempered. This type
acted as though she had "a grudge against the house and
everything in it," and if the "tone [of request wasn't] just
right, she flies into a passion and gives notice." And
give notice and depart they did. Sometimes the departure
was over a trivial issue for the woman had accepted the
position with no intention of staying on. Others did intend
to remain, but particularly foreign domestics became dis-

contented after "the democratic idea was injected." Many remained long enough to collect their pay and then departed for a better position. Of all this one employer stated, "I wouldn't care . . . if only you could get one of them to stay. But they won't. The best of them love to change. They're like birds of passage, with you for a brief season and then flitting on."[11] But recalling one of her less than pleasant working experiences and ensuing departures was the following somewhat different servant account:

> <u>November 29</u>. Mrs. Foster told me today that she did not want me any longer and that I could leave next week. I told her I would not stay with her any longer anyway as the work was too hard, and she said I was an ungrateful wretch. I was washing the dishes, and then I let a cup fall on purpose and it broke. Whew! but she was mad. Then I broke a plate. . . . She needn't have talked that way to me. I am just as good as she is, and anyway, I hate her old husband. I wasn't going to stay in the house with them another week so I left to-night, and she'll have to get breakfast her own self. . . . I wish I could get a nice place where I could stay a long time. Changing so much is hard.[12]

Whatever may have been the reasons for the negative attitudes about service work and the high turnover rates, such conditions were not conducive to union formation. Furthermore, women workers often found themselves in particularly unique as well as difficult situations, further lessening the likelihood of collective activity. First of all, many female workers were under twenty-five years of age. This was especially true of servants; as late as 1880, approximately 10 percent of all female domestics were between the ages of ten and fifteen years. This group alone made up 9.4 percent of all women servants in the nation. Many believed this pronounced youthfulness a distinct handicap since it provided females with few experienced leaders. Being young and inexperienced also tended to mean these women had not yet learned the need of col-

lective action. When faced with additional hardship, they
only sought a cheaper room or another boarder in their already crowded quarters and tried to spend a little less
each day on food. Such a "child-like and simple code of
worldly wisdom and ethics" was difficult to change. Aban-
donment of this "happy-go-lucky care-free-ness" meant a
complete revolution in their mind of ideas. Since they were
still at a "play age," it was little wonder that even after
joining a union, such women were neglectful of meetings
and their locals.[13]

Youthfulness was apt to mean other things as well.
Few young workers had attained an eighth-grade education; even if they had, fewer still had been taught anything about the labor or women's movements. This, according
to experts, made women much more susceptible to public
opinion, for not only did this make them less inclined to
join widely unpopular unions, it made them much more
hesitant about making vocal any problems or demands.
Women simply did not understand that they were within the
scope of the labor movement.[14]

Employment served many purposes for women in the
United States, but seldom did these purposes serve to
facilitate union membership. For example, in a most interesting discussion of life cycles and household structure,
Laurence Glasco discovered that domestic employment was
used by the Irish and German residents of Buffalo, New
York, for very functional purposes. Irish and German
girls left their parents' homes early to begin domestic
work (as early as age eleven). By the age of twenty-one,
virtually all Irishwomen lived apart from their parents.
Although the German girls' years in service were shorter,
the pattern established during adolescence was the same.
Native-born women did not live apart from their parents
until around age twenty-five. The ethnic pattern of employment in service provided families with increased income
and acted as a regulator of family size. This is verified
by the fact that German and Irish fertility rates were almost double that of native-born women, and although the
ethnic child-bearing period lasted about ten years longer,
immigrant families remained almost the same size as those
of their native-born counterparts.[15] These functions, and
especially the latter, meant that neither Irish nor German
women intended to remain engaged in domestic service
throughout their potential years of gainful employment.

Black women, on the other hand, not only found domestic labor their only employment option, but a necessary
one to either supplement family income or provide for family survival. In short, unlike many white women, black
women were compelled to work whether married or single.
"I will say, also, that the condition of this vast host of
poor colored people is just as bad as, if not worst [sic]
than, it was during the days of slavery. Tho today we
are enjoying nominal freedom, we are literally slaves."[16]
Furthermore, a detailed study of Philadelphia revealed an
exceptionally high mortality rate for black males. Black
men could also remarry more readily than black females
because they had more women to choose from and a greater
need to do so. And of course, men could more actively
initiate a marriage agreement. Women without means possessed little bargaining power and were less likely to attract a mate. They were certainly less able to become involved in activities like unions, which might jeopardize
their jobs. Evidence indicates this was equally true in
New York City and Boston.[17]

Nor was this true only of black women. Whether
the women were black or white, native or foreign-born,
married or unmarried, the incomes provided by working
women were often a necessary margin to fall back upon.
Few families could rely on the wage of a single provider.
Studies at the turn of the century in New York City showed
that the income of one wage earner could not sustain a
family of four. In addition, many ethnics saved any extra
money to aid those in their families still living in the land
of their birth. Others used such funds to assist in bringing family members to America.[18]

Even if their incomes had not been so essential,
many ethnic women were accustomed to being held in low
esteem and often accepted mistreatment with little complaint.
Failure to rebel in any degree may well have reflected
private doubts about its legitimacy, coupled with the fear
of losing employment. Those less fortunate women were
the least likely to act effectively or aggressively against
abusive work authorities. Consider the complexities involved with the typical ethnic female worker:

> [S]he combines the problem of the immigrant
> in industry with that of the woman in indus-
> try. The difficulties which she would
> naturally encounter as an immigrant, in

finding work in America, in becoming accustomed to new occupations and new industrial methods, and in acquiring a new language, new associations, and new customs
are greatly multiplied by the fact that she
is a woman.[19]

Thus if such women were to protest at all, the action would
probably be individualistic in nature. In fact, some writers believed the experience of women throughout history
had not been antisocial, but unsocial. Women have lived
an individualistic existence, for "as soon as the division
of early labour sent the man out to fight and kept the
woman in the house, the process began which taught men
to act in concert while women acted singly."[20]
    Whether or not women actually lived individualis-
tically remains an unanswerable question. Not at question,
however, was the fact that women did function in a sexual-
ly segregated world of work. Their labor was priced in-
dependently and thus much lower than that of men. Such
expressions as "only a girl," "a very good wage for a
girl," and "she does good work for a woman," bore wit-
ness to the all too common acceptance of lower wage standards for women. These attitudes were based on the notion
that female workers were mere "helpers-out at home."[21]
Most women had no conception of their place in the industrial world, and they all too readily accepted their wage
as an auxiliary wage--a wage which merely supplemented
the wages of others. Nor was such an attitude theirs
alone; it was the general attitude. In addition, this attitude prevailed whether or not the woman was entirely alone
as the sole wage earner or whether she had to work to
supplement the family livelihood. Many concluded that
these factors inhibited trade union activity among women.
Adding to these difficulties was the preponderance of male
organizers who did not understand or relate well to particularly female issues. To sum up, the root of the problem
with respect to organizing most women was that "no one
expect[ed] a woman to take her wage-earning seriously, or
to consider it as a future occupation."[22]
    Work as a serious consideration in one's future was
a major issue with respect to union participation. Probably without ever fully analyzing it, men, women, employers, and unions expected females to be only temporary
members of the labor force. "In other words, most women

in the industrial labor force regarded themselves as women
first and workers second."[23]   One of the most important
elements with respect to this self-definition was the expec-
tation of an eventual marriage and family life.   This ex-
pectation, fulfilled or not, would lessen the possibility of
union membership.   "Because of this they care less for organization and the sacrifices necessary to maintain it.
They become even more anxious to escape the conditions of
low-paid labor than to improve them.   Unionism offers a
present sacrifice for a future benefit.   The working girl
appears unwilling to make the sacrifice.   The ends sought
are immediate."[24]   As for domestic workers specifically,
"In the vast majority of households the maid is a maid, a
young woman of lower classes, doing this work because she
can do no other, and doing it only until she marries."[25]

The role of family and marriage with respect to
work varied according to ethnicity, race, and income.
But as Patricia Branca has demonstrated, the ultimate goal
of most female workers was to leave the workplace.   Therefore, women were less likely to see work and its attendant
conditions as of prime importance in their lives.   One
group of women, blacks, were less likely than any other
group to leave the paid work force.   Nevertheless, as
Herbert Gutman well established, this inability did not
stem from a lack of desire to do so.   In fact, the contrary was demonstrated by their preference for live-out
work.   Since married black women were far more unlikely
to be freed from their economic responsibilities than their
white counterparts, blacks tried to reconcile paid employment by continuing to run their own households.   This
helps to explain their preference to labor as washerwomen
and the eventual transformation of service work from a
live-in to a live-out occupation.[26]

Coupled with the almost absolute necessity for black
women to continue gainful employment after marriage was
their responsibility to maintain the home and family.[27]
Such a combination left these women with little thought of
union involvement.   Recent research also indicates that
black kinship systems underwent adaptations in urban settings that fostered self-reliance.   Given the kind of hiring
practices that prevailed in a city like Pittsburgh, Pennsylvania, and given the nature of racial and class subordi-
nation, young Negroes emerged from the formative years of
their lives with a strong sense of individualism.   They
possessed "a realization that survival would ultimately de-
pend upon their own personal resourcefulness."[28]

Unlike the ethnic and racial homogeneity that prevailed among American steelworkers, domestics included a
wide variety of racial and ethnic groups.[29]   Generally
speaking, union organization was difficult enough without
this tremendous diversity.   In fact, experts believed this
had made union formation more difficult in the United States
than in any other free country.   "Indeed," according to
John R. Commons, "almost the only device and symptom of
originality displayed by American employers in disciplining
their labor force has been that of playing one race against
another.   They have, as a rule, been weak in methods of
conciliation and feelings of consideration for their employees, as well as in the means of safe-guarding life and
health, but they have been strong with the weapon 'divide
and conquer.'"[30]   Complicating matters even more was the
lack of certain traditional bonds that tied the workers of
Europe together into a type of class characterized by common patterns of behavior and thought.   In fact, the workers of the United States were probably most noteworthy for
their heterogeneity.[31]

Equally diverse were religious differences.   Native
American workers were consequently contemptuous of Irish
Catholic immigrants.   Irish Catholics, in turn, looked down
upon later arriving Catholics like the Slavs, Italians, and
Poles.   Jews suspected Gentiles and vice versa.   Among
domestics one of the most common sources of conflict was
religion.   "No experience will teach employers and agencies
that Catholics and Protestants will always quarrel over
who goes to church when, starting a split that will continue down into the smallest detail of the day's work, and
that a German valet and a French chambermaid are so
much flint and steel at striking sparks."[32]

Differences in race, religion, and ethnicity were
volatile beyond the confines of the home.   Such, for example, was the competitive dilemma of blacks and Irish for
service positions.   The preference for blacks was often
predicated on the notion of their supposed submissive and
docile natures.   In fact, blacks often were compared to
white workers on such a basis.   One employer, having
tried Irish, Dutch, Canadian, Swedish, and native-born
white Americans, decided in favor of Negroes even though
"[the Negro] is not so quick as many white laborers, but
he demands so much less in the way of supplies, is more
acclimated and generally easier to get along with."[33]

Racial, religious, and ethnic cultural traditions played a far greater role in the work and potential activities of domestics than the mere fostering of long-established antagonisms. In fact, whether or not women worked outside the home (particularly in occupations like service) varied by ethnic or racial group, proclivity to job opportunity, and need.[34] As one scholar of ethnic female work patterns has discovered, there was a kind of give and take with traditional old-country values and new social contexts. Although immediate circumstances clearly limited the work choices women had, they worked within them and chose those which engendered the least familial strain. "In short, immigrants constructed and interpreted their social reality in terms of past experience."[35] Nor was this any less true of blacks, as comparisons of them with ethnics have established.

Two excellent but divergent examples of ethnics involved in domestic service are the Irish and Italians. Of all the various groups that could be examined—Jews, Poles, Russians, Slavs, Germans, Scandinavians, and so forth—none worked outside the home as frequently as the Irish. Irishwomen were not especially involved in activities related to their ethnic group. Nor did they have a particularly traditional familial life-style as did the Italians, or even the Poles. Irishwomen outnumbered Irishmen, and they also tended to marry later in life than other ethnic women. Because they had been in the United States longer than any other group, Irishwomen most resembled native-born females. Their literacy rate was high, especially by the second generation. They possessed a native understanding of English. And finally, they brought with them to the United States a service tradition: domestic labor had been the single largest occupation for women in Ireland.[36]

Italian women, on the other hand (reflecting the behavior of their group), were the least likely of all to leave home to work. They remained closest to the European tradition, which placed emphasis on the isolation of women and large families. In a historical study using Philadelphia as the test city, Italian women were found to be the most recent arrivals, and thus they had the lowest literacy and English-speaking rate. Judging by the literature, this was a long-recognized pattern. Compared to other ethnic groups, Italian women immigrants were the most varied in age. But whatever their age, they were seldom unaccompanied. One writer said of this, "The Italian girl . . . unless she has stepped beyond the confines of morality, is rarely seen in public places of amusement save in the company of an older person. No daughter is more carefully looked after than the child of Italian parents."[37] Nor was restriction confined to just the young, for despite poverty, few Italian women ever found their way into American homes to work as domestics. Italian women stayed in their own homes and engaged in homework such as the making of artificial flowers. By so doing, they were not taken away from their young, and this work was considered a comfortable extension of traditional female roles. Equally important, "By nature the Italian is most jealous and demands of his mate, not only absolute devotion, but often abstinence from almost the commonest civilities from other men." This included mingling with other men in shops and being in another man's home.[38]

Comparisons of Italian and black female work patterns reveal additional subtle cultural distinctions. In creating a controlled comparison between these two groups of women, Elizabeth Pleck sought to discover the reasons for a higher overall rate of employment for married black women. While not totally discounting any of the foregoing discussion, Pleck arrived at some slightly different variations. She suggested that black women's wage-earning characteristics were influenced by three patterns: husband-wife relations; child-rearing practices; and the degree of emphasis on children's schooling. All three of these patterns were collectively necessary to offset strong male objections to paid female employment--an objection apparently shared by ex-slave wives.[39]

Husband-wife relations emanated from a complex pattern of conflicting interactions unique to Afro-American slavery. Because of this institution, or perhaps despite it, black women believed it was the husband's responsibility to provide for his family. However, these same women doubted his ability to do so. In such cases black women assumed the responsibility and thus gained respect for their own ability as providers. Despite male objections against continuing this role in freedom, black women somehow overcame their opposition. By way of comparison and for yet unknown reasons, Italian wives were not able to do likewise.[40]

Child-rearing patterns were also an important variant between these two groups--a variant that enabled black

mothers to work outside the home more easily than Italian
women. Blacks believed in home training that fostered independence, but Italians believed in close childhood supervision. A properly raised Italian child (ben educato) was
never left alone and was encouraged to play with siblings
or relatives rather than outsiders. And the degree of
such supervision probably intensified in the New World.
For blacks, the heritage of slavery once again determined
a far different course. Since both slave parents were
often forced to work away from the home, others generally
supervised the children, and thus slave parents did not
seem to connect their physical presence to good parenting.
Even if after freedom black mothers wished to spend more
time with their children, they were seldom able to do so.
Consequently black families devised methods of child rearing that continued to train for early self-reliance.[41]

The final variant between these groups with respect
to female employment patterns has to do with parental attitudes about children's education. In turn, these attitudes were imbedded in family plans for survival, and
while both groups shared such a concern, they expressed
it through very different strategies. For example, it was
rather well known that even as slaves blacks desperately
desired to read and write.[42] This intense desire carried
over into freedom. As two leading scholars have written:

> [I]f land ownership was central to the lower
> class freedmen's wishes, close to it in im-
> portance was the desire for education.
> Identifying it with the superior status of
> white men, the freedman naturally shared
> the American passion for common school in-
> struction. Old and young flocked to the
> schools opened by the missionaries as the
> federal armies moved southward.[43]

Most simply put, the key to the future for the older generation in the family and the social mobility of their children
rested in acquiring an education. To achieve this objective, black women would sacrifice themselves by their continued presence in the work force--most often as domestics.
On the other hand, Italian children frequently had to sub-
merge their needs to those of their parents, especially
of their mothers. Thus "exploitation for family purposes
is universal among the Italians, with whom the children
are definitely considered an economic asset."[44]

Despite all these differences, most working women, including domestics, shared certain common characteristics which served to further prohibit union activity.[45]   Black or white, foreign-born or native-born Americans, women who entered the ranks as servants tended to come from a preindustrial heritage.[46]

One of the distinguishing factors of this preindustrial force of servant women was their unfamiliarity with the urban milieu.   Because of their peasantlike origins—an expression equally applicable to foreign- or native-born— one labor historian has charactrerized them as people caught between two modes of existence.[47]   In essence, they were a people living between two worlds: the old existence of the communal village and the new world of urban disorder and violence, the old world of the family versus the new world of individualism, and the old-world system of peasant and artisan work methods as opposed to the new-world system of industrial discipline and modern machinery.   Bringing these diverse elements to terms with each other often proved to be a most trying and difficult task.   In the end this process involved more resistance and adaptation and relatively little assimilation.[48]

Examples of adaptation for the various groups abound, but in general there was a frequent sense of bewilderment when city and industrial life was experienced for the first time.   Therefore, first experiences were commonly those of disappointment and homesickness:

> The streets of the city . . . [were] not al-
> ways broad and beautiful, and life not
> always gay and bright as they had hoped
> it would be.   [Furthermore,] sometimes it
> seem[ed] to the peasant girls as if they
> had exchanged the green fields and woods
> and the long, quiet winter for a hideous
> round of noise, heat, and bitter cold.[49]

Studies revealed that the first year was often the most difficult of all.   Invariably, the migrant knew no one; even if she did, the sense of responsibility felt by friends or relatives was limited in duration.   Thus she was thrown on her own, perhaps, for the first time.   Miss Terry, head of the YWCA Bureau of Immigration in New York City, drew certain conclusions based on the women she observed.   Terry believed:

> [L]oneliness . . . [was] the strongest fac-
> tor for evil during the first year here.
> In Europe, community life is strong. Yet
> most of the girls come here alone, to a
> new world. If they are lucky enough to
> escape all the dangers of landing and
> falling into the hands of dishonest runners,
> immoral surroundings in lodging, etc.,
> they may secure a situation from one of
> the immigrant homes or honest agencies.[50]

Whether these women were internal or external migrants, observers characterized them as childlike. Coming
from different conditions, sometimes ignorant of the language and customs, these workers were not always able to
overcome the temptations which they confronted. Little
wonder that this was so when past experience had so seldom prepared them for independent action or personal moral
dilemmas. A frequent first step in the wrong direction
was taking up with questionable friends. On occasion,
women escaped wiser for their experience, but others were
not so fortunate.[51] Furthermore, evidence indicates service positions were one of those least likely to provide
adequate protection for young female morality.[52]
    Not all acclimation was as disastrous and wrenching
as that of conceiving an illegitimate child. In fact, the
consequences of naiveté ran a vast gamut: from the pa-
thetic black migrant who was cheated of her hard-earned
savings to the quaint amazement of a country girl over a
city flat. At the very core of the problem was the issue
of adapting to new life-styles, with little preparation to
do so. Writing on this very issue was one dismayed urban
mistress who pondered:

> I am wondering what you would think of
> parents who send their girls of thirteen
> and fourteen, and fifteen years into our
> towns from their country homes with no
> underwear, one nightgown, one pair of
> stockings and shoes, no apron or cotton
> workdresses--in fact, only the apparel
> they have on when they arrive. They come
> to us, never having cooked or baked--nor
> seen potatoes mashed, or steaks broiled,
> or a table laid--and they expect "good"

wages with "no washing, ironing, or baking." [53]

Although work was an essential element of peasant existence, its meaning was at great variance with that of the middle class. Despite the aphorisms of Benjamin Franklin, no time like that beginning in the mid-nineteenth century would evolve a gospel of labor quite comparable in strength. The Anglo-American work ethic was heavily steeped in British prophets. Perhaps its most evangelical spokesperson was Thomas Carlyle:

> Whatsoever of morality and of intelligence; what of patience, perseverance, faithfulness, of method, insight, ingenuity, energy; in a word, whatsoever of Strength the man had in him will lie written in the Work he does. . . . Produce! Produce! Were it but the pitifullest infinitesimal fraction of a Product, produce it, in God's name.[54]

However easy or difficult it would be for middle-class Americans to retain such notions of work in an ever increasingly industrial society, the injunctions never penetrated very deeply into the urban working classes—native or foreign-born.[55]

Work—as a builder of character, a vanquisher of despair, a redeemer, a curb to animal instincts, an ingrainer of habits like self-control, fortitude, and perseverance—was hardly compatible with the Slavic conception of work as an instrument of survival. Thus for the eastern European peasant there was no relationship between the acquisition of wealth and work. The world was a source of limited goods and little, if anything, could change the situation. One worked only to survive. And although people were taught to work hard from childhood on, it was not because upward social mobility was obtainable. In fact, that was irrelevant. What mattered was survival, and that meant virtually no risk taking, no new experiences. For women this meant continuing to do those tasks that had always been done—a pattern continued by the second generation. Poles, therefore, made good factory hands and good servants.[56] As one source reported:

In these places Polish girls are chosen for
the following reasons:
1. Because they come of strong peasant
   stock, and accomplish a large
   amount of work.
2. They are very thorough in what
   they do.
3. They are willing to take low wages.
4. They are submissive, that is, they
   never protest.
5. They are ignorant in the laws of
   this country, and easily imposed
   upon.
6. They never betray their superiors,
   no matter what they see.[57]

Despite assertions to the contrary by some cliometric
historians, Afro-Americans may not have been any more
involved with the Protestant work ethic than their European
peasant counterparts.[58] Writing to a northern friend, a
southern mistress related an incident about one of her
black cooks. She awoke one morning to find that she was
without the services of this servant. The mistress had
been given no warning, no notice, and in addition, her
house was full of guests. Not one of the servants could
offer an explanation. Maid Nancy's departure remained a
mystery until her former employer happened to meet her on
the street. The former mistress demanded an explanation.
"Why did you leave me like that? What was the matter?"
Nancy replied, "No'm. Mis' Brown, nothin' was the matter
. . . only you company; they gave me eight dollars, an'
I thought I jess wouldn't work any more!"[59]
Authors frequently pointed out similarities between
the country's internal and external migrants. Like their
European counterparts, blacks often underwent an abrupt
transition from a paternalistic agricultural society to an
impersonal, extremely organized industrial life. Both
lacked education and both confronted prejudice:

As I talked with the landlords of the
neighborhood, I found that, like the Southern white man in his attitude toward the
Negro, they were indulgently tolerant of
the faults of the peasantry but were con-
vinced that these faults were due to the

> fact that the peasants were quite a differ-
> ent order of human beings from themselves.
> They laughed at us for taking the peasants
> so seriously and imagining we could make
> ladies and gentlemen of them.[60]

Both groups came from semi-feudal backgrounds and both
were thrust into a new environment. Neither group was
well prepared for the long, regular, and disciplined work
days of the industrial North. Speaking of her own situation and that of those who followed her was Jane Hunter.
In fact, her founding of the Phillis Wheatley Association
in Cleveland, Ohio, was intended to aid this very kind of
transition.[61] Of herself Hunter said, "I was undisciplined
and inefficient." Of those she sought to help, she wrote,
"Some of them, coming from the deep South, are amazingly
backward, and their reactions are conditioned by the feel-
ing of inferiority which tradition and a lack of education
have bred in them." Some, limited in ability, had an
aversion to labor. This resulted in constant tardiness and
continued requests for time off. When the training school
in Cleveland finally opened, Hunter reported that the most
wretched and poor arrived. Neglected and untidy in every
respect, even those reared in cities had never used a
bathtub.[62]

Equally difficult in the transition from North to
South was the loss of intimacy that existed in small southern black communities. Entirely new impersonal relationships had to be established in the North. There as on
board ship or in the army, efficiency depended upon discipline. The best way to establish and maintain this was
through distance, for distance prevented familiarity. This
had not been the experience of the black servant and in
some cases of the European servant. But new circumstances
and environments created confusion, for "those not reared
with negroes and thoroughly understanding them do not
find it easy to be familiar and still be distant. This is
one reason . . . why negroes make such very poor servi-
tors in the North. They are not in a congenial environment, and sometimes, like the transplanted foreign servants,
are victims of false notions as to their status."[63]

If unfortunate enough to be forced to live in, as
opposed to living out, the black woman was doubly removed
from her ties with her family and former community. In a
study of Farmville, Virginia, W. E. B. DuBois found this

could mean splitting up families. For those who remained single or childless, the northward migration uprooted ties of everyday existence. Disruption went as deep as disturbing basic dietary patterns. But clearly the alien experience was not confined to blacks alone. Concluded one writer: "It has been the confusion of the American experiment--this taking of the Irish peasant, the peasant from the fields of Europe, into the small, well-regulated, private family; to sweep, dust, and to take care of children--that most delicate of all industries. . . . Her own home has certainly not been a superior establishment for the formation and development of high industrial and domestic qualities. A woman goes out to service as into a new existence."[64]

Urban industrial civilization was one built on the prudent use of time and this, too, was foreign to the pre-industrial workers who toiled in American homes. Often incomprehensible was the pace of movement in society. Equally so were expressions like "Time is money," or "It takes not only money, but time." Reacting against industrial work routines, one Italian woman explained why Italian men did not like factory jobs. "You go to factory, you have to work just as hard as at home. Boss say 'Hurry up! Hurry up!' At home, no one say 'Hurry up!' I figure out."[65] As she so well expressed, the pace in the home was slower, but perhaps not slow enough in somebody else's home. Consequently southern black cooks were notoriously late enough in the morning to make a housekeeper feel uncomfortable about having them prepare breakfast. Writing at a considerably later time, the familiar theme persisted--the girls needed to be instilled with a sense of dependability--for as one employer said, "Colored girls were never dependable."[66] But the problem was not one of race because "most of them do not care to save themselves labor or time. If it takes them a long time to do a certain thing they will have no time to do something else. Their time is not considered their own, anyhow, so why should they save it."[67]

Although Alice Kessler-Harris was correct in shifting the onus for lack of female union membership away from the workers, the fact remains that they were difficult to organize. Seldom was this truer than with domestics. Kessler-Harris acknowledged this when she pointed out that most women worked in unskilled jobs--a third being servants--which were traditionally hard to organize. Further-

more, working women tended to come from groups without a
union tradition. About one half of them were immigrants,
or daughters of immigrants, from rural backgrounds. In
urban areas this figure could reach as high as 90 percent.
"Domestic workers," wrote another source, "are the nomads
of industry. Their lives are like their work—impermanent,
detached from others', unobserved."[68]

Of all the various factors discussed so far—attitudes
about domestic work, the unique position of women workers,
ethnic and racial variety, preindustrial background, and
antiunion attitudes—perhaps none was more important in
inhibiting union organization than the occupational mobility
and eventual decline of service work as a major employer
of women.[69] In short, women did not enter service occupations with any intention of remaining there for the duration of their productive years. For white ethnics the pattern was first established by the Irish. They began as
domestics in the 1830s, but gradually drifted into the mills
during the 1840s. Those who followed in this path were
"in many cases not unwilling to enter domestic service,
but eventually they made an effort to break away from it
in order to go into work that appears to them to be on a
higher plane."[70] This was especially true regarding their
hopes for the future of their children.[71]

This hope, the hope for a better future of their
children, was a promise of American life. Often it proved
to be a viable one for both sons and daughters. Starting
in a lowly position, that of a domestic, a daughter might
go on to become a nurse or a secretary. The rewards
were twofold: a better salary and a higher status. And
there was always the chance that she might marry well,
perhaps to a businessman or a doctor. Was this not a
powerful safety valve, one that could dissipate much discontent? Wasn't this especially so considering the following data: almost all working women in 1900 were domestics, unskilled factory workers, or farm workers. However,
by 1901, 7 percent of all employed women were typists or
stenographers. In 1920 the largest single area in which
women were employed was in clerical positions. This transition from kitchen to office seldom occurred in a single generation. But for the mother of foreign birth and for
foreign-born children, it was the American dream come
true.[72]

For many, then, servanthood was intended to be only
a temporary occupation, a stage in one's life. However

temporary it was, domestic work played a valuable function in facilitating upward mobility. Immigrant girls, for example, were often sent out at a very impressionable age, when language, cultural values, patterns of behavior, and dress were still being learned. Thus service work helped bring about and perhaps speeded up the process of acculturation. It also served a similar function for native-born women by placing them in contact with a middle-class lifestyle and a more modern environment.[73]

Since no foreign-born or white group ever formed a permanent servant class in the United States, the work was left largely to black women. At the end of World War I, the decline in the number of white servants—native and foreign born—was tremendous. During this very period black women began flooding into northern cities from the South. Previously the basis of the southern servant class, they began to fill the void left by whites in the country's largest urban areas. As this black urban population continued to decline, the growing black communities came to supply an increasing percentage of America's domestic workers. By 1920 black women comprised 40 percent of all domestic servants. Unlike white women, including ethnics, they were barred from sales and clerical work. Black women did not prefer service jobs. They had no choice but to take them. Statistics tell the story: in Chicago 3,512 black women of a total 8,880 were domestics in 1910. They constituted about 10.2 percent of the total servant population. By 1920 the black female population of Chicago had increased to 20,755 of whom 6,250 were domestics. They now constituted 23.9 percent or about one fourth of all female servants in the city. In New York City 26,352 black women were residents in 1910, of whom 12.4 percent or 14,079 worked as domestics. In 1920 black women numbered 40,484, of whom 22.4 percent or 18,996 were domestic workers. Detroit, Michigan, witnessed similar changes; in 1910 there were 960 black women in the city, of whom 415 were servants. This constituted 6.1 percent of the servant population. By 1920 Detroit had 4,969 black women, of whom 1,755 were domestics. Their percentage of the domestic work force had increased some 17 percent. Cleveland, Ohio, had 1,582 black women in 1910, and 677 of them were domestic laborers. By 1920 there were 5,118 black women and 30.1 percent of them, or 1,974, were domestics. And finally, in Philadelphia in 1910 there were 22,535 black women. Thirty-eight and one half percent or 14,278

of them were servants.   In 1920 black women in Philadelphia numbered 27,792, of whom 15,227 constituted 53.8 percent of the servant work force.   Similar increases took
place in all northern cities to which blacks migrated in
large numbers during these decades.[74]
        While the hue of the servant population grew in-
creasingly darker, the actual number of servants declined.
In 1870 more than half of all employed women were private
household workers, but by 1940 they comprised slightly
more than 20 percent.[75]   This shrinking work force, one
made up of a predominately despised racial group of poor,
uneducated, and unskilled women, was an unlikely candi-
date for organized labor unions.

NOTES

        1.   Alta, The Shameless Hussy: Selected Stories,
Essays, and Poetry (Trumansburg, N.Y.:   Crossing Press,
1980), p. 56.
        2.   Gertrude Barnum, "Fall River Mill Girls in Do-
mestic Service: A Time Strike Experiment," Charities,
February 11, 1905, p. 550; Helen Campbell, Women Wage
Earners: Their Past, Their Present, and Their Future
(Boston: Roberts Brothers, 1892), p. 240; Izola Forrester,
"The Girl Problem," Good Housekeeping, September 1912, p.
377; Elizabeth McCracken, "The Problem of Domestic Service:
From the Standpoint of the Employee," Outlook, February
29, 1908, pp. 368-73; Eugenia Wallace, "The Servant and
the New Democracy," North American Review 1920 (October
1920):537-538.
        3.   Christina Goodwin, "An Appeal to Housekeepers,"
Forum, August 1895.
        4.   "The Home Club--The Servants Side of the Servant
Question," Outlook: A Family Paper, March 16, 1895, p.
440; Helen Campbell, Prisoners of Poverty: Women Wage
Earners, Their Trades and Their Lives (Boston: Roberts
Brothers, 1887; repr. ed., Westport, Conn.:   Greenwood
Press, 1970), p. 241; Catherine Webb, "An Unpopular In-
dustry: The Results of an Inquiry Instituted by the
Women's Industrial Council into the Cause of the Unpopular-
ity of Domestic Service," Nineteenth Century and After,
June 1903, pp. 996-97; Robert A. Woods and Albert J.
Kennedy, Young Working Girls: A Summary of Evidence
from Two Thousand Social Workers (Boston: Houghton,

Mifflin, 1913), pp. 28–29; Mary E. Trueblood, "Housework versus Shop and Factories," Independent, November 13, 1902, pp. 2692–93; and Ida M. Tarbell, "Social Standing of Our Houseworkers," Ladies Home Journal, March 1913, p. 26.

5. William I. Thomas and Florian Znaniecki, The Polish Peasant in Europe and America, vol. 1 (New York: Alfred A. Knopf, 1927), p. 192. This pattern was altered by the second generation. For example, consult William M. Leiserson, Adjusting Immigrant and Industry (New York: Harper & Brothers, 1924), pp. 19–20. Also see Susan J. Kleinberg, "The Systematic Study of Urban Women," Historical Methods Newsletter 9 (December 1975):14–16.

6. Mary Heaton Vorse, "The Experiences of a Hired Girl," February 1910, Mary Heaton Vorse Collection, Archives of Labor History and Urban Affairs, Wayne State University, Detroit, Michigan, Articles and Stories, Di-Fai Box 19, February 1910, Tangier, Morocco. Consult Hasia R. Diner, Erin's Daughters in America: Irish Immigrant Women in the Nineteenth Century (Baltimore: Johns Hopkins University Press, 1983) for a very different point of view.

7. Polly Sprague, "The Hired Girl in the Home," Ladies Home Journal, September 1916, p. 54; C. Helen Barker, Wanted, a Young Woman to Do Housework (New York: Moffat, Yard, 1915), pp. 24–25; I. M. Rubinow, "The Problem of Domestic Service," Journal of Political Economy 14 (October 1906):508, 510–11; Robert Ernst, Immigrant Life in New York City 1825–1863 (New York: King's Crown Press, Columbia University, 1949), p. 68.

8. Jane Edna Hunter, A Nickel and a Prayer (Cleveland: Elli Kani, 1940), pp. 71–72; and Barbara Klaczynska, "Why Women Work?: A Theory for Comparison of Ethnic Groups," Labor History 17 (Winter 1976):84–87.

9. Lucy Maynard Salmon, Progress in the Household (Boston: Houghton, Mifflin, 1906), pp. 58–59, 70–71; ibid., "Recent Progress in the Study of Domestic Service," Atlantic Monthly, November 1905, p. 633; Webb, "An Unpopular Industry," p. 633; Marion Dutton Savage, Industrial Unionism in America (New York: Ronald Press, 1922), p. 314; Robert E. Park and Herbert A. Miller, Old World Traits Transplanted (New York: Harper & Brothers, 1921; repr. ed., New York: Arno Press and the New York Times, 1969), p. 46; The Spectator, Outlook, May 4, 1912, p. 41; David M. Katzman, Seven Days a Week: Women and Domestic Service in Industrializing America (New York: Oxford University Press, 1978), pp. 172–73; and Frances A. Kellor,

Out of Work: A Study of Employment Agencies: Their
Treatment of the Unemployed and Their Influence Upon
Homes and Business (New York: G. P. Putnam's Sons,
1905), p. 125.

10. Thane Wilson, "How We Treat Servants and How
They Treat Us: An Interview with Lida S. Seely," American Magazine, October 1923, p. 114.

11. Walt Mason, "The Dearth of Damsels," Colliers:
The National Weekly, August 7, 1915, p. 26; Kellor, Out of
Work, p. 114; "The Visiting Housekeeper," Good Housekeeping, March 1911, p. 340; Goldwin Smith, "The Passing of
the Household," Independent, August 24, 1905, p. 424; and
Elizabeth Frazer, "The Servant Problem," Saturday Evening
Post, February 25, 1928, p. 11.

12. Annie Marion MacLean, "The Diary of a Domestic Drudge," World To-Day: A Monthly Record of Human
Progress, June 1906, pp. 602-3.

13. Katzman, Seven Days a Week, pp. 71-76; George
Gorham Groat, An Introduction to the Study of Organized
Labor (New York: Macmillan, 1926), p. 161; and Alice
Henry, Trade Union Women (New York: D. Appleton, 1915),
pp. 142-43, 146-47.

14. Ibid., pp. 81-82, 148; and ibid., Women and
the Labor Movement (New York: George H. Doran, 1923),
pp. 108-35; and Lillian R. Matthews, Women in Trade
Unions in San Francisco, University of California Publications in Economics, No. 3 (Berkeley, Calif.: University of
California, 1913), p. 203.

15. Lawrence A. Glasco, "The Life Cycles and
Household Structure of American Ethnic Groups: Irish,
Germans, and Native-born Whites in Buffalo, New York,
1855," in A Heritage of Her Own: Toward a New Social
History of American Women, Nancy F. Cott and Elizabeth H.
Pleck, eds. (New York: Simon & Schuster, 1979; Touchstone
Book), pp. 279, 281-82, 284-87.

16. A Negro Nurse, "More Slavery at the South,"
Independent, January 25, 1912, p. 196.

17. Frederich A. Bushee, "Population," in The City
Wilderness: A Settlement Study, Robert A. Woods, ed.
(Boston: Houghton, Mifflin, 1898), pp. 44-45; Robert A.
Woods, "Livelihood," in Americans in Process: A Settlement
Study, Robert A. Woods, ed. (Boston: Houghton, Mifflin,
1903), p. 123; Frank F. Furstenberg, Jr., Theodore Hershberg, and John Modell, "The Origins of the Female-Headed
Black Family: The Impact of the Urban Experience,"

Journal of Interdisciplinary History 40 (Autumn 1975):226–29; and James R. Green, The World of the Worker: Labor in Twentieth-Century America (New York: Hill & Wang; American Century Series, 1980), pp. 25–26.

18. Ibid., pp. 26–27; Susan Estabrook Kennedy, If All We Did Was to Weep at Home: A History of White Working-Class Women in America (Bloomington, Ind.: Indiana University Press, 1979), p. 95; Woods and Kennedy, Young Working Girls, pp. 11–12; and Thomas L. Nichols, Forty Years of American Life (London, 1864), quoted in Historical Aspects of the Immigration Problem: Select Documents, Edith Abbott, ed. (Chicago: University of Chicago Press, 1926), p. 519.

19. Leiserman, Adjusting Immigrant and Industry, p. 297.

20. Annie Marion MacLean, Modern Immigration: A View of the Situation in the Immigrant Receiving Countries (Philadelphia: J. B. Lippincott, 1925), p. 49; Peter Roberts, The New Immigration: A Study of the Industrial and Social Life of Southeastern Europeans in America (New York: Macmillan, 1912), pp. 121, 142, 145; Jane Addams, "A Belated Industry," American Journal of Sociology 1 (March 1896):539–40; Leslie W. Tentler, Wage-Earning Women: Industrial Work and the Family in the United States, 1900–1930 (New York: Oxford University Press, 1979), pp. 52–78; and Emily James Putnam, The Lady: Studies of Certain Phases of Her History (New York: G. P. Putnam's Sons, 1921), p. xix.

21. Henry, Women and the Labor Movement, pp. 135–36.

22. Ellen C. Dubois, Feminism and Suffrage, The Emergence of an Independent Women's Movement in America 1848–1869 (New York: Oxford University Press, 1978), p. 128; Helen Marot, American Labor Unions (New York: Henry Holt, 1914), pp. 68–69, 71–73; Henry, Trade Union Women, pp. 149–50; and Henrietta Roelofs, "The Minimum Wage Conference," Woman's Press, July 1923, p. 401.

23. Robin Miller Jacoby, "The Women's Trade Union League and American Feminism," in Class, Sex and the Woman Worker, Milton Cantor and Bruce Laurie, eds. (Westport, Conn.: Greenwood Press, 1977; Contributions in Labor History, Number 1), p. 206.

24. Groat, An Introduction, pp. 160–61.

25. Henry, Trade Union Women, pp. 148–49, 217–18; and Charlotte Perkins Gilman, The Home: Its Work and

Influence (New York: McClure, Phillips, 1903), pp. 110–11; Carl N. Degler, At Odds: Women and the Family in America from the Revolution to the Present (New York: Oxford University Press, 1980), p. 375; and Peter Gabriel Filene, Him/Her/Self Sex Roles in Modern America (New York: Harcourt, Brace, Jovanovich, 1974; Mentor Books, 1976), p. 26.

26. Patricia Branca, "A New Perspective on Women's Work: A Comparative Typology," Journal of Social History 9 (Winter 1975):140–41, 147; Klaczynska, "Why Women Work?" pp. 74, 82; Kleinberg, "The Systematic Study," pp. 14–15, 17; Furstenberg, Jr., Hershberg, and Modell, "The Origins of the Female-Headed Black Family," pp. 219–23; Mary White Ovington, Half a Man: The Status of the Negro in New York (New York: Longmans, Green, 1911), pp. 140–41, 146; Lois W. Banner, Women in Modern America: A Brief History (New York: Harcourt, Brace, Jovanovich, 1974), pp. 83–84; and Herbert G. Gutman, The Black Family in Slavery & Freedom, 1750–1925 (New York: Pantheon Books, 1976), pp. 166–68, 443–45, 447–48, 451, 483–84, 508, 628–32, 635.

27. Of course, this was not a responsibility completely unique to black working women. See Marot, American Labor Unions, pp. 71–72.

28. John Bodnar, Michael Weber, and Roger Simon, "Migration, Kinship, and Urban Adjustment: Blacks and Poles in Pittsburgh, 1900–1930," Journal of American History 56 (December 1979):548–65.

29. David Brody, Steelworkers in America: The Non-Union Era (Cambridge, Mass.: Harvard University Press, 1960).

30. John R. Commons, Races and Immigrants in America (New York: Macmillan, 1915), pp. 149–50.

31. Melvyn Dubofsky, We Shall Be All: A History of the Industrial Workers of the World (Chicago: Quadrangle Books, 1969), p. 10; Henry, Trade Union Women, pp. 115, 125, 127; Robert Hunter, Poverty: Social Conscience in the Progressive Era, Peter d'A. Jones, ed. (New York: Macmillan, 1904; repr. ed., New York: Harper & Row, 1965), pp. 274–75; Roberts, The New Immigration, p. 72; and Ernst, Immigrant Life in New York City, pp. 106, 176–77.

32. Dubofsky, We Shall Be All, p. 10; and James Dymock, "The High Cost of Livery," Saturday Evening Post, July 27, 1935, p. 59.

33. Ernst, Immigrant Life in New York City, pp. 67, 104; Leon F. Litwack, North of Slavery: The Negro in the Free States 1790–1860 (Chicago: University of Chicago

Press, 1961), p. 166; Charles H. Wesley, Negro Labor in the United States: 1850-1925 (New York: Russell & Russell, 1927), pp. 197-98; and Walter L. Fleming, "The Servant Problem in the Black Belt," Sewanee Review 13 (January 1905):6-7.

34. Kleinberg, "The Systematic Study," pp. 14-17.

35. Degler, At Odds, pp. 138-39; and Virginia Yans-McLaughlin, "Italian Women and Work: Experience and Perception," in Class, Sex and the Woman Worker, Milton Cantor and Bruce Laurie, eds. (Westport, Conn.: Greenwood Press, 1977; Contributions in Labor History no. 1), p. 108.

36. Klaczynska, "Why Women Work?" pp. 76-77, 81; Katzman, Seven Days a Week, p. 69; Ernst, Immigrant Life in New York City, pp. 6, 66; and Oscar Handlin, Boston's Immigrants: A Study in Acculturation, rev. ed. (Cambridge, Mass.: Harvard University Press, 1941; repr. ed., New York: Atheneum, 1969), p. 61.

37. Jessie Fremont Beale and Anne Withington, "Life's Amenities," in Americans in Process: A Settlement Study, Robert A. Woods, ed. (Boston: Houghton Mifflin, 1903), pp. 233-34.

38. Klaczynska, "Why Women Work?" pp. 77-78; Yans-McLaughlin, "Italian Women," p. 109; Grace Abbott, The Immigrant and the Community (New York: Century, 1921), p. 68; Park and Miller, Old World Traits Transplanted, p. 146; Henry, Trade Union Women, p. 138; Louise C. Odencrantz, Italian Women in Industry: A Study of Conditions in New York City (New York: Russell Sage Foundation, 1919), pp. 27-28, 29, 32-33.

39. Elizabeth H. Pleck, "A Mother's Wages: Income Earning among Married Italian and Black Women, 1896-1911," in A Heritage of Her Own, pp. 367, 384-85.

40. Ibid., pp. 385-86. Also consult Gutman, The Black Family, pp. 146-55, 168.

41. Pleck, "A Mother's Wages," pp. 386-87; Park and Miller, Old World Traits Transplanted, p. 241; Sadie Tanner Mossell, "The Standard of Living among One Hundred Negro Migrant Families in Philadelphia," Annals of the American Academy of Political and Social Science 98 (November 1921):186; and W. E. B. DuBois, The Philadelphia Negro: A Social Study (Philadelphia: University of Pennsylvania, 1899; repr. ed., with an Introduction by E. Digby Baltzell, New York: Schocken Books, 1967), p. 111. Two excellent examples of northern white women's inability

to understand this pattern of self-reliance can be found in Frances A. Kellor, "The Housewife and Her Helper," Ladies Home Journal, June 1906, p. 22.

42. A classic, if not the best individual example of this desire, was that of Frederick Douglass. See Life and Times of Frederick Douglass (repr. ed., London: Collier-Macmillan, 1962; Collier Books), Chapter 10.

43. August Meier and Elliot Rudwick, From Plantation to Ghetto, 3rd ed. (New York: Hill & Wang, 1976; American Century Series), p. 173.

44. Woods and Kennedy, Young Working Women, pp. 46–47; Pleck, "A Mother's Wages," pp. 387–88. Examples of black women speaking to this issue can be found in Gerda Lerner, Black Women in White America: A Documentary History (New York: Random House, 1972; Vintage Books, 1973), pp. 102, 246. Herbert J. Gans illustrated how education was devalued by urban Italian-Americans in The Urban Villagers (Glencoe, Ill.: Free Press, 1962).

45. Yans-McLaughlin, "Italian Women," p. 107.

46. This notion, and its meaning, was first and best discussed by E. P. Thompson regarding the English working class. See his The Making of the English Working Class (New York: Random House, 1964).

47. Abbott, The Immigrant and the Community, pp. 66, 166; John R. Commons et al., History of Labour in the United States, vol. 1 (New York: Macmillan, 1913), p. 414; ibid., Races and Immigrants in America, pp. 64–65, 68, 72, 84–85, 87.

48. Dubofsky, We Shall Be All, pp. 149–50; and Green, The World of the Worker, p. 8.

49. Abbott, The Immigrant and the Community, pp. 61–63.

50. Forrester, "The Girl Problem," pp. 378–79; and Abbott, The Immigrant and the Community, pp. 63–64.

51. Sprague, "The Hired Girl in the House," p. 54.

52. Abbott, The Immigrant and the Community, p. 74; Henry, Trade Union Women, pp. 119, 130–31, 135–36; Roberts, The New Immigration, p. 71; William I. Cole and Rufus E. Miles, "Community of Interest," in Americans in Process, pp. 323–24; Frederick A. Bushée , "The Invading Host," in ibid., p. 70; Ovington, Half a Man, pp. 153–54; and Forrester, "The Girl Problem," pp. 380–81.

53. Hunter, A Nickel and a Prayer, pp. 139–40; MacLean, "The Diary of a Domestic Drudge," pp. 601–2; Kellor, "The Housewife and Her Helper," April 1907, p. 42.

54. Thomas Carlyle, Past and Present (1843; repr. ed., New York: Charles Scribner's Sons, 1918), p. 183, quoted in Daniel T. Rodgers, The Work Ethic in Industrial America 1850–1920 (Chicago: University of Chicago Press, 1974), p. xiv.

55. Ibid., pp. 12, 14–15, 22, 29.

56. Ibid., pp. 11–12; John Bodnar, "Immigration and Modernization: The Case of Slavic Peasants in Industrial America," in American Working-Class Culture, pp. 342–45; Park and Miller, Old World Traits Transplanted, p. 28; and Yans-McLaughlin, "Italian Women," p. 109.

57. Henry, Trade Union Women, p. 140.

58. Robert William Fogel and Stanley L. Engerman, Time on the Cross: The Economics of American Negro Slavery, vol. 1 (Boston: Little, Brown, 1974), pp. 5, 146–48, 231–32, 237.

59. Katherine Metcalf Roof, "A Plea for the Negro as Public Servant," New Outlook, September 27, 1916, p. 224; and Kennedy, The Negro Peasant, p. 120.

60. Abbott, The Immigrant and the Community, pp. 59, 79.

61. The Phillis Wheatley Association, Minutes of the Board of Trustees, 14 February 1912, bound vol. 1, pp. 3–4, Western Reserve Historical Society, Cleveland, Ohio. Hereafter referred to as the PWA Papers.

62. Hunter, A Nickel and a Prayer, pp. 31–32, 138, 145, 155–56.

63. The Spectator, New Outlook, p. 118.

64. W. E. B. DuBois, "The Negroes of Farmville, Virginia: A Social Study," Bulletin of the Department of Labor 3 (January 1898):2, 16; Katzman, Seven Days a Week, p. 211; and M. E. W. Sherwood, "The Lack of Good Servants," North American Review 800 (November 1891):547.

65. See Yans-McLaughlin, "Italian Women," p. 113.

66. PWA Papers, letter to E. Jane Hunter from Ruth Blalu, 31 May, 1937.

67. Roberts, The New Immigration, pp. 45, 293–94; Fleming, "The Servant Problem in the Black Belt," p. 6; and Mrs. J. C. Kirtland, "Servants and Labor-Saving Devices," Good Housekeeping, December 1912, p. 860.

68. Alice Kessler-Harris, "Where Are the Organized Women Workers?," in A Heritage of Her Own, pp. 344–45; and Rheta Childe Dorr, What Eight Million Women Want (Boston: Small, Maynard, 1910; repr. ed., New York: Kraus Reprint, 1971), pp. 280–81.

69. See Chapter 2, pp. 50–56, for discussion and data dealing with these issues.

70. Abbott, Women in Industry, pp. 137–39; Mary Anderson, "Domestic Service in the United States," Journal of Home Economics 20 (January 1928):7.

71. Banner, Women in Modern America, pp. 74–75.

72. Ibid. Also consult I. M. Rubinow, "The Problem of Domestic Service," Journal of Political Economy 14 (October 1906):508.

73. Branca, "A New Perspective," p. 138; Glasco, "The Life Cycles of Household Structure," pp. 287–88; Katzman, Seven Days a Week, p. 171; and Woods and Kennedy, Young Working Women, p. 29.

74. Katzman, Seven Days a Week, pp. 70–72, 77–78; Green, The World of the Worker, p. 25; Ethel M. Smith, "America's Domestic Servant Shortage," Current History 26 (May 1927):214; U.S. Bureau of the Census, Thirteenth Census of the United States, Taken in the Year 1910, vol. 4, Population (Washington, D.C.: Government Printing Office, 1914), pp. 546–47, 549–50, 554–55, 574, 590; and ibid., Fourteenth Census of the United States, Taken in the Year 1920, vol. 4, Population (Washington, D.C.: Government Printing Office, 1922), pp. 1079–80, 1086–87, 1104, 1161–62, 1196–97.

75. U.S. Department of Labor, Bureau of Labor Statistics, Women in Domestic Work: Yesterday and Today by Allyson Sherman Grossman, Special Labor Force Report 242 (Washington, D.C.: Government Printing Office, 1981), p. 18.

5

Preservers of the Status Quo: The Employers

"Lady love!   Lady Love!   wilt thou be mine?
Thou shalt neither wash dishes, nor yet feed swine!
But sit on a cushion and sew a gold seam
And feed upon strawberries, sugar and cream!"[1]

The reservations expressed by servants about domestic work
were rivaled only by those of their employers. Mistresses'
dislike of housework was displayed in a myriad of ways:
by their refusal to regard it as a serious occupation; by
their refusal to perform it whenever possible; and sometimes by their treatment of those who labored on their behalf.[2]   Since such work was characterized as menial, degrading, monotonous, demeaning, uninteresting, drudgery,
and "mere woman's work," it was little wonder that Charlotte Perkins Gilman, one of the severest critics of housework, concluded that "skilled labour and domestic service
was incompatible."[3]   Summing up all of these attitudes by
way of discussing changes made in her own home, one
writer said:

> First, . . . I changed my whole attitude
> toward her [the maid]. I dropped the dic-
> tatorial idea of ordering her around and
> feeling that she is subordinate. That is a
> false relation, and is the very heart of
> the difficult situations between mistress
> and maid. . . . But before I assumed
> this new attitude toward Katy I had also
> to assume a new attitude to my whole pro-
> fession of homemaking. I had to think of

it as worthy of my highest efforts, as not
degrading nor unimportant. Then with this
idea firmly in my mind, I could more easily
convince Katy of the dignity of her work.
Great soldiers and even great business men
say they do not ask others to do what they
would not themselves be willing to do. I
carried this same attitude into the kitchen.[4]

However slight their regard for domestic work, mistresses realized two crucial facts about it. In the first
place they recognized that the occupation was plagued with
many problems, and they wanted to be in charge of the
necessary reforms. Change, necessary as it was, should
emanate from the top down. Second, they realized their
dependence on their servants. Without Katy, Mary Ann, or
Dinah, the mistress of the home would have to perform her
own housework.[5] A familiar couplet of the times captured
this dilemma: "We may live without friends, we may live
without books. But civilized man cannot live without
cooks."[6]

Reluctance to act could lead to further complications.
Mistresses might lose control of the entire domestic situation! Would this not be the case if servants resorted to
collective action? Were servants beginning to think about
rights and to ask what those rights were? And here was
the great danger--the danger that servants would recognize
their rights and claim them! But surely the genius of
woman was able to solve this dilemma by some means short
of doing her own work. One prominent Chicago clubwoman
proposed a unique solution. She called a meeting in the
summer of 1901 so that the mistresses of servants could
organize. Professing that her object was not to antagonize
a recently formed Servant Girl's Union, Mrs. Charles Henratin believed it was best "to determine with them the
rules to be observed."[7]

But Mrs. Henratin stood alone. Movements directed
at encouraging collective action, even as conservative as
this, were routinely condemned. Perhaps responding to
the Chicago ladies, one irate mistress wrote to a popular
weekly periodical exclaiming, "I think women have seen
enough of other unions to dread them. I don't see how
anyone who has to hire help would set such a thing on
foot if she had horse sense!"[8] Precedents and numbers
were apparently in support of "horse sense," for almost a

unanimous chorus of uniformity spoke out against union maids. Many authors advocated undertaking the necessary changes at home before the maids took matters into their own hands through unions and strikes. Although some remained dubious about their servants' abilities to organize themselves effectively, most were concerned enough to believe it possible. If it was possible, "It is better after all to incur some of the evils of individual contract and want of it—than to be bound by servant trades unionism, which fixes the prices for work."[9]

Fear of servants forming regular trade unions was not confined to the twentieth century. Nor were those opposed concerned exclusively with the issue of wages. Lamenting all the deficiencies of the butler and the chambermaid, a New York Times editorial of 1873 warned that the worst was yet to come. The worst would of course arrive when servants no longer lacked organizations. Pointing to a servant strike in Dundee, Scotland, in 1872, the paper reported the even more ominous news of a trade union formed by the domestics of Ottawa, Canada. What if the contagion should jump across the border and land in New York? What if the servant girls of New York should strike for six Sundays in the week, or a 50 percent advance, or possibly even the right to vote? "They would march through the streets like an army, terrible with brooms and skillets, or, following the amiable example of their male prototypes, go about from house to house, 'rattening,' or 'doing' for their substitutes; blowing them up with powder in the cooking-stove, destroying their kettles and stewpans, broiling them on their own grid irons, or even hanging the luckless non-society girls out-right on the door-posts."[10]

Prevention was the best course of action. But prevention had to be based on an understanding of the problems that so beleaguered service occupations. Generally speaking, the problems are best categorized under two broad subheadings: servant causation and mistress causation. These two simple divisions are encompassing enough to include the vast variety of factors that were considered contributing elements to disorder and unhappiness in American homes. In reality, the problems of the maid and mistress were limited only by the number of homes in which they lived and worked. This reality stemmed from the highly individual nature of domestic work, with one or perhaps two servants working in separate homes. Probably

no aspect of housework made successful reform less likely
than this fact. Maybe that was why one writer commented
that "the servant problem is like the weather in that
everyone is always talking about it but practically no one
does anything about it."[11]

Seldom without explanation for the woes of domestic
service, employers often zeroed in on their servants' unfamiliarity with American life. Foreigners in the home
were wasteful and ignorant. "There remains for us, the
majority of housewives, the riffraff of the nations of the
earth: underdeveloped or degenerate; irresponsible; restless; untaught and generally unteachable creatures."[12]
They fed their relatives from the spoils of the pantry.
Since they came from European hovels, it was no wonder
they broke dishes and never learned to bathe! How could
they possibly know a dustpan on sight? Little question
that they burned and broke things at will. Little wonder
that they stopped up the drains with no remorse. And
still they demanded high wages![13]

While some writers, mistresses, and reformers considered such problems universally true of all domestic help,
others attributed certain less than desirable characteristics to specific races or ethnic groups. Thus blacks were
racially inclined to petty thievery. To others this was a
habit originating in the southern practice of toting--carry-
ing off all the kitchen leftovers at the day's end. Nevertheless, blacks drank, were lazy, used drugs, and were
basically unsuited to work in the North. "Now, the good
servant seldom if ever has to leave the South. It is only
the restless, worthless negro woman that wants to break
home ties and sunder old associations. . . ."[14] Even if
this was not true, many expressed the belief that southern
black domestics could not adapt to northern work, habits,
life-styles, and standards of competent service. Verification seemed apparent when northerners moved South and
neither they nor their newly hired southern servants could
make each other happy.[15]

Nor could relief be found by looking to the southwestern Mexican peons. True, they had the reputation of
being hard-working and they were a source of cheap labor.
But once across the border, they became afflicted with
grandiose dreams in the land of promise, leaving the mistress with no option but the Negro. On the other hand, in
a choice between black and oriental, one had to admit
from the start that neither was congenial or capable of

being transformed into a real household member. No doubt, one writer professed, the oriental was smarter and very adept in combining many skills. Yet about the Asiatic there was something positively alien.[16]

Initially the Irish were at a disadvantage as servants because of anti-Catholic sentiment. Since they were disliked and even feared, they shocked Americans by their propensity for drunkenness. As a group, they seemed turbulent and impulsive. Comparing Irish to black service, one commentator believed that with rare exception the former rendered highly unsatisfactory work.

Bridget, declared another, was above all things temperamental. This was a major drawback because of all occupations housework called for people in possession of their tempers. And coming from Ireland, these Bridgets were singularly lacking in regular economy and regular habits.[17]

Undoubtedly when middle-class employers brought women of different cultures, classes, races, and religions into their homes, the disparities between the groups were greatly accentuated. In that sense no woman available for domestic service would have proven satisfactory to the American homemaker. Perhaps no one captured the sense of this irony better than Mr. Dooley in the following jeu d' espirit:

> What naytional' ties to ye hire? says I.
> I've thried thim all, he says; an, he says,
> I'll say this in shame, he says, that the
> Irish ar-re th' worst, he says. Well,
> says I, ye need have no shame, I says,
> f'r 'tis on'y th' people that ar-re good
> servants that'll niver be masthers, I says.
> Th' Irish ar-re no good as servants be-
> cause they ar-re too good, I says. Th'
> Dutch ar-re no good because they ain't
> good enough. No matter how they start,
> they get th' noodle habit. I had wan
> wanst, an' she go an' she put noodles in
> me tay, I says. Th' Swedes ar-re all-
> right but they always get married th'
> sicond day. Ye'll have a polisman at th'
> dure with a warrant f'r th' arist in ye'er
> cook if ye hire a Boheemyan, I says.
> Coons'd be allright, but they're liable f'r

to hand ye ye're food in rag-time, an' if
ye ordher pork-chops f'r dinner, an' th'
hall is long, 'tis little ye'll have to eat
when th' platter's set down, I says.[18]

Another problem frequently discussed by American
homemakers was the general level of incompetence of their
servants. Although reared in homes, they seemed to know
nothing of the rudiments of good housekeeping. Their ignorance of the simplest kinds of work was both appalling
and astonishing. Practically every kind of food they
touched was ruined. Homemade bread from their ovens
would have made better paving material than hardened
brick. They fried beefsteak and saturated all other foods
with grease. Although always glad to take their money,
they only half-performed their part of the contract. In
short, servants often gave the "impression of being ungrateful, stupid, and a number of other things . . . ugly
and disagreeable."[19]
    Ungrateful, ugly, and disagreeable were but three
of many charges made about the temperament of domestics.
Collectively these accusations went by the name of tyranny--
"the tyranny of 'servant-galism' with which all housekeepers are familiar. They have learned by bitter experience
the folly of resistance, the hopelessness of any contest
with the autocrat of the kitchen, who, like Horace's hero,
if by no means 'impiger,' is at least 'iracundus, inex-
orabilis, acer.'"[20] Everywhere, so it was charged, servants grew more impudent, insubordinate, showy, idle, and
independent. Their behavior was so bad that in despair
families were seeking refuge in hotels and boarding houses.
Servants had become the lawgivers. The end result was
that in many instances the servant came to hold the domi-
nating position. Proving her point, one dismayed housewife related that in all her thirty-nine years of homemaking her cook had always been called Mary. Imagine the
shock, then, when one uppity maid objected and boldly
stated she preferred to be called "Miss [Rose] Mundy, if
you please. . . ." But as soon as Miss Mundy's new employer could recover her composure, the servant was told,
"Well Rose . . . I don't please. You'll never be called
miss in this house--not while I'm alive."[21]
    Another frequently cited shortcoming of domestic
workers was unreliability. Discontent led to instability.
The resulting tendency was a propensity for constant

change. Servants simply vanished without giving reason or warning. Invariably they departed at the very times they were most needed.[22]

Servants were terribly ungrateful. This was certainly unfair because most mistresses believed they had endeavored to be helpful, kindly, and thoughtful. But look what happened to homemakers who attempted to practice the credo of equality! Their servants were suspicious of their motives. Suspicion led to impudence which, in turn, left the employer no alternative but to discharge her spoiled help. Consider the kindly mistresses who provided their maids with large, airy rooms. What thanks did they receive--rooms in constant disarray unless inspected daily! Why some servants had the audacity to lock their doors for no reason but to conceal their untidiness! When it came to advising the help about their dress, reading habits, or friends, servants regarded the advice as impertinent. Domestics also rejected efforts to regulate their work. Certainly, employers believed, it was a totally untrue charge that they imposed more work when a spare hour or so had been secured through diligence. And of course it was a well-acknowledged practice for mistresses to pay for extra work, while at the same time seldom deducting wages for unfinished tasks, summer vacations, or sickness.[23]

Servants complained about their hours and thus, whenever possible, avoided domestic employment. They also disliked being called "servants" rather than "help." But how else could one who wore inharmonious shades of green, who knew nothing of the refined value of the taste of olives or grapefruit be regarded? Since they cared nothing for the homes in which they worked, their sole objective seemed to be doing the least work for the most pay in order to squander it on the most fashionable clothes. Wasn't it true servants ended up spending far more money on clothes than those for whom they worked?[24]

Despite all the faults attributed to servants, employers were not so self-righteous as to hold themselves totally above reproach. In fact, many realized that bad servants could very likely mean bad mistresses. "Perhaps, a few maxims, as applicable to the employer as to the employed, could be of service. They were as follows: 'Good masters make good servants,' and 'servants will not be diligent where the master's negligent,'. . . ."[25]

Early on in the history of service, Catherine Beecher had admonished homemakers in the United States to use more

patience, self-control, wisdom, and principle when dealing
with their employees. Likewise, she urged them not to be
fretful, exacting, or too hard to please. At all times
they should manage their children so that the youngsters
were not ungoverned and constant vexations to the help.
Work should never be so burdensome that no time or energy
was left for relaxation and care of personal matters, such
as a wardrobe.[26]

However wise such advice was, employers had a tendency to misrepresent their demands with respect to hours,
privileges, conditions, and even the number of family members. On top of this, employers demanded that their employees be more than human. A girl had to be strong,
neat, capable, quick, well-trained, nice-looking, good-
tempered, well-mannered, strictly sober, and chaste. She
was expected to take care of the rooms, cook, wait on the
table, use good judgment, skill, discretion, and practice
all the economies of the owner. Others were required to
wear a cap, belong to the family's church, and be religious. Did such people exist, especially in light of the
fact that the maid was "expected to consider herself a
menial?"[27]

Although Ida Tarbell attributed the problems in the
household to a lack of democracy, others were equally persuaded mistresses spoiled their servants. Thus one writer
exclaimed, "For Heaven's sake, do be mistresses in your
home!"[28] Clearly this was the mistress's right and responsibility as the educated and mature individual in the
employer-employee relationship. The mistress should be
the wiser and clearer thinker in their dealings, especially
considering the domestic's limited experience, antecedents,
and immaturity. In many ways servants were like little
children. If men had been in charge, they would long
ago have dealt squarely with the issues. A woman in
charge of her girls seldom had trouble. However, most
women "have compromised, we have become philanthropic
and sympathetic, and then we have of a sudden [sic] insisted on our rights, until even archangels would have left
us without a week's notice."[29]

In 1871 an unsigned New York Times editorial criti-
cized the city's employers for another unsound practice
when it wrote: "So long as there is a large mass of
housekeepers who will run in crowds after servants all
over the City, and who will take them without characters
and give them characters to which they are not entitled,

and who have the money to pay high wages . . . good servants, as a rule, cannot be looked for."[30] Servants had no need or no incentive to work hard or well. As long as the servant could secure a good reference, she would be able to find another position. This fact was especially true in light of the great demand for help. Only mistresses could alter this situation by changing the reference system. Until they were willing to do so, poor servants could only become worse and the good ones would only remain tolerable.[31]

Those who examined the problems of household labor realized that servants were not the only ones ignorant of domestic work. Many potential servants avoided service because they did not want to work for women who lacked understanding of the work that had to be done. Both employer and employee were in need of training. Until this was accomplished, domestic service could never be run on a professional basis. Until service was put on a professional basis, there would be no fixed requirements for admission to its ranks. As it was, "Some women made housekeeping a fine art, and some women permit[ted] it to lapse into a kind of protracted picnicking. In the one case it becomes something more; and in the other something less than a profession."[32]

The fact that domestic service was regarded as something less than a profession allowed mistresses to act capriciously. Because there were no standards, each employer was a law unto herself. She was free to impose her own standards, her own hours, and her own terms for the payment of wages. "In no other occupation in which so large a number of women is engaged does the employer have so much personal option."[33] Conditions such as these made servants the most discontented of all wage earners. Furthermore, as long as housekeeping continued to function in such a fashion, confusion and isolation would reign supreme.[34]

Capricious and individual behavior, confusion, isolation, lack of adequate training, and nonprofessionalism combined to prevent service from ever being run on business methods. This allowed employers to exploit young women (greenhorns) because they saw a chance to profit from the greenhorns' ignorance. As long as mistresses allowed these conditions to prevail, service work would never become truly honorable. Speaking to this issue, one turn-of-the-century writer said, "When we have made the service

of the hand in the kitchen as honorable as the service of
the hand with the typewriter, or the broom, or the counter,
or the piano, or the pen, then, and not till then, may we
expect to have ideal conditions of service, and not till
then can we expect young women of ability, of ambition
and power to enter the home for service as readily as they
now enter service in other departments of human labor."[35]

    Indicative of the lack of business methods in do-
mestic service was the absence of a custom of long contracts. This was not the case in England, where servants
were hired by the year or by the quarter. As a general
rule, American housewives did not have a large enough
sense of responsibility or active enough interest in the employee to use an extended contract. Few employers had
qualms, especially those in cities, about casually dismiss-
ing help when the summer vacation time rolled around.
Yet, as Charlotte Perkins Gilman commented, "We expect of
our house-servants that they be 'attached,' 'loyal,' 'faith-
ful,' 'respectful,' 'devoted,'. . . . Attachment is especially valued. If only we could still OWN them! Then
there would be that pleasant sense of permanence and security so painfully lacking in our modern house-service."[36]

    Here then was a long and impressive array of prob-
lems existent in the domestic/mistress relationship: general servant incompetence coupled with unfamiliarity with
American life-styles; servant tyranny and unreliability;
mistress misrepresentation of demands and expectations;
the spoiling of servants; the abuse of the personal reference system; mistress ignorance of domestic service; the
lack of business methods in the home, like the absence of
long contracts; and the capricious nature of mistress behavior. How could the American homemaker resolve these
issues so as to prevent the likelihood of servant unionization?

    Perhaps the oldest proposed solution to the foregoing
problems was paternalism. Paternalism in the home frequently went by the expression "Make them one of the family," or by called-for applications of the Golden Rule--
"Treat your servant as a member of the family, as an
equal." This call to the heart of sentimentalists was
thrilled by the humanism of Walt Whitman's homily that
said, "He that sweeps the walks and empties the cesspools,
To him do I give the family will and him do I greet as
brother."[37]

One of the earliest and most thorough espousers of this solution was Catherine Beecher. Appealing to the better nature of the homemaker, Beecher called upon employers to put themselves in the place of the domestic. In so doing, she believed the mistress would be less likely to expect any more of her servant than she would of herself. Here was a way for the woman to cultivate a habit of regarding her help with forbearance and sympathy, as much as she would wish for herself or her own daughter. The more unfortunate the circumstances of the domestic's background, the greater the claim there was for compassionate forbearance. "They ought ever to be looked upon, not as the mere ministers to our comfort and convenience, but as the humbler and more neglected children of our Heavenly Father, whom he has sent to claim our sympathy and aid."[38]

A way to further enhance the life of the servant was for the mistress to take the necessary pains required to make the residence of the domestic agreeable to her. She should endeavor to attach the servant to her family through the cultivation of affection and gratitude. Few employers who pursued such a course of action had difficulty in finding or keeping good, steady help. Their domestics had no reason to leave for the simple reason that they knew they could not better their existence. The servants' realization of this went beyond the mere existence of good food, comfortable rooms, presents, and privileges. Real, true attachment resulted from expressions of benevolent and friendly concern over servant comfort and improvement. This concern should incorporate a vast gamut of matters, including the wise supervision of social and leisure activities; instruction in the skills necessary to make and properly care for clothes; guarding the servants' health; supplying the servants with proper reading material; and, if necessary, teaching them to read. In short, the mistresses' function was similar to that of a parent. When this is done, "They grow to love her and to kiss the hem of her garments." And in the end "The mistress will not receive an eye-service, a perfunctory service, a mechanical service, but a real service."[39]

Beecher also discussed the common resentment domestics felt against the label "servant." While granting the need for allowance and consideration on this issue, Catherine Beecher believed the origin of this problem was the fact that from their earliest years children were trained to abhor the idea of servitude as applied to themselves.

It was believed the greatest of all possible degradations and shames. The very term "servant" and its duties harkened to many minds the label "slave." In other words more than simple pride was involved in the application of the word "servant." Yet granting the origin of the problem, Beecher went on to advocate the necessity of educating the domestic in the value of labor. All labor was worthwhile, regardless of its kind and regardless of what class performed it.[40]

Another important aspect of the paternalistic solution was its method of dealing with domestic deficiencies in the performance of household duties. Because of servant origins and class, many of them had never been properly trained to perform domestic work. How unreasonable, then, to expect work to be properly done. Great patience and benevolence was called for in this respect. Proper methods needed to be demonstrated by going round with the novice on her first days and repeating correct methods over and over again. This was a skill built on the great Christian principles of patience and meekness, not on excessive faultfinding and criticism. After all, it should be remembered that one of the duties of the mistress--by reason of her greater intelligence--was to aid her less fortunate sister. "A servant may be stupid, yes, but after all, stupidity is a misfortune: not a crime. It rests with those who have intelligence to give a hand to those who are less gifted."[41]

Maternal benevolence advocated by Catherine Beecher and others could serve purposes beyond that of resolving domestic/mistress problems. Certainly if the employment of servants could fulfill many social purposes, it could also fulfill psychological ones. In fact, not all mistress/servant love was maternal. Some evidence indicates women were concerned for one another within the mutual bonds of womanhood. Other lonely women might have been seeking a platonic companionship.[42] In neither case was the objective really achieved. The cultural, class, ethnic, religious and, even more so, racial discrepancies were too expansive to bridge. Beyond all of the above was the overriding basis of the relationship--the work relationship of employer and employee.[43]

If paternalism as a panacea possessed considerable longevity, so too did the belief that education would lessen the woes of servant and mistress. In fact, the two overlapped each other in the early years. One author main-

tained that mistress and servant could and should learn
together and from each other. If the mistress ceased to be
a mere criticizing onlooker, this would act as a tremendous
encouragement to the learning domestic. The key was to
establish a give and take--the natural and spontaneous
giving of mutual assistance and exchange of courteous
acts. On the other hand, what better place than the
American home for those new to democratic life to learn
how they could function as free, independent individuals?
Was this not one of the highest functions of the American
homemaker? Was this not a most compelling reason for the
homemaker to develop her business to the highest possible
level?[44]

The new approach to housework, tied as it was to
the professionalization of motherhood, had its tenuous roots
during the last quarter of the nineteenth century. It began
with the establishment of a few cooking schools in large
American cities, with marketing and recipes in the columns
of women's magazines, and with some midwestern universities offering home economics courses. By the turn of the
twentieth century, these efforts gathered momentum into
something of an evangelical movement. Home economics,
more commonly called "domestic science," was its name.
Now women's organizations established courses, even entire
schools, to teach cooking, budget making, marketing, nutri-
tion, and the efficient use of household appliances. Publication of new journals like Domestic Science Monthly began.
One fifth of all public high schools offered home economics
courses by 1917. Some two hundred universities and col-
leges taught 18,000 students this new discipline. Also the
American Home Economics Association was created as a national body designed to coordinate various proliferating
activities. Finally, the Smith-Hughes Act (1917) was
passed. Smith-Hughes included housekeeping education in
its vocational appropriations to the Office of Education.
Along with this, the U.S. Congress approved the new subject by defining "homemaking" as a basic vocation for
women. Little wonder popular public opinion held "that
schools for the training of domestic servants would do
more than anything else to solve the domestic service
problem."[45]

But long before this movement was under way, popular writers and reformers were arguing the various virtues
of education. For example, "Education or training is the
first step in raising a workman in esteem,"[46] and "the

spirit of the times, the sentiment of the trades-unions, the opinion of the employers, [were] all in the same direction--that more education and more training [was] necessary. . . ."[47] YWCAs were in the forefront of a like-minded philosophy. First established in 1866 in Boston, the Young Women's Christian Association soon had chapters in virtually every American metropolis. Among their many goals was that of aiding young girls in their search for respectable employment. For the Y, this usually meant some form of domestic service. One way of achieving this objective of respectable employment was to offer the necessary training classes. This the nation's Ys did.[48]

Like paternalism, training or education fell short of the desired goals. One reason for this failure was that in many instances only half of the women ignorant of housework were educated. If training for servants was necessary, it was equally essential for many mistresses. Reform, stressed one writer, must come from above and below. No one versed in the problems of the mistress/servant relationship could deny the need of trained servants, but even more than trained servants America needed trained mistresses. Not only would this bring about a vast improvement between the two, it would give the employer a general respect and appreciation for service work. Then the mistress would be able to put aside individual conceptions of domestic labor and enter into agreement with her employee. "When a little professional interest has been imbued into both mistress and maid there will be less problems. After all, housekeeping is a profession; good living is an art; why should we beggar it so?"[49]

The most important reason training schools failed to resolve the problems of domestic service was because servants refused to attend. Many believed training was a waste of time. "I can get just as good without it. Shure, now, why should I be l'arnin' when I kin shove me oar in anywhere and get a good job."[50] Others were certain that if they knew more, more would be expected of them, although their pay would remain the same. But the fundamental problem of the numerous training institutions was that the schools did not meet the needs of the servants. In one random examination of a half-dozen training school announcements, no courses could be completed in a reasonable period of time. Courses such as "household values, chemistry of cooking, bacteriology, and food manufacture" held little value or appeal to the semi-literate, illiterate,

or non-English-speaking woman. The failure of training
schools like the Woman's Educational and Industrial Union
in Boston, the Woman's Domestic Guild of New York, and
the Girl's Union of San Francisco testifies to the fact that
servants' educational needs were not being met.[51]

Closely related to the professionalization of motherhood and housework and their emphasis on training or
education was the goal of making housework a business.
One of the basic principles of this new solution was to
show how very faulty the older concepts of paternalism
were. Perhaps better than any other advocate of reform
Lucy Maynard Salmon contrasted the old concept with the
new one. Salmon strongly believed considerable confusion
existed in the understanding of the terms "paternalism"
and "democracy." Mutually constructive and active relationships developed from democracy, while paternalism forced
one side of the mistress/servant relationship to be receptive and passive. "With all its benevolence of aspect and
of demeanor, paternalism is often but a guise of an uncon-
trolled love of power and of authority that seeks an outlet for itself rather than the real welfare of the object of
its apparent solicitude. Democracy and paternalism are
mutually exclusive, as are democracy and love of authority." For Salmon, then, no improvement in the affairs of
the household could come before attitudes of mind underwent
a radical change.[52]

An essential part of this radical change of mind
dealt with the attempted inclusion of the domestic employee
into the family. This inclusion was impossible. Furthermore, in all the history of service work there had never
been anything more than a semblance of such a relationship. Now even that semblance was gone! The servants
came and went, but the family unit lived on without them.
Obviously the domestic was not essential to the family. In
fact, the domestic may have contributed somewhat to the
destruction of family integrity. This was possible because
"family life presupposes the existence of congenial tastes
and sympathetic relationships. It argues nothing against
domestic service as an occupation that those engaged in it
are rarely those who would be chosen as life companions
or even as temporary companions by those with whom the
accident of occupation has thrown them."[53]

Clearly the answer was to stop pretending that domestic service and the servant/mistress relationship were
something they were not. The answer was to admit the

basic commercial spirit of Americans and realize that the
relationship between maid and mistress was, before all
else, a money relation. In order to bring the servant
question out of the dark and into the light, all had to
admit that the governing principles were not those of Christian charity or poetic sentiment. The governing principles
were the love of gain and independence: straight business
principles. All other labor relationships had come to this
recognition. It was time for woman's work, housework, to
cease being the economic cipher.[54]

Authors discerned several factors forcing domestic
service to establish itself on business principles. First
was a reported "revolt" of servants--a movement developing
in the household similar to the labor movement as a whole.
Second was the development of domestic science. Related
to this were the rising standards for domestic work, such
as specialization. Third, other nations, especially those
in Europe, were far ahead of the United States in establishing business methods. Although in social status the
European domestic was behind the American, industrially
she was recognized as an economic unit. She was protected through the implementation of service books, courts
of domestic service, and certificates of excellence. Fourth,
domestic service was way behind other economic enterprises
in adapting itself to the new business principles. And
fifth, because domestic service remained behind the times,
other industrial employments were opening up to women and
drawing more and more of them away from service occupations. Thus, summed up one writer, "Incorporating the
household on a business basis is the only intelligent solution of the problem. Factory and office regulations must
eventually take the place of the present confusion in the
home. Capitalists, large manufacturers and employers of
the working class in general have found it to their ultimate
advantage to meet the just complaints of their employees in
some such equitable compromise. Why should the plan not
work equally well at home?"[55]

Numerous private and philanthropic organizations
jumped aboard the "housework on a business basis" band-
wagon. Under its auspices the Young Women's Christian
Association issued a number of publications advocating that
employers should operate their households on business principles. Work was to be systematized, hours were to be
regulated, and the worker was to be granted adequate
time and freedom so as to live a normal social and family

life. Educators and girls would work together to meet the
demand for trained service. Likewise, the Phillis Wheatley
Association of Cleveland, Ohio, began pushing for some
definite standards. The association would establish standards and send domestics out to homes only if the employers agreed to them. In 1919 the U.S. Employment Service
began a seven-week experiment designed to see if housework could be adapted to a regular business work day--
eight hours. Private funding allowed for the completion
of the last four weeks because the government cut off funds
after only three weeks. Earlier, in August of 1903, the
Domestic Economy Committee of the Woman's Educational
Association of Boston created a Household Aid Company.
Its stated objective was "to bring together the housekeeper
and the household worker on a business basis that shall
be satisfactory to both."[56] Finally, in cooperation with
the Central Branch of the YWCA in New York City, a group
of prominent women, spurred by the publication of C. Helené
Barker's book, Wanted, A Young Woman to Do Housework,
founded the Home Assistants Committee. It, too, desired to
recruit workers for homes that would be run and organized
on a businesslike basis.[57]

Extending over a forty-some-year period, advocates
of business methods in the home offered a wide variety of
points in their programs. Almost invariably, they agreed
on at least one ingredient: the relationship of mistress
and servant should be placed on a business basis. Generally most agreed that a definition of a day's work should
be determined and mutually understood. Usually this point
incorporated a restriction on hours. The actual number of
hours proposed varied over the years. Many also advocated a written contract. While domestics continued to live
in, it was believed business terms should include decent
accommodations and food. Offensive aspects of service life
like livery and tips were to be eliminated. Some stressed
the importance of guest privileges and meeting places other
than the kitchen. Additional aspects of the business relationship varied from the specialization of tasks to a reduction in the work load to an increase in salary; all wages,
including overtime, should be paid in cash. Days off,
vacations, and holidays were other issues sometimes addressed by reformers.[58]

The diversity of objectives and the extended time
period that encompassed the business-methods-in-the-home
philosophy allowed reformers to isolate ways to structure

the mistress/servant relationship on a business basis. Two
important examples of this isolation process were proposals
to move either the work or the worker out of the employer's
home. This second alternative, believed Jane Addams,
would eliminate the "servant" attitude from the household
industry. The female domestic was just as entitled to a
full social and home life as the male window washer working in an office building. In fact, some writers were
quick to point out that certain workers were already operating under such a system. A prime example was the
female post-office clerk. But an even more important illus-
tration was the black servant woman. "Southern ladies
will possibly be shocked at the suggestion that the unreliable colored servant girls are working for the progress
of society." Yet in reality they were the makers of a
quiet revolution for "the colored servant's dislike to live
[sic] in the house of the employer (and perhaps the employer's dislike to have her live there) are progressive
forces for which the destruction of this old custom and the
strongest impetus is given to a normal regulation of the
hours of labor; and the strongest foundation of the master's despotism, which extends over and beyond the working-
hours, is destroyed thereby."[59]
     This single change in the residential patterns of
the domestic would bring about a geometric rather than an
arithmetic step in achieving the implementation of business
practices in the home. Here, in one swoop, was a way to
regularize hours, destroy medieval relationships, and upgrade the quality of servants. Surely, if all of these
goals were accomplished, the better sort of woman would
be attracted to service work.[60]
     The other important example of restructuring in the
home to implement business methods--moving the work out
of the home--had been under way since the late nineteenth
century.[61] A humorous reflection of this transformation's
meaning for the American housewife was revealed in the
following college song and its revision:

Original

> Can you brew, can you bake
> Good bread and cake?
>   Before my love I utter.
> Can you sew a seam?

Can you churn the cream
    And bring in the golden butter?
What use is refraction?
Chemical reaction, biologic protoplasm,
Psychologic microcosm?

Would you be my weal,
You must cook the meal--

You shake your head--
You I'll not wed--
And so, Farewell!

Revised

Are you up on the pure food laws affecting the
    manufacture of canned soup?
Can you assure me that you know the conditions
    governing the sanitary production of pastry?
Can you bring enough influence to bear on
    public opinion so that the family clothing
    will not have to be made in a sweatshop?
Do you know how to get honest Government
    inspectors appointed, to assure the purity of
    the milk and butter you promise to serve me?

What use is knowing
Everything of sewing,
All of pickling and preserving
All of washing and serving?

Would you be my weal,
Do not cook the meal,--

You shake your head,--
You I'll not wed,--
And so, Farewell![62]

    In accordance with such sentiments, reformers of
various shapes pushed for the removal of more and more
tasks from the home. These tasks included cooking, baking, window washing, carpet cleaning, rug beating, child
and sick care as well as the more routine daily duties
like dusting, lamp trimming, and dish washing. Invariably these functions were to be subsumed by cooperative

kitchens, public laundries, hospitals, public nurseries, and kindergartens. In some cases it was proposed that individual family members be held responsible for their own rooms, and that hired specialists should enter the home to perform only those functions that could not be done outside it. "That which remains," wrote one author, "will be performed by persons no longer servants, but persons trained to do well, specific things, and having, therefore, the independence and self-respect of the professional class. Much of beauty and excellence there was in the old relation at its best, but in the new relations there will be a new excellence, and that fairest, as it is also the latest and the rarest, product of social evolution--justice."[63]

The most thorough, articulate, and radical advocate of this line of thinking was Charlotte Perkins Gilman. As a result of her contention that all female roles derived from woman's sexual functions, Gilman argued that true freedom could be achieved only when women gained economic equality with men. Gilman argued that this could not occur so long as the home remained the sole domain of women. Society had, therefore, to evolve mechanisms that would allow every individual to cultivate his or her potential. From such a premise Gilman's solution was clear: all women, married and single, needed to work not at home but outside it. In order for married women to begin paying jobs, Gilman proposed to totally reorganize the traditional home. Domestic cooking was to be abolished along with housework and much of domestic child rearing. The old individual family home would be abandoned. The services it once performed were to be done in rows and blocks of professional catering, cleaning, and nursery facilities.[64]

Except for proposals to make the servant one of the family, no program to inhibit the rise of domestic unions through reform was more comprehensive than welfare capitalism. And although welfare capitalism reflected the new trends and tendencies of the early twentieth century--organization, rationalization, and cooperation in industry--no plans except the oldest and the newest were more akin to each other. Like its early predecessor, welfare capitalism, stripped of all the verbiage attached to it, was at its very core nothing but paternalism.[65]

A working framework of the various ingredients that came to constitute welfare capitalism were put forth in September 1915 in the Colorado Industrial Plan or the

Rockefeller Plan. Proposed for Rockefeller's Colorado Fuel
& Iron Company, the plan resembled company unionism, or
industrial democracy, as it had been first introduced at
the Philadelphia Rapid Transit Company in 1911 and at
the Packard Piano Company in 1912. Implicit in the diversity of these companies was the awareness that the basic
concepts of welfare capitalism were broad and all-encom-
passing enough to embrace a wide spectrum of occupations.
Included among those essential ideas labeled "welfare capitalism" were the undesirability and eradicability of conflict, human understanding through improved communication, and harmony of interests in shop and community.
The earlier Christian ethic in human relations was gradually phased out and replaced by a type of group psychother-
apy. As one prominent labor historian has written, Christ
was replaced by Freud.[66]
        In accord with these essential ideas, various plans
of welfare capitalism were devised by specific industries.
But however varied the plans, they shared many common
characteristics. These included the following more specific
terms: management structure with respect to labor relations, employee organization, hours of work, welfare, and
wage determination. Uniquely both the general ideas and
more specific terms of welfare capitalism were adaptable to
the home.
        In line with the idea that conflict was undesirable
and eradicable, mistresses formed management structures in
the home to deal with their servants. Both home and industrial managers believed this kind of initiative and
structure should be imposed from the top down.[67] Such an
example was that of Mrs. Richard Boardman. Living in a
New Jersey suburb in 1915, Boardman determined to place
her own household system on a higher plane. She therefore
adopted the role of a household engineer and replaced the
careless house servant with someone she labeled a "home
assistant." When the Boardman family moved to New York
City, Mrs. Boardman found her system very adaptable to
apartment life. Maintaining her position as a professional
household efficiency engineer, Boardman established a type
of placement bureau for employers and employees in agreement with her concepts. Likewise, in 1920 club women in
numerous eastern cities came together under the National
Civic Federation for the purpose of organizing interclub
employment bureaus. A Boston survivor of this plan placed
all types of women in various occupations. The maids the

federation placed lived at home, in boarding houses, or at
the Young Women's Christian Association. The Boston organizer established regular hours for the women for whom
she found work. Hours included one thirty-minute lunch
period for each working day. Each worker provided her
own food or paid her employer thirty cents a meal if it
was supplied. Every day the worker prepared a report
specifying her hours of arrival and departure and a log
of the work completed. Wages varied according to job
type and skill.[68]

As was the case for its industrial counterpart, the
goal of welfare capitalism in the home was to promote
human understanding. Once again the direction and course
were to come from the top down because "it is not sufficient that we should think well of our maids; they must
also think well of us, and for this we are alone responsible."[69] Thus it was the responsibility of the mistress to
open channels of communication. One way to open channels
was to make the worker feel that she shared in the plans
and responsiblties of the employer. This might be achieved
by discussing the grocery and gas bills as well as the
general business of housekeeping. Equally important was
the need to establish personal contact and personal interest in the maid. Unlike the old mentality of making her a
part of the family, the new thrust was based on the most
businesslike of attitudes. This new business attitude was,
therefore, not a sentimental or curious one. Instead, it
was a healthy, respectful recognition of the maid as an
individual with personal aspirations. In short, the new
business attitude was based on a genuine interest in her
as a human being. In fact, it was the "practical application of the psychology of handling maids."[70]

Such businesslike techniques lessened the likelihood
of conflict, promoted human understanding, and improved
the channels of communications. All of the above could be
further enhanced through open and frank discussions about
the conditions of employment. At all times the mistress
and servant should give reasonable consideration to each
other's wants and needs. It should be recognized that
servants are working at a trade. Consequently they should
be paid by the hour, supplied with the best labor-saving
devices, and have their duties clearly defined prior to
their employment. Capricious behavior was no longer a
part of the mistress/servant relationship. All talk of employer social superiority was to be eliminated. Furthermore,

all business objectives were best achieved through the implementation of scientific management. Scientific management principles were the best vehicle to promote a harmony of interest between the mistress and servant. Now Katy would be motivated to do more work at a higher standard for a bonus. The end product would benefit both employer and employee, whereas before only the employer gained.[71]

The highly individualized nature of domestic service prohibited the formation of anything even resembling company unions. Consequently the only type of collective activity fostered by the mistress was the social club. In this sense servant clubs were one dimension of the household version of social welfare. Clubs were intended to provide the servant access to a normal social life. Such facilities might house a library, a parlor where educational classes could be held, a reading room, and recreational equipment. In all of this, the mistress was encouraged to assume an active interest. If clubs were not established, the employer would attempt what he or she could by way of intellectual stimulation.[72] Other ingredients of welfare like vacations, sick pay, bonuses, and long continuance were entirely in the hands of the individual employer.[73]

In the wake of radicalism and labor unrest in the post–World War I world, a conference of engineers, economists, and employers was held to determine the causes and solutions of the national labor crisis. Professor Irving Fisher of Yale University drew up a list of seven basic "instincts" common to humanity. Under proper guidance Fisher held these "instincts" were as applicable to the home as to the factory. By carefully examining the following list authored by Professor Fisher, one can easily see how they reflect the concepts included in welfare capitalism:

1. The instinct of self–preservation. This demands not only living–wages, but healthy working conditions and the lightening of drudgery wherever possible.
2. The instinct of workmanship. Pride and joy in individual creation, and personal expression through one's work; good work must have scope and be rewarded by praise and recognition.
3. The instinct of self–respect. This is encouraged by treating people as individuals, giving them credit in advance for skill and trustworthiness, and, in the

home, abolishing the false notions of social caste that
are still prevalent in domestic service.
4. The instinct of loyalty. This is based on justice, mutual consideration, respect of other's [sic] people's
rights and wishes, putting extra effort on a volunteer
basis, and putting oneself in another's place generally.
5. The instinct of play. All work and no play makes
Katie a dull girl--and probably a Bolshevik.
6. The instinct of love. In industry it is now recognized
that the worker reflects his family life in output. Domestic service is undertaken by so many women working
to keep a home or a family together that this must be
considered.
7. The instinct of worship. This finds an outlet, not
merely in opportunities for church-going but in ideal-
ism, humanity and the spirit of service. Every man
and woman has something in the way of religion though
it be vaguely formulated, and this, given as an opportunity, will be reflected in his or her daily work.[74]

Precisely how much mistresses' attitudes about service work and their solutions to its problems contributed
to the failure of unionization is virtually impossible to determine. But to the degree that one of their major objectives was to retain absolute control over their homes and
their servants, they largely prevailed. Beginning with a
paternalistic mentality, and returning to it (perhaps never
abandoning it), they seldom encouraged a spirit of self-
respect, self-reliance, or independence in those who toiled
on their behalf. Perhaps in that respect they were more
successful than they might ever have imagined!

NOTES

1. Charlotte Perkins Gilman, The Home: Its Work
and Influence (New York: McClure, Phillips, 1903), p. 223.
2. Ibid., pp. 121-22; C. Helené Barker, Wanted, a
Young Woman to Do Housework (New York: Moffat, Yard,
1915), pp. 2-3; Helen Campbell, Prisoners of Poverty:
Women Wage-Workers, Their Trades and Their Lives (Boston:
Roberts Brothers, 1887; repr. ed., Westport, Conn.: Greenwood Press, 1970), pp. 229-230; and Christina Goodwin,
"An Appeal to Housekeepers," Forum, August 1895, p. 755.

3. "Below Stairs: Master's Problems," Literary Digest, July 10, 1937, p. 22; Frank Crane, "How Do You Get Along with Your Hired Girl?" American Magazine, October 1924, p. 61; Mary Roberts Smith, "Domestic Service: The Responsibility of Employers," Forum, August 1899, pp. 688–89; A Mere Man, "The Servant Question," Woman's Home Companion, October 1911, p. 74; and Annie Nathan Meyer, ed., Woman's Work in America (New York: Henry Holt, 1891), p. iv.

4. Christine Frederick, "The New Housekeeping," Ladies Home Journal, December 1912, p. 16.

5. Annie L. Vrooman, "Social Evolution of the Servant Question," Arena, June 1901, p. 645.

6. Mary Anderson, "Domestic Service in the United States," Journal of Home Economics 20 (January 1928):9.

7. "The Appeal to Women," Harper's Weekly, October 18, 1902, pp. 1506–7; and "A Servant Employer's Union," New York Times, 23 August 1901, p. 1. Also consult the Chicago Tribune, 28 July and 23 August 1901.

8. Marion Harland, "One Housewife's Protest," Independent, March 6, 1902, p. 564.

9. Kate Gannett Wells, "The Servant Girl of the Future," North American Review 157 (December 1893):719; Inez A. Godman, "A Nine-Hour Day for Domestic Servants," Independent, February 13, 1902, p. 398; Jane Seymour Klink, "Put Yourself in Her Place," Atlantic Monthly, February 1905, pp. 170–71; Edith J. R. Isaacs, "My Servants and Yours," Delineator, November 1911, p. 380; Sara J. Wardel, "Who'll Wash the Dishes?," New Outlook and Independent, January 30, 1929, pp. 170, 200.

10. "A Servant Girl's Trade Union," New York Times, 17 March 1873, p. 4.

11. Judith Alden, "Help!" Literary Digest, September 11, 1937, p. 18.

12. Juliet Everts Robb, "Our House in Order," Outlook, June 18, 1910, p. 356.

13. Frances M. Abbott, "How to Solve the Housekeeping Problem," Forum and Century, February 1893, pp. 784–85; Barker, Wanted, a Young Woman to Do Housework, pp. 4, 11–12, 14; and Catherine Beecher, A Treatise on Domestic Economy (New York: Marsh, Capen, Lyon, and Webb, 1841; repr. ed., New York: Schocken Books, 1977; Studies in the Life of Women), p. 197.

14. Roy L. McCardell, "Help! Help! Help!" Everybody's Magazine, October 1906, p. 480.

15.   Josephine Daskam Bacon, "We and Our Servants," American Magazine, February 1907, p. 355; "Below Stairs," p. 21; Harris Dickson, "Help! Help! Help!: The Bogy That Darkens the Sun of Southern Domesticity," Delineator, July 1912, pp. 66–67; Walter L. Fleming, "The Servant Problem in the Black Belt," Sewannee Review 12 (January 1905):13.

16.   "Below Stairs," p. 21; and Goldwin Smith, "The Passing of the Household," Independent, August 24, 1905, p. 424.

17.   Bacon, "We and Our Servants," p. 355; Robert Ernst, Immigrant Life in New York City 1825–1863 (New York: King's Crown Press, Columbia University, 1949), pp. 66–67; Annie Payson Call, "The Spoiling of Servants," Century Magazine, April 1913, p. 917; and "Report" by Mr. Francis Clare Ford on the Condition of the Industrial Classes in the United States, December 31, 1869, in Great Britain, Foreign Office, Reports from Her Majesty's Diplomatic and Consular Agents Abroad respecting the Condition of the Industrial Classes in Foreign Countries, 1870 (London, 1870), pp. 317–18, quoted in Edith Abbott, ed., Historical Aspects of the Immigration Problem: Select Documents (Chicago: University of Chicago Press, 1926), p. 385.

18.   Finley Peter Dunne, "Mr. Dooley on the Servant Problem," Harper's Weekly, February 17, 1900, p. 160.

19.   Walt Mason, "The Dearth of Damsels," Colliers: The National Weekly, August 7, 1915, p. 26; and Augusta Kortrecht, "Put Yourself in Her Place," Good Housekeeping, November 1910, p. 588.

20.   "Kitchen vs. Parlor," New York Times, 29 November 1872, p. 4.

21.   "Domestic Servants," New York Times, 15 December 1872, p. 5; Amelia E. Barr, "The Servant-Girl's Point of View," North American Review 154 (June 1892):729; Elizabeth Frazier, "The Servant Problem," Saturday Evening Post, February 25, 1928, p. 10; Christine Terhune Herrick, "Duties of the Maid of All Work," Harper's Bazaar, November 1904, p. 1116; and M. E. W. Sherwood, "The Lack of Good Servants," North American Review 153 (November 1891): 546.

22.   Beecher, A Treatise on Domestic Economy, pp. 198–99; "Who Is More to Blame: Servant or Mistress?" Ladies Home Journal, January 1909, p. 3.

23.   Ibid.; Annie Payson Call, "The Spoiling of Servants," p. 917; and Christine Terhune Herrick, "The Other Side of the Shield," North American Review 164 (April 1897):510.

24. Klink, "Put Yourself," pp. 169–70, 173; "Mistress and Servant," Living Age, January 15, 1898, p. 213; Isaacs, "My Servants and Yours," p. 380; (Mrs.) S. W. Mead, "Home Life, Not Business," Outlook, September 14, 1912, p. 71.

25. "Servants," New York Times, 10 September 1871, p. 3.

26. Beecher, A Treatise on Domestic Economy, pp. 196–97, 199.

27. Wright, "Why We Have Trouble with Our Servants," p. 22; Crane, "How Do You Get Along?" p. 61; Bolton Hall, "The Servant Class on the Farm and in the Slums," Arena, September 1898, p. 374; and Frances A. Kellor, Out of Work: A Study of Employment Agencies: Their Treatment of the Unemployed, and Their Influence Upon Homes and Business (New York: G. P. Putnam's Sons, 1905), pp. 110–11.

28. M. A. Tyrell, "Fear in the Home and the Household," Nineteenth Century and After, March 1908, p. 450.

29. Ida M. Tarbell, "The Woman and Democracy," American Magazine, June 1912, pp. 217–18; Call, "The Spoiling of Servants," p. 915; and Wells, "Servant Girl," pp. 716, 721.

30. "Housekeepers and Servants," New York Times, 15 October 1871, p. 4.

31. Herrick, "Other Side," pp. 511–12; and Sherwood, "The Lack," p. 553.

32. Wright, "Why We Have Trouble with Our Servants," p. 22; "Below Stairs," p. 22; Helen Ester March, "A School for Housemaids," Journal of Home Economics 7 (October 1915):37; and McCracken, "The Problem: From the Standpoint of the Employer," p. 372.

33. Smith, "Domestic Service," p. 684.

34. "Mistress and Servant," p. 213; Wells, "Servant Girl," p. 719; Fleming, "The Servant Problem in the Black Belt," pp. 14–15; Robb, "Our House in Order," p. 357; Klink, "The Housekeeper's Responsibility," p. 372; and ibid., "Put Yourself," p. 172.

35. Charles M. Sheldon, "Servant and Mistress," Independent, December 20, 1900, p. 21; Barr, "Servant Girl's," p. 731; Martha McCullock-Williams, "The Logic of the Servant Problem," Harper's Bazaar, November 1908, p. 1146; Lucy Maynard Salmon, Progress in the Household (Boston: Houghton Mifflin, 1906), pp. 28–29; ibid., "Democracy in the Household," American Journal of Sociology

17 (January 1912):442; and ibid., "Recent Progress in the Study of Domestic Service," Atlantic Monthly, November 1905, p. 634.

36. Kellor, "The Housewife and Her Helper," June 1907, p. 30; and Gilman, The Home, p. 109.

37. Quoted in I. M. Rubinow and Daniel Durant, "The Death and Breadth of the Servant Problem," McClure's Magazine, March 1910, p. 581.

38. Beecher, A Treatise of Domestic Economy, pp. 197–98, 206. An opposing view maintained that such acts of kindness were all too often misunderstood and one-sided for "the better you use them, the worse they treat you. . . ." See "Servant Girls," New York Times, 6 December 1872, p. 5.

39. Beecher, A Treatise on Domestic Economy, pp. 199–200; Isabel Kimball Whiting, "The General Housework Employee," Outlook, August 15, 1908, p. 851; and Sherwood, "The Lack," p. 554.

40. Beecher, A Treatise on Domestic Economy, p. 201.

41. "Who Is More to Blame," p. 3; Beecher, A Treatise on Domestic Economy, pp. 203–5; Crane, "How Do You Get Along," p. 168; Goodwin, "An Appeal," pp. 757–59; and Kortrecht, "Put Yourself in Her Place," p. 589.

42. This need and the search for maternal and/or womanly love was best discussed in a seminal article by Carroll Smith-Rosenberg. See "The Female World of Love and Ritual: Relations between Women in Nineteenth-Century America," Signs: Journal of Women in Culture and Society 1 (Autumn 1975):1–29.

43. Anne Ellis, The Life of an Ordinary Woman (Boston: Houghton Mifflin, 1929), pp. 58–59; Katzman in Seven Days a Week, pp. 156–59, 161–63, 199, 200–201.

44. Tyrell, "Fear," pp. 451–52; and Ida M. Tarbell, "Social Standing of Our Houseworkers," Ladies Home Journal, March 1913, p. 26.

45. Salmon, Progress in the Household, p. 67; and Peter Gabriel Filene, Him/Her/Self: Sex Roles in Modern America (New York: Harcourt, Brace, Jovanovich, 1974; Mentor Books, 1976), pp. 41–42.

46. Abbottt, "How to Solve," p. 786.

47. Klink, "The Housekeeper's Responsibility," pp. 376–77.

48. Sheila M. Rothman, Woman's Proper Place: A History of Changing Ideals and Practices, 1870 to the Present (New York: Basic Books, 1978), pp. 75–76. Typical of the national pattern was the Cleveland, Ohio, YWCA

chapter. Consult Unbound Records, 1878–1908, Container 1, Folder 1, YWCA, Cleveland, Ohio, Western Reserve Historical Society, Cleveland, Ohio. Hereafter referred to as the Cleveland Y Papers.

49. "The Visiting Housekeeper," Good Housekeeping, March 1911, p. 342; "An Unsettled Question," Outlook: A Family Paper, July 7, 1894, pp. 59–60; Eugenia Wallace, "The Servant and the New Democracy," North American Review 212 (October 1920):539–40; Campbell, Prisoners of Poverty, pp. 237–38; Goodwin, "An Appeal," p. 755; Klink, "Put Yourself," p. 174; Sherwood, "The Lack," pp. 551–52; and Whiting, "The General Housework Employee," p. 854.

50. Kellor, Out of Work, p. 130.

51. Ibid., pp. 130–32; Lillian R. Matthews, Women Trade Unions in San Francisco, University of California Publications in Economics, no. 3 (Berkeley, Calif.: University of California, 1913), p. 5; and U.S. Industrial Commission Report, 18 vols., "Domestic Service" by Gail Laughlin, vol. 14 (Washington, D.C.: Government Printing Office, 1900–1902), pp. 761–62.

52. Salmon, "Democracy in the Household," pp. 456–57; and Progress in the Household, pp. 98–99.

53. Ibid., pp. 113–14.

54. Flora McDonald Thompson, "The Servant Question," Cosmopolitan: A Monthly Illustrated Magazine, March 1900, pp. 521–22.

55. Wardel, "Who'll Wash the Dishes?" p. 170; Campbell, Prisoners of Poverty, p. 241; Izola Forrester, "The Girl Problem," Good Housekeeping, September 1912, p. 380; "Nine-Hour Day for Domestic Help," Literary Digest, April 12, 1919, p. 123; Alden W. Quimby, "Housekeeper's Stone," Forum and Century, June 1901, p. 456; I. M. Rubinow, "The Problem of Domestic Service," Journal of Political Economy 14 (October 1906):517.

56. Priscilla Leonard, "Boston Housework Experiment," Harper's Bazaar, March 1905, p. 225.

57. "The Seven Weeks Experiment by the Committee on Household Assistants," Journal of Home Economics 2 (December 1919):548–53; Anderson, "Domestic Service in the United States," p. 8; and PWA Papers, 1 February 1926, Container 8, Folder 20.

58. Barr, "Servant-Girls," p. 732; Campbell, Prisoners of Poverty, pp. 239–40; Christine Frederick, "Why Should Our Servants Live with Us?" Ladies Home Journal, October 1915, p. 98; Caroline L. Hunt, "More Life for the Household Employee," Chautauquan, January 1903, pp. 392–96.

59. Addams, "A Belated Industry," _American Journal of Sociology_ 1 (March 1896):540–41; Rubinow, "The Problem of Domestic Service," p. 515; ibid., "Household Service as a Labor Problem," _Journal of Home Economics_ 3 (April 1911): 138–39; and _The Spectator_, July 16, 1892, p. 92.

60. Rubinow, "Household Service as a Labor Problem," p. 138; and ibid., "The Problem of Domestic Service," p. 515.

61. Some of the literature discussing this movement includes Filene, _Him/Her/Self_, Chapter 1; Rothman, _Woman's Proper Place_, pp. 14–21. Consult all of the following by Rose Schwartz Cowan: "The 'Industrial Revolution' in the Home: Household Technology and Social Change in the 20th Century," _Technology and Culture_ 17 (January 1976): 1–23; "Two Washes in the Morning and a Bridge Party at Night: The American Housewife between the Wars," _Women's Studies_ 3 (1976):147–72; and "A Case Study of Technology and Social Change: The Washing Machine and the Working Wife," in _Clio's Consciousness Raised: New Perspectives on the History of Women_, Mary S. Hartman and Lois Banner, eds. (New York: Harper & Row, 1974; Harper Torchbooks), pp. 245–53.

62. Martha Bensley Brueré, "The New Home-Making," _Outlook_, March 16, 1912, p. 595.

63. "A Vanishing Relation," _Independent_, August 23, 1906, p. 467.

64. To fully understand the comprehensive nature of Gilman's program, see _Women and Economics: The Economic Factor between Men and Women as a Factor in Social Evolution_ (Boston: Small, Maynard, 1898; repr. ed., New York: Harper & Row, 1966, with an Introduction and edited by Carl Degler; Harper Torchbook); Filene, _Him/Her/Self_, pp. 56–58; Daniel T. Rodgers, _The Work Ethic in Industrial America 1850–1920_ (Chicago: University of Chicago Press, 1974), p. 190; and William H. Chafe, _The American Woman: Her Changing Social, Economic, and Political Roles, 1920–1970_ (New York: Oxford University Press, 1972), pp. 7–10.

65. Irving Bernstein, _The Lean Years: A History of the American Worker 1920–1933_ (Boston: Houghton Mifflin, 1966; repr. ed., Baltimore: Penguin Books, 1970), pp. 186–87.

66. Ibid., p. 169.

67. Bernstein, _The Lean Years_, p. 170.

68. "'Home Assistants' as a Solution of the Servant Problem," _Literary Digest_, June 19, 1920, p. 82; Smith,

"Domestic Service," p. 688; and Anderson, "Domestic Service in the United States," pp. 11–12.

69. Barbara—The Commuter's Wife, "Why Domestic Service Is a Problem," New Outlook, October 1, 1904, p. 303.

70. Mildred Maddocks Bentley, "The Psychology of Servants," Ladies Home Journal, December 1925, p. 159.

71. T. W. Hotchkiss, "Advice to Employers," Good Housekeeping, September 1909, p. 244; and Frederick, "The New Housekeeping," p. 16.

72. Smith, "Domestic Service," p. 688; Klink, "The Housekeeper's Responsibility," p. 380; and "Our Own Times," Reader: An Illustrated Monthly Magazine, December 1907, p. 109.

73. A Thankful Husband, "How My Wife Keeps Her Maids," Harper's Bazaar, December 1909, p. 1231.

74. James H. Collins, "Woman's Mishandling of Labor," Ladies Home Journal, October 1920, p. 142.

6

Preservers of the Status Quo: Organized Labor

"They would march through the streets
like an army, terrible with brooms and
skillets. . . ."[1]

As historian William H. Chafe once observed, the American labor movement "held the key to the condition of women in industry."[2] Chafe's observation was not intended to minimize the general plight of workers, but in the case of women the collective problems of labor were intensified by the onerous burden of sex discrimination. Relegated to the least skilled jobs, granted the fewest opportunities for advancement, and regarded as the most expendable members in the work force, female workers in the United States more than any others needed a "powerful protector" to insure their rights.

Seldom were these observations truer than for the domestic worker. Invariably the servant was female and unskilled. In addition, large numbers of servants were members of ethnic or racial minorities. Thus it is necessary to examine organized labor's attitude toward women and the unskilled. Perhaps then it will be possible to understand why labor was so reluctant to embrace this most numerically significant segment of the female work force.

Despite the fact that the Industrial Revolution cut across old lines of demarcation, the sexual barrier remained fundamentally intact. Some scholars have argued that throughout the nineteenth century the sexual division of labor, which determined women's inferior place, was the central fact of those gainfully employed females.[3]

Nevertheless, women were part of the trade union movement
from a very early date. One of the earliest examples involved the tailoresses of New York City, who formed a
union in 1825. Still 1866 is often regarded as the date of
the first significant female entry into the foray of union
activity. This was when the National Labor Union was
established.[4]

In fact, the National Union is an excellent place to
begin because it was the first attempt to create a new
unity within the labor movement. This unity was to include women while previous organizations had endeavored
to exclude females at all costs. Examples of the former
abound, but possibly one of the earliest to set precedence
was the Typographical Society of Philadelphia. Fearing
the impending employment of women, the union demanded
that the machines be operated by journeymen printers
trained in the trade. Few women were journeymen and the
union was powerful enough to keep it that way. Officials
in other trade unions frequently modeled their exclusionary
policies on those of the printers. The specific motive was
the same--to prevent the employment of women in their respective trades.[5] The hostility of these early unions to
female membership was based on a variety of assumptions.
One common belief was that women actually lowered the
wage standard. In conjunction with this notion was the
idea that for every woman who was employed, a man went
without a job. Equally important, many believed women
were only transient workers and, consequently, poor union
material. Others held that even when women formed labor
unions, they were seldom of long duration. Much of the
accuracy of this last charge was due to the fact that the
greatest number of women were employed in unskilled occupations such as domestic work. These were generally the
most difficult to organize. An important additional assumption was the notion that female labor was a moral and physical danger to women. Above all, women belonged in the
home.[6]

In fact, the accuracy of such assumptions was less
significant than the tenacity of their duration. All the
more amazing was it that women should have continued to
form unions and that, under the influence of William Sylvis,
the National Labor Union adopted a progressive attitude
toward female workers. As early as 1866 the union pledged
to support factory operatives, serving women, and other
daughters of toil. In so doing, the union made it abun-

dantly clear that its action did not stem solely out of
sympathy for working women.   It was also acting in what
it perceived to be the ultimate best interest of working
males.[7]

Even so, President Sylvis appointed the chief director of the Collar Laundry Workingwomen's Association of
Troy, Kate Mullaney, as the assistant secretary for the
National Labor Union.   Her basic duty was to correspond
with and aid in the creation of working women's associations throughout the nation and to affiliate them with the
National Labor Union.   In addition, the National Labor
Union encouraged women's trade unions and welcomed their
delegates to its yearly congresses.[8]

One such organization created by nineteenth-century
feminists was the Working Women's Association.   Because
their concern for women was centermost, the feminists challenged the labor movement to broaden its conception of
workers and their needs beyond men.   The feminists came
to believe this was particularly important after confronting
trade union hostility to women.   The Working Women's Association was created to force labor to join forces with
feminist reforms, especially since the suffragists claimed
that the enfranchisement of women was compatible with the
aims of labor reform.   Another important reason for the
establishment of the Working Women's Association was to
provide Susan B. Anthony with the necessary credentials
for her acceptance as a delegate to the 1868 National Labor
Congress.[9]

The cordiality of the National Labor Union and the
suffragists lasted through the September 1868 Congress.
Once there, Susan B. Anthony and the women she brought
with her, Mary Kellog Putnam, Mary McDonald, and Elizabeth Cady Stanton, were granted delegate status.   The
only woman to whom the union objected was Stanton since
she represented the Woman Suffrage Association of America.
Since none of these women truly represented a bona fide
labor union, the real objection to Stanton was the thorny
issue of woman suffrage.   Only after Susan B. Anthony
spoke on behalf of Stanton was the latter seated as a delegate.   However, a resolution was added asserting that the
NLU was not committing itself to, or endorsing, female suffrage.   Thus the seating of Stanton as a delegate was
separated from the organization and issues she actually
represented.[10]

But the issue was not resolved.   In fact, it reap-
peared in a far uglier fashion in August 1869 when John

Walsh from Local No. 6 of the National Typographical Union challenged Susan B. Anthony's credentials. He claimed the Working Women's Association was not a true labor organization, and even more significant, that Anthony had acted as a recruiter for strikebreakers. Anthony could not deny this charge, and instead tried to explain and justify her course of action. In the end the National Labor Union rejected her credentials.[11]

Even though all women were not excluded from the 1869 NLU convention, the Anthony debate soured relations between the organization and feminists. The incident clearly revealed some of the male labor world's deep-seated opposition to female suffrage. It also intensified the enmity of those who already opposed women in industry. Thereafter, the National Labor Union's suspicion of the woman's rights movement was easily noted. As one source commented, the NLU "steadfastly refused to let the discussion of woman's suffrage lead the organization away from its primary work."[12] Thus, in general, male support for female trade unions declined and by 1872 most women's labor organizations had vanished.[13]

By the time the National Labor Union had passed into history in 1873, no endorsement of woman suffrage had occurred. Despite this fact, the NLU had adopted the most progressive stand on the question of female labor to date. In a way the union made labor history by affirming and then reaffirming its position in support of certain rights for working women. Foremost among these was the right of women to receive equal pay for equal work.[14]

Even as the NLU gasped its last breath, partly impaled by the feminists' insistence on electoral equality, a new organization was born. Conceived in secret by nine blacklisted Philadelphian garment cutters, the Noble Order of the Knights of Labor came into being in 1869. Although imbued with advanced notions on numerous issues, the Knights' founder, Uriah H. Stephens, was obsessed with the significance of secrecy and the sexist view that women could not keep secrets. As a consequence, women were excluded from the Knights for more than a decade.[15]

Time, plus a combination of factors, drove the Knights to change their policy with regard to women. In the first place the Roman Catholic clergy would not countenance secret oaths. Second, secrecy was discredited by the so-called Molly Maguires. Named for a legendary Irish revolutionary, the Mollys were believed to exist in the

mining regions of Pennsylvania. They were accused of
plotting the assassination of the mine superintendents and
others with whom they disagreed. Perhaps of even greater
importance was the rate of increase for women over the
age of fifteen actively employed in manufacturing. The
census of 1880 disclosed that, while the population of the
country had increased by 30 percent in the preceding decade, the number of males employed in manufacturing had
grown by less than 24 percent. On the other hand, the
number of women so employed over the same decade had
increased by 64 percent.[16]

Although in semblance the Knights gave lip service
to the establishment of a community of all workers, these
societal attitudes and changes forced them to adopt policy
changes significantly affecting women. Indication of such
change occurred during the first national convention held
in January 1878. Here, in addition to calling for an end
to child labor in mines, workshops, and factories, the
Knights proposed to secure equal pay for equal work. A
similar call went out at the Knights' second national convention in 1879. Stephens made it clear that the formulation of such a stand was being put forward in the interest
of male wage earners. On this point he was quoted as
having said, "Perfected machinery persistently seeks cheap
labor, and is supplied mainly by women and children.
Adult male labor is thus crowded out of employment and
swells the ranks of the unemployed or at least the under-
paid."[17] In addition, at the second national convention
of the Knights of Labor a representative from Ohio put
forth a resolution allowing working women the right of
membership and the right to form their own assemblies
under the same conditions as men. The committee on laws
supported the resolution by a vote of fourteen to six and
then laid it on the table for the next annual convention.[18]

All these issues came to the forefront when the new
master workman, Terence V. Powderly, opened the General
Assembly meeting in Detroit, Michigan, in September of
1881. Here the delegates voted to abolish oaths and all
other secret aspects of the organization by the beginning
of the next year. Although Powderly had been authorized
to convene a committee to prepare for the ritual and induc-
tion procedure of women, he never did so. He later explained that such separateness would imply inequality.
Actually this meeting proved unnecessary. In early 1881
the male shoemakers of Philadelphia Local Assembly 64 re-

fused to accept a wage cut, and management turned to
nonunion females. Management then proceeded to cut wages
an additional 30 to 60 percent. Taking up the mantle of
leadership, Mary Stirling organized the women who went
out on strike. Thus the first Knights' local composed entirely of women, Garfield Assembly 1684, came into being
in September of 1881.[19]

In 1882 several new unions were added and female
membership increased steadily thereafter. The high point
was probably reached in May of 1886 when twenty-seven
all-female locals joined the ranks of the Knights of Labor.
(Appendix A provides a breakdown of these locals.) After
that date the great decline within the organization began
and during the next half-dozen years virtually the entire
strength of female unionism in the Knights of Labor vanished.[20] For example, in 1888 total female membership in
the Knights was believed to be less than 12,000. A short
two years earlier, during an eighteen-month period more
than that number of women joined the organization in the
single state of Massachusetts. However, it should be understood that the Bay State contained about one seventh of the
total number of female Knights. Granting the preponderance of women in the union from Massachusetts, best estimates claim about 50,000 female Knights in the organization's peak years.[21]

Although there can be little doubt that the Knights
of Labor deserved their reputation as "the first labor organization to place women on an equal footing with men,"
the meaning of this reputation needs some further clarifi-
cation.[22] Opinions vary widely. For instance, although
the Knights stood firmly behind the idea of mixed assemblies because they believed this intermingling of individuals from various trades and occupations would cultivate
an appreciation of labor solidarity, they never insisted on
an intermingling of the sexes.[23]

It is also interesting to contemplate what might
have happened if Philadelphia Local Assembly 64 had accepted its proposed wage cut and not forced management to
hire nonunion women shoe workers. While that course of
events was altering history, the fifth regular session of
the General Assembly was meeting in Detroit, Michigan,
and voting down a resolution of Representative Cuno of New
York. This resolution called for the admission of women
into the Knights and commissioned them to become union
organizers.[24]

Reports also vary about the Knights of Labor and its willingness to recruit female members. Some experts believed the Knights were motivated by highly idealistic goals that were intended to aid all who honestly toiled for a living. The following observation taken from the Los Angeles Union, and reprinted in a prominent labor periodical reflects this more positive view of the Knights and women workers. The author wrote, "The Knights of Labor is the only organization we know of which encourages the membership of ladies; demands for woman exact equality and insists on giving her equal pay for equal work. Throughout the North, East, and West the Order embraces within its ranks thousands of ladies."[25]

Others were not so positively inclined. A contemporary of the Knights discussed the issue of female recruitment and union interest at considerable length. His discussion was put forth at a most crucial time, 1886, the peak year of female Knight membership. George Brown's observations have additional meaning because this was also the year that the union made labor history by being the first organization to create a Department of Woman's Work and placing at its head an enthusiastic Knight and excellent female orator named Leonora M. Barry[26]:

> Women--Geo. R. Brown thus writes: There is an immense reserve force awaiting an opportunity to join hands with the Order of the Knights of Labor--a force that will double its members and increase its power threefold, add to its effective working, be a bond of union, and add a new growth to an already vigorous young giant. The force referred to are our wives and daughters, of the female portion of the toiling millions. . . . While the Order admits women, it has never made any concentrated move to induce them to join; many times have we seen strikes, induced by the employment of girls or women, and no effort made to bring them into the union.[27]

Wherever the Knights of Labor stood on the active recruitment of female members, their position vis-à-vis women was somewhat rectified by the creation of the Department of Woman's Work. The department grew out of a report drawn up by Mary Hanaflin, a member of the Committee on Woman's Work, which had been authorized at the Hamilton, Ontario, 1885 General Assembly meeting. The findings of the committee's questionnaire, which were sent to all local assemblies with female members, revealed gross abuses in the working conditions of women and children. On the basis of these findings, Hanaflin advocated sweeping investigations to locate the most serious problem areas for female workers. It was hoped that such investigations would provide the data for a strong public campaign to disclose the working conditions of women and help bring them into the Knights. Hanaflin's report led directly to the creation of the Department of Woman's Work. The directive of the department was "to investigate the abuses to which the female sex is subjected, and to agitate the principles which our Order teaches of equal pay for equal work, and of the abolition of child labor."[28]

However necessary and noble the intention of this department, it is paramount to examine closely the Knights' commitment to it and to its stated objectives. Unfortunately, the Knights of Labor fell short in their devotion to women, to the Department of Woman's Work, and to the department's director, Leonora M. Barry. For example, as labor historian Philip Foner has pointed out, numerous male Knights resented the hard and diligent work undertaken by Barry and refused to work with her. Most noteworthy in this category were certain Catholic priests, one of whom actually engaged in a name-calling attack. Terence V. Powderly supported Barry, not the priests. He encouraged her to continue her work, but not to spend time organizing or lecturing to men.[29]

But the strongest indictment of the Knights' commitment to the Department of Woman's Work came from Leonora Barry herself. Reporting to the General Assembly after one year in office, Barry admitted her own and the Knights' lack of understanding about the real plight of working women. She challenged the order to live up to the twenty-second plank of their platform, which demanded equal pay for equal work, or strike it from the page. She claimed that in the history of the order this section of the platform had been nothing but a cruel mockery. And how sad it was to "make a farce of one of the grandest principles of our Order."[30]

Condemning the selfishness of the males in their local orders, Barry went on to say:

> Within the jurisdiction of our District As-
> semblies starvation and sin are knocking
> at, aye, and have gained entrance at the
> doors of thousands of victims of underpaid
> labor. And the men who have pledged
> themselves to the "assistance of humanity"
> and the "abolition of poverty" are so en-
> grossed in the pursuit of their own ambi-
> tious desires, that upon their ears the wail
> of woe falls unheeded, and the work of
> misery and destruction still goes on.[31]

Undaunted, Barry's enthusiasm remained intact up
to the time of the 1889 General Assembly meeting. By then
the Knights were in a state of general decline. Sensing
demise and her own failure, Barry recommended an end to
the Woman's Department and advocated that all efforts be
directed toward educating and organizing women in the order. Furthermore, she had come to believe that all workers should be members of the Knights of Labor without dis-
tinction of sex. Only then would it be "incumbent upon
all to work more earnestly for the general good, rather
than for sex, Assembly or trade."[32]
Barry's recommendation was not accepted, and both
she and the department continued to function. However, in
November of 1889 Powderly notified her that, due to strait-
ened economic circumstances, she would have to restrict
her travel and center her activity on the Philadelphia
area. She followed this directive until the following November. Upon her marriage to fellow Knight, Oliver R. Lake,
Barry tendered her resignation in 1890. But at the same
time she urged the delegates to select a successor. An
effort was made in this direction, but when the single
woman delegate to the 1890 convention, Alzina P. Stevens,
declined, the Woman's Department of the Knights of Labor
ceased to exist.[33]
Although this same fate was not in store for the
Knights, by 1890 they were no longer a strong national
force. Local assemblies continued to exist throughout the
1890s and on into the twentieth century, but the course of
organized labor and the future of women workers were to
be determined by new organizations. Yet despite all its
weaknesses and shortcomings, the Knights did provide many
women with their first taste of union work, their first experience in organizing the unskilled, and their first ex-

perience as strikers. Furthermore, however bound by the constrictions of thought concerning the proper role for women in American society, the Knights proved to be far more progressive than some of their successors.[34]

The most significant of these immediate successors was the American Federation of Labor. First organized in 1881 as the Federation of Organized Trades and Labor Unions of the United States and Canada and then reorganized and renamed in 1886, the new union gave early indication of an interest in committing itself to working women. In fact, prior to adopting the name, American Federation of Labor, members meeting at a labor convention in Washington, D.C., in 1885 introduced the following significant resolution: "Resolved, That we call upon and advise the working women of this country to protect themselves by organizing into unions of their respective trades or callings, and the legislative committee is hereby authorized to render such assistance whenever opportunity offers."[35]

A short two years later, AFL President Samuel Gompers in his first annual report wrote on how women were employed, in the workshops and factories of the nation, only to reduce the wages of men. Thus Gompers went on to strongly advocate the organization of women. "First and foremost we should lend our energies to the organization of laboring women in trade unions and to secure education for their children."[36] One year later, after several organizations of working women had been founded, Gompers again stressed the importance of trade unions among women. Only through such action could women hope to improve their condition as workers.[37]

Because Samuel Gompers was the first president of the AFL and the head of the organization every year until his death in 1924 (the exception being 1895), his views on women in unions were of utmost significance. Biographers have frequently asserted that Gompers showed an early interest in the relationship of women to the labor movement and in their problems as workers. Evidence was often based on the fact that Gompers urged the labor world to acknowledge the common identity of working men and women. Furthermore, early in the twentieth century, he appointed a number of female organizers. But all the while that he urged women to organize and advocated the principle of equal wages, he believed the proper place for the American woman was in the home.[38]

In fact, despite all the public pronouncements to the contrary made by Gompers and the AFL, there is sparse evidence of any real desire to aid working women. In short, the leaders of the American Federation of Labor really wanted and really believed a woman's place was in the home. Again and again and again, the official AFL voice, the American Federationist, printed articles condemning the employment of women in American industry. Typical of this stance was an article written by Edward O'Donnell. O'Donnell was secretary of the Boston Central Labor Union, an AFL affiliate, and his article was entitled, "Women as Bread Winners--the Error of the Age."[39]

Nor did the position of the AFL change much over time. For example, from 1890 to 1910 the number of women gainfully employed increased from 4,005,532 to 8,075,772. But in this very same period women remained a relatively insignificant part of organized labor. Experts estimated that 73,000 women were union members in 1910. This number constituted only 0.9 percent of all wage-earning women in the United States. This 0.9 percent broke down approximately as follows: (1) 20 to 30 percent of the 2,407 women employed in the beverage and liquor industries were unionized; (2) 333,000 women were employed in the printing, bookbinding or clothing industries--of these, 20 to 30 percent were organized; (3) 5 to 10 percent of the 145,870 women employed in tobacco and cigar factories or leather industries were unionized; (4) 1 to 5 percent of 415,000 women engaged in the textile, furniture, or lumber industries were organized; and (5) the remaining 7,180,000 women were less than 1 percent organized. Even by 1920, the high point for union membership in the United States until the late 1930s, only 6.6 percent of all the nonagricultural female labor force was organized.[40]

Irrespective of these facts and their momentous meaning, the AFL continued blithely about its business. Reflecting its backward-looking position on the employment of women was an article published in the American Federationist in 1910. Speaking for the union, the author wrote, "We stand for more than this. We stand for the principle that it is wrong to permit any of the female sex of our country to be forced to work as we believe that the man should be provided with a fair wage in order to keep his female relatives from going to work. This man is provider, and should receive enough for his labor to give his family a respectable living."[41]

Further indication of the union position is the fact that in 1898 and then again in 1914 the AFL annual conventions almost passed resolutions against women working in the paid labor force of the nation. One international leader summed up the federation's position very well when he said, "Keep women out of the trades and if not, out of the union."[42]

And keep them out of the union they did! Of course other factors worked to check the growth of female membership. Undoubtedly some of this can be correctly attributed to the hostility displayed by many craft unions toward female artisans. But essentially American working women failed to join the trade union movement because, at least until the 1930s, they were not invited. Union leaders were certain that women did not belong and to that end they deployed numerous techniques to prevent them from joining.[43]

One simple technique used by the AFL was to disallow women members. Usually this was achieved through the use of constitutional clauses. However, this was only the most direct method instituted to bar the admittance of women. Therefore, some unions admitted women employed by certain of their branches, but not those employed by others. Invariably they were excluded from the main branches of the trades. In addition, virtually all AFL unions denied new employment opportunities to women. In this way females were confined to unskilled jobs. Almost all apprenticeship programs restricted female entrance. Moreover, most AFL unions denied women the opportunity for on-the-job training and/or promotions. The net result was that women were generally unable to acquire additional skills or put any such skills to use.[44]

Correctly the AFL leadership could point to the fact that numerous international unions did not discriminate against women workers. In some cases these internationals went so far as to pass regulations reducing both fees and dues for women. Some even adopted resolutions favoring apprenticeship training for females and equal pay for equal work. On the other hand, there were international unions which did discriminate against women, refusing to admit them as members even though women were actively employed in those trades. In 1922 the Women's Trade Union League, first established in 1903, sought ways around this problem. The league reported an instance where another group in 1921 had asked the AFL to pass an amendment to its constitution denying affiliation to any international union that discriminated on account of sex. No such amendment was passed.[45]

Perhaps equally important was the fact that there tended to be a tremendous gap between the practices of the internationals and the practices of local unions. This was especially crucial because local unions had the final say in implementing policy. Many simply disregarded their national's declarations. Others denied admission to female applicants. Still others refused to grant special charters for a woman's local, and frequently rejected female applicants who held transfer cards.[46]

Nor did the AFL make extensive use of woman organizers. Only under pressure from women did the federation appoint Mary E. Kenny as an organizer in 1892. When her term of office expired later that year, she was not rehired or replaced. Furthermore, between 1903 and 1923, a period of tremendous expansion in women's employment, the American Federation of Labor hired only thirty female organizers and used many of them for only very brief periods of time.[47]

Essentially, whatever effort was expanded to organize and assist women workers came from a small phalanx of dedicated females. These dedicated individuals were social workers, leisure-class reformers, or rank-and-file laborers. The most significant of the various labor reform organizations--one which attempted to combine all of these elements--was the Women's Trade Union League, which was established in 1903. In these early years the league concentrated its efforts directly on organizing. In so doing, it established a very close relationship with the general trade union movement. But since its membership was not limited to wage earners, it was associated with the "woman movement" in a much broader sense. Nevertheless, the league had fraternal delegate representation in Federal Conventions, State Federations, and City Centrals. In both the local leagues and the national body, there was a requirement that a majority of the Executive Board had to be trade unionists of good standing. In 1924 there were seventeen centers in industrial locations of the nation. These centers, or local branches, had at least twenty-five members from at least three trade unions. National League headquarters was in Chicago. In addition, the league had two official publications, Life and Labor and Life and Labor Bulletin.[48]

The founders of the Women's Trade Union League attempted to deal with three fundamental problems confronting working women in the United States.[49]   These problems included: (1) unionizing women; (2) educating unions about the need of unionizing women; and (3) enacting protective legislation for children and women.   Although not truly affiliated with the AFL, the league's constitution included the following statement: "To assist in organizing women into trade unions . . . such unions to be affiliated, where practicable, with the American Federation of Labor."[50] Although the AFL welcomed this venture politely, the leaders gave the league only lip-service support.   Very little was ever done to encourage the WTUL in its work.   Furthermore, various international affiliates and the AFL Executive Council threw roadblocks in the league's path.[51]

One final indication of the federation's lack of commitment to women workers is the fact that seldom were they found in leadership positions.   Even when women were active members of the AFL, they seldom had much to say about policy determination.   Women were even less likely to hold union office.   One sympathetic source wrote of the AFL that "the discrimination against women is within rather than without the membership."   She verified this by pointing out that "women are discouraged from taking an active part in the executive affairs of organization.   There are no women among the national officers or the national executive of the American Federation.   In the 111 national unions there is but one woman president.   It would be rare to find women presiding over a city or state organization."[52]

The conservatism of the AFL was matched by the radicalism of a rival organization founded on June 27, 1905.   Gathered together on that day were anti-AFL unionists, anarchists, workers from the Western Federation of Miners, and socialists.   Calling themselves the Industrial Workers of the World, these organizers believed in one big union for all laborers in every section and region of the nation.   Furthermore, William Haywood, secretary of the Western Federation of Miners and chair for this first meeting, called for the creation of "a working class movement in possession of the economic powers, the means of life, in control of the machinery of production and distribution without regard to capitalist master's."[53]

In the beginning it seemed that the IWW's attitude about women would differ some from that of the AFL.   For

example, at the founding convention twelve female delegates were present. Of these twelve women, at least
three went on to hold positions of importance at the convention. Nonetheless, the Executive Committee was an all-
male preserve.[54]

Unlike the AFL, the Industrial Workers made important use of female organizers. Leaders in this crucial activity were Matilda Rabinowitz, whom it was said the local
police dreaded; Vera Moller, one of many Wobbly songwrit-
ers; and Katie Phar, a cripple who possessed a beautiful
singing voice. Phar's organizing activities invariably included the use of this talent. However, none of these important female organizers was of equal stature to Elizabeth
Gurley Flynn.[55]

Young, intelligent, vibrant, and beautiful, Flynn
was not only an excellent organizer, speaker, and union
member, she also became known as "Miss IWW." Exposed
to reformers, radicals, revolutionaries, socialists, feminists, and anarchists throughout her formative years,
Flynn became a member of the General Executive Board of
the IWW. To the present day no position of comparable
importance has been held by a woman in the AFL or its
successor organization, the AFL-CIO. Flynn's importance
to the organization is perhaps best symbolized by the fact
that she became immortalized in song by Wobbly Joe Hill.
Hill's "The Rebel Girl" was written for Flynn in 1915.[56]

Other women who played active roles in the union
included Lillian Forberg, a delegate to the first convention. An active agitator, Forberg was an organizer in
the Chicago textile industries. In addition, she served on
the Chicago General Advisory Board and on her local Executive Board. In Portland, Oregon, the IWW made Nina Wood
an organizer. The Portland General Executive Board also
granted volunteer organizer credentials to Ester Niemien in
1909.[57]

The IWW recognized that women were in the work
force to stay. Consequently the union was determined to
recruit women and to support their participation in organized labor. They also sought not to discriminate
against women as the AFL and other labor groups had
done and were continuing to do. Thus at their second
convention the Wobblies lowered female dues beyond the
rates that had been previously established. Since female
dues were already below male rates, the discrepancy became even greater because the scale for men remained the

same. The union also endeavored to pay special attention
to any and all activity undertaken by its female members.[58]

Since the IWW kept few records, the exact number of
female members, especially during the pre-World War I
years, is all but impossible to determine. What is clear
is that the union was considerably more successful in recruiting women in the East than in the West. Women workers tended to be concentrated in the eastern textile factories. Western labor was dominated by migratory workers,
lumberjacks, and miners. These were male occupations
which existed in a predominately male world--the world of
mining, construction, and migratory camps of the American
West. The great Swedish-born Wobbly songwriter Joe Hill
commented on this very characteristic. He remarked on the
freakish, one-legged, male animal of a union that existed
in the western IWW. Hill strongly recommended that female
Wobbly organizers be used exclusively to build up a strong
female following in the organization. However seriously
the union took his suggestion, there is little evidence to
suggest that much of anything was done in this regard.[59]

As the failure to implement Hill's suggestion implies,
how truly committed to the female worker was the IWW?
How significantly different were they from the AFL and
those unions which had gone before? Generally it is be-
leved that after the 1907 IWW convention when the Western
Federation of Miners voted to withdraw from the organization, the Wobbly leaders turned their attention mainly to
industries in which migratory labor was dominant. These
were the same male provinces of harvesting, lumbering,
and railroad construction.[60]

Closer examination of this evidence leads directly
to the fact that the IWW actually contradicted itself on
issues relating to women workers. Although union organizers were seeking to convince women to join and carry the
message to other females, and although the IWW expressed
the belief that women were in industry to stay, they really
wanted women in the home. Women were not to bear the
onus for the damaging effects their employment might have
on working conditions and wages. After all, they, like
men, were slaves and victims of the capitalist system.
All the more reason to organize everyone. Nor did the
Wobblies hold to the position that women could not be organized. Yet the ultimate solution lay in organizing men
so that the system could be changed and women could return to where they truly belonged--the home. Therefore,

organization was really to apply to young, unmarried
women. The young industrial worker of the day would
become the supportive wife of a union husband in the
future.[61]

But what of married women workers? Solidarity
answered that question very clearly in a November 23,
1918 article. While justification for single, young women
could be maintained, the union was rather aghast at married women leaving their children and homes to work.
These females were not to be in the work force of the nation.[62] Furthermore, the IWW never really resolved the
question of whether or not the wives of union members were
eligible for membership. Views and inaction such as this
incurred the wrath of some working women, especially those
in the IWW. Calling herself "A Woman Toiler," one such
female union member wrote the following letter:

> Fellow Worker Man Toiler: You say you
> want us girls to keep out of the factory
> and mill so you can get more pay, then
> you can marry some of us and give us a
> decent home. Now, that is just what we
> are trying to escape. And aren't you a
> little inconsistent? You tell us to get into
> the I.W.W., an organization for wage work-
> ers only. We haven't heard of any House-
> hold Drudge's Union. . . . Going from the
> factory back into the home means only a
> change in the form of servitude, a change
> for the worse for the woman. The best
> thing that ever happened to woman was
> when she was compelled to leave the narrow
> limits of the home and enter into the indus-
> trial life of the world. This is the only
> road to our freedom. . . . So we will stay
> in the factory, mill, or store and organize
> with you in the I.W.W. . . . so we can
> provide ourselves with decent homes, then
> if we marry you, it will be because we
> love you so well we can't get along without
> you, and not give you a chance to pay our
> bills, like we do now.[63]

Possibly an even more telling aspect of IWW incon-
sistency was the hostility women organizers met when they

went ahead on their own and organized women workers.
At least in the West such women had to combat the opposi-
tion and chauvinism of both their employers and the male
IWW leaders. This was the fate of Jane Street, secretary
and founder of IWW Local No. 113, a Denver Domestic
Worker's Industrial Union.[64]

Street's extensive organizing in Denver led to secret
meetings where domestics gathered, expressed their feelings,
made their demands for improved working conditions, and
formed their union on March 31, 1916. Then followed regular weekly meetings--business and social. Hoping to avoid
the regular employment agents (called "employment sharks"),
Street established her own agency for Denver's domestics.
Most impressive was the fact that after one year of existence, the local had personally interviewed 1,500 to 2,000
women. They were informed about the IWW and eventually
approximately 1,000 were placed in domestic positions.
These positions were facilitated through the establishment
of a card file that contained all the potential domestic
openings in Denver. Recalcitrant employers would have a
difficult time securing help if they refused to meet union
demands. Street also secured a rented clubhouse for her
members. Costs eventually drove her to abandon this
dream.[65]

In fact, so successful was the Domestic Worker's
Industrial Union, IWW Local No. 113, that it came to meet
ever increasing opposition. The opposition in Denver consisted of the obvious interests, mainly "the employment
sharks whose business the union has seriously disrupted;
the mistresses of Denver; and the YWCA."[66] Intimidation
failed to weaken the domestics and knowing one of the organization's great sources of strength lay in the card file,
these collected enemies responded accordingly. Solidarity
carried the following report after the disappearance of the
card file:

> The loss to the Union is inestimable as the
> card list contained data on practically
> every job in town where domestics are em-
> ployed, and represent over seven months
> work. . . . The cards bore information
> obtainable as to working conditions, wages
> and all other data of interest to the work-
> ers seeking a job in the private homes of
> the masters. . . . By its use the House-

maids had practically cornered the labor
market for general housework.[67]

Despite the loss of the card file, the union did not
fold and Jane Street began to attack the male Wobblies in
Denver. Furthermore, she warned women in the process of
organizing domestics not to establish their headquarters in
connection with other IWW locals because "sex can come
rushing into your office like a great hurricane and blow
all the papers of industrialism out the windows."[68] Street
also believed the Denver mixed locals had caused her organization more harm than all her other enemies combined.
She held them directly responsible for slandering the domestics' local and her. She believed they were involved
in cutting her organization off from outside donations and
from other locals. Street accused the mixed local of caus-
ing dissension among union women, of giving her clubhouse
a bad name, of tearing up the domestic local's charter,
and of personally assaulting her.
Of particular concern to Street was Phil Engle, who
was also a Wobbly. Street claimed Engle had warned her
months before the card file incident that his objective was
to see her outside the union. According to her, Engle had
spent much of his time trying to destroy the domestic
workers' organization and he was working "with maniacal
fervor toward" the objective of forcing her out of the IWW.[69]
In a remarkable letter to Mrs. Elmer F. Buse, another domestic attempting to organize workers in Tulsa,
Oklahoma, Jane Street professed that her accusations were
not strictly personal in nature. The issues were far more
serious. Street believed this type of opposition confronted
all domestics' locals in the IWW. "For domestic workers'
local [sic] to spring up anywhere and achieve success is
a monument to their treachery and false prophecy against
us, and they therefore discourage them in an effort to
protect themselves."[70] Apologizing, Street concluded by
expressing the hope that bitterness had not colored her
remarks. "But when one looks upon the slavery on all
sides that enchain the workers--these women workers sentenced to hard labor and solitary confinement on their
prison jobs in the homes of the rich--and these very men
who forget their I.W.W. principles in their opposition to
us--when we look about us, we soon see that the Method
of Emancipation that we advocate is greater than any or
all of us and that the great principles and ideas that we
advocate is greater than any or all of us and that the

great principles and ideas that we stand for can completely overshadow the frailties of human nature."[71]

The experience of Jane Street and the Denver domestics, coupled with the fact that the IWW hierarchy believed women belonged at home, clearly indicates that the Wobblies were not as different from the AFL in their views about women as they would like to have believed. The similarities between the two labor unions are further strengthened by the failure of the IWW to resolve the issue of membership status for the wives of male Wobblies. Even the otherwise sympathetic interpretation of labor historian Philip Foner is tempered by these realities.[72] Thus in varying degrees labor organizations, beginning with the craft unions, never completely or truly ceased to be sexist institutions.

Intimately bound up with and inseparable from the issue of sex was the issue of unskilled versus skilled labor. Clearly revealing this relationship is Table 1.1, which lists the ten leading female occupations during the decades 1870 to 1940.[73] With the few exceptions of teaching, nursing, and secretarial-related occupations, all the other women's occupations were unskilled. Furthermore, domestic service ranked first from 1870 to 1940.

Another way of comprehending the relationship between labor organization, occupation, and sex is the fact that the first collective attempts were established by skilled mechanics in order to preserve and protect their own standard of living. As for women, William Chafe wrote, "To some extent, the low degree of female participation in the labor movement reflected the type of work females performed. Most women in industry were clustered in low-paying, unskilled jobs. . . . In addition, the labor movement had historically concentrated its efforts among the skilled workers. The majority of its members came from the mining, construction, and transportation industries—areas with few female employees." Simply put, as Chafe concluded, "Women workers were grouped in occupations which fell outside the mainstream of organized labor's concern, [and consequently] they were largely ignored."[74]

Despite the close relationship of unskilled labor and sex, the latter proved to be of greater significance in the history of American female workers. Verification of this statement is illustrated by the simple fact that at least two of the labor organizations under consideration—the Knights of Labor and the Industrial Workers of the World—were industrial rather than craft unions.

The significant difference between an industrial
union versus a craft union is clearly illustrated by the
January 1905 Manifesto. Its authors were thirty prominent
socialists and labor radicals, many of whom later comprised key elements in the IWW's attack on the capitalist
system. Those in attendance clearly spelled out numerous
labor grievances--many of which related to the craft sys-
tem--and called for a new organization of workers.[75]
Labor organization, as it existed, failed to offer relief to
those bound in "wage slavery." In part, this was because
the separation of one craft from another prevented financial
and industrial solidarity. Jealousy among crafts fostered
the establishment of trade monopolies. Crafts tended to
cultivate political ignorance among the workers. Consequently, as a group workers were divided in the shop,
mine, and factory as well as at the ballot box. Historically craft unions were used to aid employers by establishing monopolies which, in turn, raised prices. In such
fashion one set of workers was used to make the conditions
of life harder for another set of workers. Furthermore,
craft divisions inhibited the development of worker class
consciousness. In so doing, they fostered the idea of a
harmony of interests between the employing exploiter and
the employed slave. Eradication could be achieved:

> only by a universal working class movement.
> Such a movement of the working class is impos-
> sible while separate craft and wage agree-
> ments are made favoring the employer
> against other crafts in the same industry,
> and while energies are wasted in fruitless
> jurisdiction struggles which serve only to
> further the personal aggrandizement of
> union officials.
> A movement to fulfill these conditions
> must consist of one great industrial union
> embracing all industries,--providing for
> craft autonomy locally, industrial autonomy
> internationally, and working class unity
> generally.[76]

To these ends the International Workers of the World
was founded in 1905. They were to be the champions of
the unskilled. The objectives were reflected in the motto
of the organization which read, "An Injury to One Is the

Concern of All."[77]   Much like the Knights of Labor before
them, the Wobblies stressed being a worker before all other
things--Catholic or Jew, black or white, male or female,
skilled or unskilled. This course of action was an attempt
to create a true sense of labor solidarity and brotherhood.
As one author said of them, the IWW was trying to teach
"something that was not so, in the hope that sometime it
would be."[78]

Much the same can be said about the Knights of
Labor and the unskilled. For example, the constitution of
the Knights stated that three fourths of every assembly
had to be composed of wage earners. This aided in making
the Knights one of the largest and strongest labor organizations for the semi-skilled and unskilled from 1879 to
1886. Equally important was the order's principle of organization, which was directly opposed to uniting the membership of a single craft in individual locals. Instead,
the Knights endeavored to include representatives of many
callings and trades in their locals. These mixed assemblies' primary concern was to center around interests common to all productive workers. Through association of this
type, the Knights hoped diverse groups could better recognize the fundamental principle of the order: "That is the
most perfect government in which an injury to me is the
concern of all."[79]

A somewhat different and special case existed for
the National Labor Union, which grew out of certain post-
Civil War conditions in the United States. Union growth
during this period was facilitated by inflation and a
shortage of workers. The combination of these factors led
directly to the establishment of new local and national
unions. This loose organization included trade assemblies,
Workingmen's Unions, Eight Hour Leagues, national unions,
local unions, and city centrals. Destined to last for six
years, the National Labor Union urged the organization of
all who remained unorganized--skilled and unskilled. Additional recommendations advocated the formation of unions
in all trades and localities where none existed. Every
branch of the industry was also encouraged to form an international. Fully cognizant that most of the unskilled
would not be welcomed into the existing trade unions, the
National suggested they be organized into a general Workingmen's Association. In turn, this association would be
affiliated with the National Labor Congress and granted
representation in that body.[80]

Thus even though the National Labor Union was essentially composed of skilled trade elements, it recognized and supported the needs of the unskilled. Such was not the case with the American Federation of Labor. And despite the position of these other labor organizations, the attitude of the AFL was the most crucial. Speaking directly on this issue, historian Philip Foner asserted that the AFL, early on in its history:

> had to deal with the accusation that it
> was interested solely in the organization
> of skilled craftsmen and actually objected
> to organizing the unskilled. The Federa-
> tion was often characterized in labor
> circles as a "business organization of the
> skilled mechanics of the country."[81]

There is little evidence to dispute either this accusation or characterization of the AFL. Of course, Samuel Gompers vigorously maintained that his organization encouraged all workers, skilled or unskilled, to organize. His conception of the trade union movement would seem, on the surface, to have supported his assertions. Gompers saw the movement as a well-organized, stable, and comprehensive spokesperson for workers. Logically this conception would be weakened if any group were to remain outside the fold. For example, no trade could maintain wages above the average if it were not organized. Moreover, the wages of the organized skilled worker would be directly affected by the wage scale of the unorganized unskilled.[82]

Despite the logic and the rhetoric, there is considerable reason to question Gompers's commitment to the unskilled. The long-standing position of the AFL held that it was much easier and more fruitful to organize the skilled worker. They were the workers with the greatest bargaining power. Possibly even more significant was the craft structure of the AFL. This structure virtually excluded the unskilled who comprised the vast majority of the work force. Still the AFL refused to organize among them. This refusal was aided and abetted by the federation's opposition to industrial unionism. Furthermore, had Gompers ever been truly committed to organizing the unskilled, he would have been hampered by notions of voluntarism, autonomy of trade internationals, and a recurrent shortage of AFL organizational funds. As one labor historian poignantly wrote:

> The American Federation of Labor has never
> failed at its annual convention in declaring
> for the necessity of organizing the unor-
> ganized, but there has never been a sin-
> cere, nation-wide, energetic campaign to
> organize these masses. The trade unions
> have remained the monopoly of the skilled
> section of the working class, a fortress to
> a very great extent, against any attempt
> of the unskilled upon the privileges of the
> skilled.[83]

Because the typical domestic worker was unskilled
and female, she had little chance of being included in the
AFL. This fact was bluntly acknowledged in a 1905 American Federationist article. Conceding that service and related occupations included a million and a quarter workers,
the author acknowledged that those employed in private
residences had never been successfully organized. Furthermore, they probably would not be for some time to come.
Only those employed in laundries, hotels, and restaurants
had been able to achieve some degree of organizational
success. Therefore, he concluded that "in these classes of
employment . . . it is seen that the association of a considerable number of persons under a single employer is
necessary for successful organization."[84]
    Early in the twentieth century, the AFL had at
least one opportunity to organize a group of domestics in
New York City. All the preliminary work had been accomplished by a Mrs. St. Justin Beale. She spoke to interested city domestics, planned a series of educational lec-
tures for them, and invited the federation to come and
speak to the women about organizing. When AFL organizer
Herman Robinson arrived, he informed the women that "he
did not quite see how the trade union movement could be
applied to the servant girls' union."[85]
    The simple truth of the matter was that the AFL had
no real interest in organizing these women or any other
group of unskilled women. This most excluded group of
female workers, those who toiled at housework, were not
represented by the federation because it did not wish to
represent them. Yet when reflecting on his years in the
labor movement, Samuel Gompers held the unskilled workers
responsible for their own exclusion. The unskilled were
unorganized because they lacked the requisite intelligence.

In his Autobiography Gompers defended the federation's
failure to exert itself among the unskilled because of their
"lack of courage, lack of persistence, [and] lack of
vision."[86]
 Being female and unskilled were the two most significant impediments which tended to discourage organized
labor from including domestic workers. Other contributing
factors might have been their ethnic or racial origins.
Here, too, the record of labor unions tended to be a mixed
and spotty one, sometimes good, sometimes not so good.
But none of the major labor organizations were able to
hurdle all the obstacles presented to them by domestic
workers. Even the glimmering rays of hope offered by the
International Workers of the World and the Knights of
Labor were inadequate. In the end they remained workers,
not necessarily without a home, but workers without a
union.

NOTES

 1. "A Servant Girl's Trade Union," New York Times,
17 March 1873, p. 4.
 2. William H. Chafe, The American Woman: Her
Changing Social, Economic, and Political Roles, 1920-1970
(New York: Oxford University Press, 1972), pp. 67-68.
 3. Norman J. Ware, The Labor Movement in the
United States 1860-1895: A Study in Democracy (New York:
D. Appleton, 1929), p. 73; and Ellen C. Dubois, Feminism
and Suffrage, The Emergence of an Independent Women's
Movement in America 1848-1869 (New York: Oxford University Press, 1978), p. 128.
 4. U.S. Congress, Senate, Report on the Condition
of Women and Child Wage-Earners in the United States, 19
vols., Doc. 645, 61st Cong., 2nd Sess., 1911, History of
Women in Trade Unions by John B. Andrews and W. D. P.
Bliss, vol. 10 (Washington, D.C.: Government Printing
Office, 1911), p. 11.
 5. Edith Abbott, Women in Industry: A Study in
American Economic History (New York: D. Appleton, 1910),
pp. 250-51, 257-58, 260. Consult John R. Commons et al.,
History of Labour in the United States, 4 vols. (New York:
Macmillan, 1918), pp. 595-96 for examples of other unions
and exclusionary policies used in the 1850s.

6. Abbott, Women in Industry, pp. 207–8; Chafe, The American Woman, pp. 68–69; Commons et al., History of Labour, p. 436; Alice Henry, The Trade Union Women (New York: D. Appleton, 1915), pp. 8–9, 38–39, 59, 146–47; Alice Kessler-Harris, "Where Are the Organized Women Workers?" in A Heritage of Her Own: Toward a New Social History of American Women, Nancy F. Cott and Elizabeth H. Pleck, eds. (New York: Simon & Schuster, 1979; Touchstone Book), p. 349.

7. Philip S. Foner, Women and the American Labor Movement: From Colonial Times to the Eve of World War I (New York: Free Press, 1979), pp. 126–27; George Gorham Groat, An Introduction to the Study of Organized Labor (New York: Macmillan Company, 1926), p. 152; Commons et al., History of Labour, p. 128; and Congress, Senate, Report—History of Women in Trade Unions, pp. 15, 87.

8. Commons et al., History of Labour, p. 128; and U.S. Congress, Senate, Report—History of Women in Trade Unions, p. 87.

9. Dubois, Feminism, pp. 120, 126.

10. Commons et al., History of Labour, p. 133; and Foner, Women and the American Labor Movement, pp. 135–36.

11. Joseph G. Rayback, A History of American Labor (New York: Free Press, 1966), p. 121.

12. U.S. Congress, Senate, Report—History of Women in Trade Unions, p. 87.

13. Foner, Women and the American Labor Movement, pp. 136–37; Rayback, A History of American Labor, pp. 121–22. Also consult Dubois, Feminism, pp. 126–27.

14. Foner, Women and the American Labor Movement, pp. 140, 160.

15. Ibid., p. 185; U.S. Congress, Senate, Report—History of Women in Trade Unions, p. 113.

16. Foner, Women and the American Labor Movement, pp. 185–86.

17. Uriah H. Stephens, quoted in U.S. Congress, Senate, Report—History of Women in Trade Unions, pp. 114–15.

18. Ware, The Labor Movement in the United States, p. 346; and U.S. Congress, Senate, Report—History of Women in Trade Unions, pp. 114–15.

19. Foner, Women and the American Labor Movement, pp. 186–87; Alice Hyneman Rhine, "Women in Industry," in Woman's Work in America, Annie Nathan Meyer, ed. (New York: Henry Holt, 1891), p. 299; and U.S. Congress, Senate, Report—History of Women in Trade Unions, pp. 16–17.

20. Foner, Women and the American Labor Movement, Chapter 11, and especially pp. 207-12.

21. U.S. Congress, Senate, Report--History of Women in Trade Unions, pp. 17, 115, 128. Also see John Swinton's Paper, p. 14, 21 February 1886.

22. Foner, Women and the American Labor Movement, p. 211; and U.S. Congress, Senate, Report--History of Women in Trade Unions, pp. 16-17.

23. Rosalyn Baxandall, Linda Gordon, and Susan Reverby, eds., America's Working Women: A Documentary History--1600 to the Present (New York: Vintage Books, 1976), p. 120.

24. Proceedings of the Fifth Regular Session of the General Assembly, held at Detroit, 1881 (Philadelphia, 1881), pp. 288, 311.

25. Reprinted in John Swinton's Paper, 4 October 1886, p. 3; and Richard T. Ely, The Labor Movement in America, rev. ed. (New York: Macmillan, 1905), pp. 82-83.

26. W. Elliot Brownlee and Mary M. Brownlee, eds., Women in the American Economy: A Documentary History 1675 to 1929 (New Haven, Conn.: Yale University Press, 1976), p. 209; Groat, An Introduction, pp. 154-55; and Foner, Women and the American Labor Movement, pp. 198-99.

27. John Swinton's Paper, 21 March 1886, p. 3.

28. Proceedings of the Tenth Regular Session of the General Assembly, held at Richmond, Virginia, 1886 (Philadelphia, 1886), p. 952; and Foner, Women and the American Labor Movement, pp. 198-99. Also consult U.S. Congress, Senate, Report--History of Women in Trade Unions, pp. 115-16.

29. Foner, Women and the American Labor Movement, pp. 199-200.

30. Proceedings of the General Assembly of the Knights of America, Eleventh Regular Session Held at Minneapolis, Minnesota, 1887 (Philadelphia, 1887), p. 1581.

31. Ibid., pp. 1581-82.

32. Record of the Proceedings of the General Assembly of the Knights of Labor, 1889 (Philadelphia, 1889) in Brownlee and Brownlee, eds., Women in the American Economy, pp. 209-10.

33. Foner, Women and the American Labor Movement, pp. 206-7; and Groat, An Introduction, pp. 154-55.

34. Baxandall, Gordon, and Reverby, eds., America's Working Women, p. 120; Brownlee and Brownlee, eds., Women in the American Economy, p. 209.

35. Quoted in U.S. Congress, Senate, Report—History of Women in Trade Unions, p. 155.

36. Ibid.

37. Ibid., pp. 155-56; and Groat, An Introduction, p. 155.

38. Bernard Mandel, Samuel Gompers: A Biography (Yellow Springs, Ohio: Antioch Press, 1963), pp. 142, 233-34; Philip Taft, The A.F. of L. in the Time of Gompers (New York: Harper & Row, 1957); Samuel Gompers, "Should the Wife Help Support the Family?" American Federationist 12 (January 1906):36.

39. American Federationist 4 (October 1897):186-87; and Baxandall, Gordon, and Reverby, eds., America's Working Women, p. 167.

40. Philip S. Foner, History of the Labor Movement in the United States, vol. 3: The Policies and Practices of the American Federation of Labor, 1900-1909 (New York: International Publishers, 1964), pp. 222, 232; and Leslie W. Tentler, Wage-Earning Women: Industrial Work and Family Life in the United States, 1900-1930 (New York: Oxford University Press, 1979), pp. 14-15; Grout, An Introduction, p. 173.

41. W[illia]m J. Gilthrope, "Advancement," American Federationist 17 (October 1910):897.

42. Quoted in Baxandall, Gordon, and Reverby, eds., America's Working Women, p. 167. Also see Kessler-Harris, "Where Are the Organized Women Workers?" pp. 347-48.

43. Foner, vol. 3: The Policies and Practices of the American Federation of Labor, 1900-1909, p. 225; and Chafe, The American Woman, p. 69; and Foner, Women and the American Labor Movement, pp. 214-15.

44. Baxandall, Gordon, and Reverby, eds., America's Working Women, p. 167; and Foner, vol. 3: The Policies and Practices of the American Federation of Labor, 1900-1909, pp. 222, 226-27.

45. Ibid.

46. Ibid., p. 227; and Life and Labor Bulletin, August 1922, p. 3.

47. Baxandall, Gordon, and Reverby, eds., America's Working Women, p. 167; and Foner, Women and the American Labor Movement, pp. 226-30.

48. Foner, vol. 3: The Policies and Practices of the American Federation of Labor, 1900-1909, p. 227; and Groat, An Introduction, p. 156.

49. Robin Miller Jacoby, "The Woman's Trade Union League and American Feminism," in Class, Sex, and the

Woman Worker, Milton Cantor and Bruce Laurie, eds. (Westport, Conn.: Greenwood Press, 1977; Contributions in Labor History, Number 1), pp. 203-4.

50. Quoted in Foner, vol. 3: The Policies and Practices of the American Federation of Labor, 1900-1909, pp. 229-30.

51. Ibid., pp. 228-30. Also consult Foner, Women and the American Labor Movement, Chapter 17; and Barbara Mayer Wertheimer, We Were There: The Story of Working Women in America (New York: Pantheon Books, 1977), pp. 284-86.

52. American Labor Unions, pp. 67-68; and Groat, An Introduction, p. 161.

53. Wertheimer, We Were There, pp. 353-54; and Joyce L. Kornbluh, ed., Rebel Voices, an IWW Anthology (Ann Arbor, Mich.: University of Michigan Press, 1968), p. 1.

54. Foner, Women and the American Labor Movement, p. 393.

55. Wertheimer, We Were There, pp. 354-55.

56. Foner, Women and the American Labor Movement, p. 395; and Wertheimer, We Were There, p. 355. Also consult Elizabeth Gurley Flynn, I Speak My Own Piece (New York: Masses & Mainstream, 1955).

57. Foner, Women and the American Labor Movement, p. 395.

58. Foner, vol. 4: The Industrial Workers of the World, 1905-1917 (New York: International Publishers, 1965), pp. 127-28; Paul F. Brissenden, The I.W.W.: A Study of American Syndicalism (New York: Columbia University Press, 1919), p. 42; and Foner, Women and the American Labor Movement, pp. 394-95.

59. Foner, vol. 4: The Industrial Workers of the World, 1905-1917, pp. 128-29; and Wertheimer, We Were There, p. 354.

60. Helen Marot, American Labor Unions (New York: Henry Holt, 1914), p. 149.

61. Foner, Women and the American Labor Movement, pp. 397-400.

62. Solidarity, 23 November 1918.

63. "From a Woman Toiler," Solidarity, 25 June 1910.

64. Foner, vol. 4: The Industrial Workers of the World, 1905-1917, pp. 127-28; Daniel T. Hobby, "We Have Got Results": 'A Document in the Organization of Domestics in the Progressive Era,'" Labor History 17 (Winter 1976):103; and Foner, Women and the American Labor Movement, p. 407.

65. "House Maids Form a Union in Denver," Solidarity, 1 April 1916; "Denver House Maids Join IWW," Solidarity, 22 April 1916; and Hobby, "We Have Got Results," p. 104.

66. Elizabeth Gurley Flynn, "The I.W.W. Call to Women," Solidarity, 31 July 1915.

67. C. W. Sellers, "Denver Housemaids' List Stolen," Solidarity, 11 November 1916.

68. Hobby, "We Have Got Results," p. 106.

69. Ibid.

70. Ibid., pp. 106–7.

71. Ibid., p. 107.

72. Foner, Women and the American Labor Movement, pp. 411–12.

73. Ibid., Chapter 1, 4.

74. Chafe, The American Woman, p. 68; and Commons et al., History of Labour, pp. 104–5.

75. Proceedings of the First Convention of the Industrial Workers of the World (New York, 1905), cited in Kornbluh, ed., Rebel Voices, pp. 7–9.

76. Ibid. Also see Philip S. Foner, Organized Labor and the Black Worker: 1619–1973 (New York: International Publishers, 1976), p. 107.

77. Foner, vol. 4: The Industrial Workers of the World, 1905–1917, p. 37.

78. Melvyn Dubofsky, We Shall Be All: A History of the Industrial Workers of the World (Chicago: Quadrangle Books, 1969), pp. 12–13, 86–87; William M. Leiserman, Adjusting Immigrant and Industry (New York: Harper & Brothers, 1924), p. 179; and Marion Dutton Savage, Industrial Unionism in America (New York: Ronald Press, 1922), p. 150.

79. U.S. Congress, Senate, Report—History of Women in Trade Unions, pp. 113–14; Commons et al., History of Labour, pp. 346–47, 533–34; Ware, The Labor Movement in the United States, pp. xviii, 72; and William Kirk, "The Knights of Labor and the American Federation of Labor," in Studies in American Trade Unionism, Jacob H. Hollander and George E. Barnett, eds. (New York: Henry Holt, 1912; repr. ed., New York: Arno & the New York Times, 1969), pp. 355–56.

80. Foner, vol. 1: From Colonial Times to the Founding of the American Federation of Labor, pp. 370–72; and Albert Rees, The Economics of Trade Unions, Cambridge Economic Handbooks (Chicago: University of Chicago Press, 1962), p. 6.

81. Foner, <u>Organized Labor and the Black Worker</u>,
p. 82.

82. Ibid.; and Fred Greenbaum, "The Social Ideas
of Samuel Gompers," <u>Labor History</u> 7 (Winter 1966):41.

83. Anthony Bimba, <u>The History of the American</u>
<u>Working Class</u> (New York: International Press, 1927), pp.
226-27; Greenbaum, "The Social Ideas of Samuel Gompers,"
p. 42; Foner, vol. 3, <u>The Policies and Practices of the</u>
<u>American Federation of Labor, 1900-1909</u>, pp. 280-81.

84. W[illia]m English Walling, "Field of Organization for Women Workers," <u>American Federationist</u> 12 (September 1905):625.

85. "Grievances of Servant Girls," <u>New York Times</u>,
6 December 1900, p. 5.

86. Clara Helene Barker, <u>Wanted, a Young Woman</u>
<u>to Do Housework</u> (New York: Moffat, Yard, 1915), p. 62;
Foner, vol. 3: <u>The Policies and Practices of the American</u>
<u>Federation of Labor, 1900-1909</u>, p. 281; and Samuel Gompers,
<u>Seventy Years of Life and Labor: An Autobiography</u>, vol.
1 (New York: E. P. Dutton, 1925; repr. ed., New York:
Augustus M. Kelly, 1967), pp. 147-48.

7

Against All Odds

The Maid's Defiance

We are coming all together, we are or-
    ganized to stay.
For nigh on fifty years or more we've
    worked for little pay,
But now we've got our union, we'll do it
    never more.

Chorus:

It's a long day for household Mary, it's a
    long day's hard toil.
It's a burden too hard to carry, so our
    mistress' schemes will foil.
For we're out for a shorter day this summer,
Or we'll fix old Denver town.

We've answered all your door bells, and
    we've washed your dirty kid.
For lo—these many weary years, we've done
    as we were bid,
But we're going to fight for freedom, and
    for our rights we'll stand.
And we're going to stick together in one
    big Union band.

Chorus

We've washed your dirty linen and we've
    cooked your daily foods;

We've eaten in your kitchens, and we've
    stood your ugly moods.
But now we've joined the Union and or-
    ganized to stay,
The cooks and maids and chauffeurs in one
    grand array.

Chorus

You've paid the wages, that's what kept
    us on the run.
You say you've done your duty, you cranky
    son-of-a-gun.
We've stood for all your crazy bunk, and
    still you wave and shout,
And call us insufficient and a lazy gad-
    about.

Chorus[1]

Granting the apparently insurmountable obstacles to domestic worker unionization--the individual nature of the work,
the low economic and social status of the workers, the intense competition among them, their isolation from one another, their ethnic and racial origins, the low value placed
on service occupations, and the historic indifference of organized labor--could domestics engage in collective activity?[2]
    Contrary to what may have seemed feasible, domestic
servants did struggle against the odds and did, on occasion, overcome them. They did organize within mainstream
unions whenever possible. Furthermore, they formed numerous independent organizations. When neither of these options proved possible or desirable, domestics engaged in
various forms of personal rebellion as their principal means
of bettering their working conditions.[3] In certain of their
endeavors, domestic workers were aided by concerned employers and social reformers. This was particularly true
of various social and benevolent societies founded in the
late nineteenth and early twentieth centuries. Thus, individually or collectively, inside or outside of organized
labor unions, with or without assistance, each of these
forms of domestic action needs further examination so as to
better understand the role of the domestic worker and her
place in the American labor movement.

Seldom did organized labor actively seek out and embrace the domestic servant, but when it did, some women were ready to seize the opportunity. This was the case with all mainstream labor organizations, even that one least likely to include domestics, the American Federation of Labor. Because the AFL had no international, there were scattered all across the nation numerous local unions chartered directly by the federation. Many of these locals included women and some were composed entirely of females. Among these various organizations were those composed of domestic workers. Specifically, the AFL reported ten domestic unions located in the following cities: San Diego and Los Angeles, California; Chicago and Glencoe, Illinois; Brunswick, Georgia; New Orleans, Louisiana; Beaver Valley, Pennsylvania; and Harrisburg, Denison, and Houston, Texas. In addition, there were ten domestic locals in various southern cities that were affiliated with the Hotel and Restaurant Employees of the International Alliance and Bar Tenders' International League of America, AFL. Unfortunately all these organizations were short-lived and at best locally effective.[4]

However, the bulk of organization (if it can ever be called such) was that which occurred inside the ranks of labor organizations such as the Knights of Labor and the Industrial Workers of the World. Unlike the AFL, these unions were industrial, not craft unions. Consequently they tended to be more receptive to unskilled workers such as domestics and women in general. Verifying this statement is the following analysis of the ninety-one female Knights assemblies found in 1886: nineteen shoe workers; seventeen mill operators; twelve housekeepers; five each of tailoresses, laundresses, and sewers; four each of collar and shirt ironers, dressmakers and cloakmakers, and knitters; two each of hatters, paper-box makers and weavers; and one each of bookbinders, cigar makers, carpet makers, feather curlers, farmers, rubber workers, gold cutters, and lead-pencil workers. In Chicago there was one assembly composed of Bohemian women, and scattered throughout the country there were an additional fifteen assemblies of black women. These assemblies located in Philadelphia, Pennsylvania; Norfolk, Virginia; Wilmington, North Carolina; and Washington, D.C., included farmers, chambermaids, laundresses, and housekeepers.[5]

Domestics were equally, if not more, visible in the IWW. Although it is not possible to compare the number of domestics in the Wobblies with the number in the Knights, IWW women did form numerous and colorful unions.[6] Perhaps typifying both of these attitudes best was Domestic Workers Industrial Union, I.W.W. Local No. 113. Founded on March 31, 1916 in Denver, Colorado, by Jane Street, the union demanded shorter hours, workless Sundays, better treatment, and twelve dollars a week. The union charged an initiation fee of one dollar and dues of 50 cents per month. However, all domestics were encouraged to join whether they could afford to pay or not.[7]

These goals were not what made IWW Local No. 113 unique. What did was the attitude that characterized its leadership and the tactics developed by the local. For example, the membership believed it knew the weaknesses of the Denver mistresses and could capitalize on them. "We have the bulge on the rich women of Denver because they won't wash their own dishes. We can rule the women of Capitol hill through this failing of theirs."[8] This distaste for greasy dishwater was the vehicle the union would use to prevail over Denver mistresses. No general strikes would be necessary. Instead, union members would be specially trained to wear down the nerves of the employers. In so doing, the society ladies of the city would be taught how they should treat their maids. This educational process would be undertaken by a series of domestics who would "leave once a week, serve meals late, take no back talk and demand the privileges for which they [had] been ask[ing] in vain."[9]

No woman would be excluded from union membership because she was incompetent or lazy. Actually large numbers of lazy women were particularly desirable because they would be the best type to teach the Denver mistresses about their proper place. But lazy or not, the plan would be carried out by the union women in training. Residing in a house rented by the local, they would not be dependent on their employer for a place to live. Furthermore, their mobility would be enhanced because they could store their belongings in the house, and if they had children, the children would be cared for while the domestics were working.[10]

As isolated and diverse women, domestics could not use the typical means of organizing.[11] Therefore, Street developed her own unique technique for bringing the women together. Working through her own method for three months, she described the process as "very tedious." But by use of the following process she collected three hundred names:

> I worked at housework for three months,
> collecting names all the while. When I
> was off of a job I rented a room and put
> an ad in the paper for a housemaid.
> Sometimes I used a box number and some-
> times I used my address. The ad was
> worded something like this, "Wanted, House-
> maid for private family, $30, eight hours
> daily." I would write them letters after-
> wards and have them call and see me. If
> they came direct I would usually have an-
> other ad in the same paper, advertising
> for a situation and using my telephone num-
> ber. I would have enough answers to sup-
> ply the applicants. Sometimes I would en-
> gage myself to as many as 25 jobs in one
> day, promising to call the next day to
> everyone that phones. I would collect the
> information secured in this way. If any
> girl wanted any of the jobs, she would go
> out and say that they called her up the
> day before.12

By the end of the year, Street had successfully conducted 1,500 to 2,000 personal interviews. In the process
she informed the women about the IWW and believed the
women had become more receptive to union membership.
She also placed about 1,000 women in domestic positions.
Yet after all of this work, only 155 women actually became
Wobblies. Of these Street conceded a sparse eighty-three
were truly active union participants. "A great many girls
leave town and some of them in town drift away and we
are unable to locate them. In lining up girls through an
employment office there are a large number who pay at
50¢ or perhaps $1.00 on their initiation fee and whom we
never get a chance to reach again. They agree to join
and think favorably of the union while here but their interest is not sufficient to hold them."13
     Thus the real strength of IWW Local No. 113 was not
its method of organization, and certainly not its eighty-
three members. Its real strength lay in the operation of
its employment office. Established prior to April 22, 1916,
the office was a free employment agency. Initially several
Denver housewives cooperated with the office. The eventual
objective of the agency was to control the market for do-

mestic employment by driving the "sharks" out of business
and by establishing control over the working conditions in
Denver homes. In line with their objectives a warning
went out to the Denver mistresses:

> Speak gently to your cook from now on un-
> less you wish to prepare the meals for
> your family and scrub the kitchen floor.
> Because cross and undesirable mistresses
> are going to be black listed by the union.
> At the office to be opened downtown as soon
> as the place can be found, there will be a
> long list including every employer of house
> servants in Denver. And opposite each
> name, its owner's character will be de-
> scribed without mincing words. How many
> rooms there are in your house will be set
> down, how many children you have and
> how well or ill-trained they are.[14]

The key to operation of the employment was the extensive card file established by the local. The cards
carefully listed every domestic position advertised in the
Denver papers. The volume of the cards grew rapidly from
about 300 in March to 2,000 in May and 6,000 by November.
The information on the cards was gathered by union women
who would answer the newspaper ads. Employers were unaware the prospective employee was affiliated with the IWW.
Once interviewed, the domestic would return and note wages
and size of the family and house. With the employment
"sharks" crippled and the card file as their ally, the employer would be unable to secure help unless she met union
demands. Thus if the domestic decided to shorten hours
or not clean the furnace or vacuum the house, she would
be retained until a replacement was found. But how to
find the replacement without the employment "sharks" and
while the union was carefully scanning the newspaper ads?
When the employer ran her ad, the union sent out a new
girl who refused to perform the same tasks or work under
the same conditions. As Jane Street wrote, "If you have a
union of only four girls and you can get them consecutively
on the same job you soon have job control. The nerve-
wrecked, lazy society woman is not hard to conquer."[15]
The union achieved considerable success despite its
few members because the women believed they had real

power to bring about change. Large membership rolls
were not necessary because once the organization owned a
telephone, it could use it systematically to raise wages
throughout the city. For example, to raise a job from $20
to $30, two dozen women would answer a single ad and
demand $30. Another tactic employed was to simply re-
spond to an ad by telling the employer $20 was an accept-
able wage. Since the employer believed the position was
filled, she would run no ad the following day. However,
the domestic would never report to work. She would call
the following day and ask for $25. Once $25 was agreed
upon, a promise to report to work would be made, but
again the following day would bring a no-show. By the
third day the employer would be ready to discuss the issue. In the end the domestic would receive $30 plus
"shortened hours and lightened labors as well." Furthermore, benefits would accrue to all. Jane Street believed
they had. "We have raised wages, shortened hours, bettered conditions in hundreds of places. This is not merely
a statement. It is a fact that is registered not only in
black and white on the cards in our files in the office
but in the flesh and blood of the girls on the job."[16]

The accomplishments of IWW Local No. 113 were significant enough to inspire the formation of other domestic
locals.[17] IWW worker locals were reported to exist in
Duluth, Seattle, Salt Lake City, Chicago, and Cleveland.[18]
Based on information in a Jane Street letter to a Mrs.
Elmer Buse, there was some union activity in Tulsa, Oklahoma. Despite this fact, all of these organizations perished
when the Wobblies were brutally oppressed by the U.S. federal government. Utilizing the Espionage Act during World
War I, the government all but destroyed an organization
employers were delighted to see eliminated. Since these
efforts were especially repressive in the American West,
all the maids' unions, along with other IWW organizations,
ceased to exist.[19]

If organizing within the American labor movement
proved less than successful or less than enduring, domestics could and did establish their own unions. In some
instances these organizations took the form of benevolent
or social societies. More correctly labeled "clubs" than
unions, the domestics were often aided by concerned reformers and employers in these types of collective endeavors.
Their aim was to provide the servant woman with a social
life and companionship free from employer restrictions. An

excellent example of this kind of servant organization was the Progressive Household Club. Located in Los Angeles and founded in 1915, it was run and operated by domestics. The club provided a variety of services to its reported 500 members. Domestics owned their clubhouse, which housed a laundry room, kitchen, and recreational facilities. The clubhouse was the site of sponsored cultural and social functions. In addition, the club ran an employment service for its members, offered low-rent rooms to its unemployed, and provided storage space for its members' personal belongings. All of these benefits were paid for by member dues, loans, and fees from other club services.[20]

Numerous earlier counterparts to the Progressive Household Club had existed. For example, the Household Auxiliary Association was established in the summer of 1892. Essentially, this organization attempted to improve domestics' working conditions. Rather than calling themselves domestics or servants, members of the Auxiliary Association wished to be hired as lady-helps. Furthermore, as lady-helps, they were no longer to endure certain living or working conditions. Lady-helps were not to eat their meals or room with the other workers. Nor were they to perform "rough" work like blacking boots, carrying heavy weights upstairs, and scrubbing. In short, this classification of domestic was to constitute a new elite within the confines of paid household labor.[21]

Even more elaborate and comprehensive was an association that evolved out of a Chicago, Illinois, May 1893 Woman's Congress. Particularly interesting was the fact that both the employee and employer met and discussed the important issues, and the rights and wrongs of domestic work. The workers developed an impressive list of employment conditions under which they hoped to work in the future. First and foremost, they wanted to be relieved of the heaviest types of labor. In return for this alteration, they were willing to accept an appropriate deduction in salary. Domestics wanted to be addressed and treated as though they, and their occupations, were equally as respectable as other trades. Whenever possible, the women wanted certain hours of absolute personal freedom. If the workers in a particular home objected to the use of livery, it was to be eliminated. The women wanted decent living accommodations, including a proper eating place. Finally, they wanted the freedom to see personal friends--male or female. In particular, they wanted this privilege to occur

in a room other than, and better than, the kitchen. Furthermore, personal visiting was to be free of family "espionage." Related to this final request was the proviso
that evening hours had proper and fair restrictions placed
upon them. Evening hours were to begin only when all
required tasks had been completed.[22]

Reformers were often involved in, or at least supportive of, these kinds of collective activities. For some
they were an alternative to more militant labor organizations.[23] But not all reformers shied away from the notion
of bona fide labor unions for domestic workers. Some did
temper their support by arguing that the Servant Girls'
Unions should be countered by Associations of Housewives.[24] Others argued that despite the servants' weaknesses, inefficiency, and lack of intelligence, the demand
for servants so greatly exceeded supply that they could
change the conditions of their employment. Therefore, domestics should unite much as the carpenters, bricklayers,
and plumbers had done before them. A union of domestics
under the leadership of those who possessed powers akin
to those of the old craft guilds would best direct the women
into the positions for which they were most qualified. Furthermore, a general sense of self-uplift would occur when
the servant woman "puts on her hat to attend a meeting of
the International House Operatives' Union Local 27 . . . .
[For then] even the memory of her serfage will vanish."[25]

Perhaps the most comprehensive analysis of and ar-
gument for domestic worker unionization was one that put
the question in the context of labor history. Arguing that
industrial labor had discerned but two effective methods
for redressing labor grievances--cooperative efforts in the
form of unions and compulsory regulations--common assumption seemed to hold neither were applicable to domestic service. This was not correct, for despite the special circumstances of this type of labor, the obstacles to collective
action were not insurmountable. In fact, large institutions
like rooming houses, hotels, and restaurants had already
paved the way for the personal household domestic. Granting the various differences in these kinds of institutions,
the similarities were more striking and essential. For instance, the basic services performed were identical. Furthermore, both collective residences and private homes
were supplied by identical sources of labor. Therefore,
the private home was not unlike the small shop of earlier
times. Despite the assertions that these businesses could

not survive labor unions or legislative regulation, they had managed to do so.[26]

Whatever the degree of similarity and amount of co-operation between the large institutions and private house-holds, the unionizing of domestics would not be easy. Domestic unions would encounter the very difficulties con-fronting all the other labor organizations involving women. Still the beginning was embodied in the achievements of the collective institutions. Because of their accomplish-ments, certain ideal standards had already been estab-lished. In the future protective legislation and direct union action would further enhance the permanence of such standards in private homes. "In short, equalization in the status of the household worker with that of the worker in other industrial fields is the requirement which labor presents, as yet unconsciously, but the demand will become clear and conscious in the future."[27]

Certainly agreeing with much of the preceding argu-ment, especially as it applied to women workers in general, was the Women's Trade Union League. Established in 1903, the league was a coalition of trade union women, social reformers, and settlement house residents. As a national organization, the league continued to exist until 1950. In addition, it had numerous eastern and midwestern local branches. However, its influence and activities declined considerably after the mid-1920s. WTUL membership was composed of working women and their supporters—leisured women who were sympathetic to the issues confronting women workers. The league had numerous goals, all of which were carried out with varying degrees of success. Included among these goals was the general objective of improving the working condition of women laborers by lobby-ing for legislation to regulate working conditions and hours, educating women from all walks of life (including working women and union men), and organizing women into trade unions. The educational activities were directly related to this last goal because they were intended to make all groups understand and appreciate the value of female labor organization.[28]

Indicative of these objectives was a call issued by Margaret Dreier Robins, president of the WTUL from 1907 to 1922. When the 1915 New York Times article quoted below appeared, the league had established eight local organiza-tions in various large cities. Maintaining working condi-tions had been bettered in these cities through organization

and legislation, the league was appealing to the working
women of the nation for both their own and the general
good. Furthermore, through education the WTUL had con-
vinced its own membership of the necessity of cooperation
and organization. Thus the Times wrote, "Margaret Dreier
Robins, President of the Women's Trade Union League, yesterday issued a call to the 7,000,000 women workers in the
United States, 3,000,000 being under 21 years of age, to
organize for better working conditions and to become affiliated with the American Federation of Labor."[29]

True to this appeal, the league concentrated on organizing women workers during the first twelve years of
its existence. Orchestrated by a national policymaking
group, and supported by various local chapters in cities
like St. Louis, Chicago, Boston, and New York, the WTUL
supplied funds, advice, publicity, and political support
for women struggling to unionize around issues of working
conditions. Working with the American Federation of Labor,
the WTUL offered financial assistance to the federation so
that it would pay heed to those women too difficult or expensive to organize.

Achieving a spectacular success in the 1909-1910
strike of New York City's garment industry, the league was
equally active and successful elsewhere. As one scholar
has written of the league, "In essence the WTUL attempted
to do for women workers what male labor unions had long
done for their male counterparts."[30]

However dedicated, however committed to the plight
of working women, the league had at least two major obstacles with respect to domestic workers. In the first
place, the early years of the WTUL's existence (national
and local) were plagued by a tenuous relationship with the
AFL. Cordial relations were first established between these
two organizations shortly after the league was founded.
Initially league leaders hoped this relationship would grow
and prosper. Hopes in this direction seemed well-founded,
especially after Samuel Gompers spoke before a WTUL-spon-
sored conference in 1905. At the First National Conference
on Women in Industry, Gompers praised the league for
broadening the horizons of organized labor and encouraging
the assistance of sympathetic men and women. But the
words of Gompers were mere platitudes. Despite this fact,
the league linked itself to the AFL and made it clear the
two organizations would adhere to the same policies.[31]

Spending much time and effort trying to appease federation leadership, the WTUL hoped that tangible results would eventuate. At one point Gompers allowed the league to print an AFL endorsement on WTUL letterhead. This led to a burst of league enthusiasm and an actual redefinition of some organizational objectives in the 1907 constitution. Crucial to domestic workers was the fact that the WTUL would assist in organizing female workers into trade unions. However, when possible and practicable, these women were to become affiliated with the American Federation of Labor. Since the federation was seldom, if ever, truly interested in organizing women, especially unskilled and minority women, the league could hardly force them to do otherwise.[32]

This does not imply that the WTUL was unaware of, or totally unconcerned with, the plight of domestic workers. At one point the league approached the secretary of labor and urged that there be a reorganization and reclassification of the household trades. The league recommended they be placed on a par with other occupations. At the same time the WTUL advocated a government investigation of domestic service. In line with such thinking, Margaret Dreier Robins urged implementation of standardized hours and the adoption of live-out service. However, the role foreseen by Robins for the WTUL in these reforms appears to have been a passive one. In some form, in some fashion, change would occur. "Every branch of industrial labor is affected by the progress of others, and domestic service is but one branch of the great social evolution of our times. It is working out its own answer."[33]

Limited by this passive philosophy of change and tied to the coattails of the AFL, the league was also mired down in internal differences. The differences stemmed from the varied backgrounds of WTUL members. In essence, the problem was whether or not women of different economic and social backgrounds could unite on the issues of feminism. Specifically the leisured women, who made up the bulk of league membership, shared the basic mentality of the Progressive Movement. Only through their involvement in other reform activities had they developed an awareness of the problems confronting working women. On the other hand, women workers had become involved in the league because they found it to be the only organization interested in improving their lot. At least in principle, the WTUL was committed to including women workers in the accomplishment of the necessary reforms.[34]

Joining the WTUL with greatly varying backgrounds and consequently sometimes with different objectives, the various members were often at odds with one another. True female solidarity was probably never achieved. In no instance was this more so than with domestic workers. Afternoon dances and teas, English classes, outings, parades and picnics, folk dancing, working women's choruses, union label campaigns, and library rooms were no substitute for union organizing. Yet the league and its numerous local branches were often bogged down in these cultural and social activities. Not only did these programs expend much time and energy, they did little to attract working women into the league. As Ida Tarbell pointed out, this was especially true with respect to the domestic worker:

> Feminine circles everywhere have been convulsed with sympathy for shop and factory girls. Intelligent and persistent efforts are making to reach and aid them. This is, of course, right, and it would be a natural calamity if such organizations as the Woman's Trade Union League and the Consumer's League should lose any of their vigor. But the need of the classes they reach is really less than the need of household workers.35

Regardless of the WTUL, regardless of other groups or individuals, domestics could and did form their own independent labor organizations. Such organizations extend as far back in time as the early nineteenth century. In 1835 day washerwomen in New York City formed an organization and went on strike. A few years earlier Marie Stewart, possibly the first black woman to speak in public and become active on behalf of black working women, addressed the Afro-American Female Intelligence Society of Boston in 1832. She stressed the need for black women to find other and better employment opportunities than those currently available: domestic service and washerwomen. Furthermore, she urged them to organize.36

In 1864 the Working Women's Protective Union was formed in New York City. Initially established to examine the charges brought by domestics and seamstresses regarding the nonpayment of wages and salary deductions, the union broadened its scope. For example, efforts were undertaken to train women in other occupations and to prevent crowding in the various trades. Although the Protective Union found jobs for several thousand women, its major emphasis and success was in securing legal protection for working women. Almost single-handedly the union successfully saw the passage of a law providing for the imprisonment of employers who failed to pay working women their wages. Unlike the group of Newark, New Jersey, female servants, who grouped together shortly after the Civil War to demand a ten dollar minimum wage per month, the Protective Union remained in existence until the 1880s.[37]

The ultimate collapse of these, and virtually all, early female attempts at unionization led to the formulation of certain conclusions about the history of women in the trade union movement. First and foremost, female labor organizations were ephemeral in nature. Often growing out of a strike, they disappeared after a settlement had been reached. Second, female organizations more than male organizations were influenced and developed by leadership outside the rank and file. External leadership was both a strength and a weakness of the union movement among women. Although the strengths were important, the weaknesses were probably more so. "External leadership has often worked injury to the trade-union women by drawing them away from plans for immediate advantages, to the consideration of more remote and less tangible schemes for universal reform."[38]

Conclusions and failures of the early unions aside, domestics continued their attempts to improve their lot through organization. In the 1880s and 1890s popular periodicals and newspapers made mention of domestic unions and strikes. At one point such groups as the Domestic Servant's Union of New York City, the Servant Girl's Union in Toledo, Ohio, and the Household Union in Holyoke, Massachusetts, were all active. Greenville, Pennsylvania, domestics collectivized in 1886 and demanded a fifty-cent weekly wage increase. Furthermore, they threatened to boycott any servant who refused to join their organization. Shortly thereafter, in 1889 Bibb City, Arkansas, black women, including domestics, staged a work stoppage because of ill treatment.[39]

Two late-nineteenth-century servant unions (one black and one white) are of particular interest. Both groups illustrate the determination, but ultimately the inability, of servant organizations to survive. Nowhere was

this more poignantly revealed than by the Atlanta washerwomen in 1881. They went on strike demanding a dollar
per dozen pounds of laundry. Cooks, child nurses, and
servants eventually joined the three thousand washerwomen
who went on strike. Other issues soon superseded labor
relations, however, because the white community of Atlanta
flexed its muscles to destroy the movement. Thus city
landlords threatened to raise the rents of women who had
gone out to strike. The city council of Atlanta passed a
bill requiring all members of the union to pay an annual
twenty-five dollar license fee. This was the same fee
levied on city businesses. Finally, the police moved in
and eventually eight strike leaders were convicted for disorderly conduct.[40]

The crucial factor for these Atlanta women and other
southern workers in general was their excess number. Few
occupational opportunities were open to black women.
Most were forced to work in order to earn a living or
supplement the low wages paid to their parents or spouses.
Young women enlarged this pool of unskilled workers even
further because they had virtually no educational opportunities. Thus, as Walter Fleming aptly noted, southern
strikes were doomed to fail because "the country darkies
will come in and take the plac= of some of the strikers."[41]

Sixteen years later a young woman named Mary
Hartropp organized the American Servant Girl's Association
in Kansas City, Missouri. Within a period of two weeks it
was reported that thirty locals had been established with
a membership total of approximately 5,000. In May of
1897 Hartropp arrived in Duluth, Minnesota, to set up another local. From Duluth she planned to move on to Superior,
Ashland, and other reasonably good-sized towns in Wisconsin.
Her ultimate destination was Chicago, where she estimated
she would remain for approximately six months.[42]

A domestic herself, Mary Hartropp developed and
used an interesting technique. Before her arrival in
Duluth, she sent postal cards to all the women she could
find listed in the city directory as servants. In this way
she prepared and advised them of the forthcoming meeting
and its purpose. One hundred and seventy-five women,
many from various ethnic groups and employed in the
boarding houses, hotels, and private homes of the city, attended the organizational meeting. The women gathered in
Silver Hall, heard Hartropp's address, and formed the
Duluth chapter of the American Servant Girl's Association.

In accordance with the wishes of Hartropp, all activities were carried out secretly. Neither the general public nor the city papers were aware of the gathering's intent.[43]

Secrecy was not to be a permanent feature of the union. The intention was to keep things quiet for several weeks "until the National Organization had gained sufficient strength to come out boldly and assert itself to the world."[44] Hartropp told the members of the chapter that their initiation fee was twenty-five cents and their monthly dues were twelve cents. Half of the initiation fee went to National headquarters and the rest to the local. Another meeting was scheduled for the following week so that members could pay their fees and elect permanent officers. In the meanwhile Hartropp emptied her satchel and passed out books, cards, and pamphlets which set forth all the regulations, rules, objectives, and benefits of the union. Reportedly every member in attendance took home a bountiful supply of these documents for further examination during her leisure hours.[45]

One of the items was a pamphlet issued for use in recruiting new members. The pamphlet contained the objectives of the organization and included the following goals:

> To advance the social standing of the laboring girl. To secure for the servant girl a better appreciation of her services on the part of the employer.
>
> To protect the servant girl against the infamous blacklisting system adopted by mistresses generally.
>
> To secure for the servant girl a revised system of household duties and payment of a fair remuneration for her services.
>
> To secure for servant girls the consent of all employers for a general half holiday each week, and for the privilege of enjoying freedom from bondage on the Sabbath day.
>
> To provide a means of concerted action whenever occasion required such action.
>
> To furnish employment for unemployed members and to care for them when disabled.[46]

Assessing all these union goals, Mary Hartropp believed that the last one was the most significant and most substantial feature of the organization. Although not fully in place, Hartropp projected that a well-developed insurance department would be completed within a matter of months. Through this department Hartropp proposed to provide her members with insurance at a comparatively minor cost. The policies were to provide benefits in case of injury, sickness, or death. She believed every servant woman would "avail herself of the opportunity to provide for a rainy day when the plan was ready for promulgation."[47]

Unfortunately for the servant women, Mary Hartropp was wrong. Like those numerous domestics organizations that had gone before hers, the American Servant Girl's Association vanished from the scene as quickly as it had emerged. However, three short years later another attempt was made to organize household workers. Mrs. St. Justin Beale of New York City sparked the initiative and tried to sustain what Mary Hartropp had failed to keep alive. Beale told the women that she had long been interested in the plight of servants. Her interest and investigation had led her to conclude that servants were frequently overworked, badly housed, and badly fed.[48]

Operating from her Second Avenue home, Beale proposed to charge union members a one dollar initiation fee and twenty-five cents monthly dues. She said the money would be used to establish a fund for a union headquarters, a reading room, a free labor bureau, and free sacred Sunday concerts for members. Whatever Beale promised seemed to have had little appeal because only twelve domestics were there to hear her. Nevertheless she persisted, addressed the women, scheduled another meeting for the following week, and persuaded six women to enroll in the Domestic Servant's Union. The women discussed future meetings and threatened a general strike of New York City servants. But the tenacity of Mrs. Beale was not enough to sustain an organization. It, too, vanished from the labor scene before moving much beyond the talking stage.[49]

Although the International Socialist Review reported that Mother Jones was organizing domestic workers in Scranton, Pennsylvania, the next really significant attempt at union formation by servants occurred in Chicago in late July of 1901. The day following the founding of the Workingwomen of America, the Chicago Tribune ran a front-page feature discussing the group. The paper proclaimed woe

was in store for the mistresses of the city once the new
organization had formalized its existence. Heretofore,
there would be "rules of the range" because "above the
cook stove may hang printed instructions for those who pay
wages."[50]

When organized, the union had three hundred members. They adopted a wage scale and a set of rules governing working conditions. For example, housekeepers and
cooks were to receive $5 to $7 per week, general and second girls $4 to $5 per week, and young and inexperienced
girls $3 to $4 per week. The governing rules were far
more complex and explicit. In a general way the rules
were an expression of long-standing discontent, as well as
an eagerness to elevate domestic work to the status of a
trade. The rules included the following:

> Rule I.—Work shall not begin before
> 5:30 a.m. and shall cease when the eve-
> ning's dishes are washed and put away.
> Two hours each afternoon and the entire
> evening, at least twice a week, shall be
> allowed the domestic as her own.
> Rule II.—There shall be no opposition
> on the part of the mistress to club life on
> the part of the domestic. Entertainment of
> friends in limited numbers shall not be
> prohibited, provided the domestic furnishes
> her own refreshments.
> Rule III.—Gentlemen friends shall not
> be barred from the kitchen or back porch.
> Members of the family shall not interrupt
> the conversations arising during said visit.
> Rule IV.—Domestics shall be allowed
> such hours off on Monday as will permit
> them to visit the bargain counters of the
> stores and enjoy on that day the same
> privileges enjoyed by the mistress and her
> daughters.
> Rule V.—All complaints shall be made
> to the business agent of the union. The
> question of wage shall be settled at the
> time of employment and no reduction shall
> be allowed.[51]

The women who convened in Chicago that summer in 1901 proceeded to elect officers for their union. All the home addresses of these officials were kept secret until the organization had 1,000 members. One of the elected members turned out to be a Miss Ellen Lindstrom. Lindstrom was a delegate of the Custom Clothing Makers' Union, and had been approached by several domestics on issues relating to union formation. Only two weeks after she had been consulted, the International Union Label League took over, held meetings, and the Workingwomen of America was eventually born. The organizers referred to their group as a "gumshoe" agitation. "They are working so secretly, so softly, that not a matron in all Chicago is expected to know whether her roof is sheltering a union girl till the time comes to make known and hang the framed rules over the kitchen range."[52]

Later in the summer of 1901, two of the officers and founders were interviewed in a lengthy Tribune article about the Workingwomen of America. When one of the women was questioned about the viability of the union, she replied that domestics were "interested enough to meet once a week." Furthermore, social gatherings would be held to acquaint the women with one another and in order to "learn from each other."[53]

The financial secretary, Margaret Keehan, also discussed why the women had chosen to call themselves the Workingwomen of America rather than the Servant Girl's Union. Her response was an excellent reflection of the organization's desire to elevate the standing of domestic service. Keehan believed the word "servant" had subsumed the meaning of the word "slave." "'Servant girl,' she is only a 'kitchen mechanic,' that's what many people say. We hear the way the clerks in the stores and the way everybody sneers at the girl in the kitchen. We are cooks, and waitresses, and housemaids—those names are good ones, and they all come under our title of working women."[54]

Recording Secretary Stella Wendt, originator of the union, developed this idea even further. Claiming her own awareness of union benefits originated with her uncle, who had been responsible for organizing the bottlemakers, Wendt foresaw several positive outcomes that would eventuate from the Workingwomen of America. From her perspective these would bring positive results to both the domestic and her mistress. One benefit would be a general upgrading of servants through proper training. Second, order and system would be established in housekeeping. Thus the women would organize themselves, they would discuss methods of procedure, and they would systematize their tasks. Once all these changes had occurred, the mistresses would realize the positive attributes of unionization.[55]

The moderate tone of union officials (Wendt put her emphasis on comfortable sleeping accommodations and a ten-hour day) seemed sometimes at variance with numerous rank-and-file members. For example, one militant Irishwoman held that the union was needed to protect the women from mistresses who had no concern for the physical or mental welfare of their employees. She believed domestics were treated more like machines than people. "I must join the union and I will be the first one to start a strike." Another member stated, "We'll have our nights off when we want them and we'll have something to say about washing day too." A commonly expressed remark was, "We'll show them."[56]

Perhaps because of these philosophical differences between union leadership and union rank and file, initial enthusiasm for the organization diminished. The hundreds of members represented a very small segment of Chicago's 35,000 domestics. Nor was the group ever able to secure a charter from the American Federation of Labor. Many Chicago domestics remained unaware of the union, and when they were informed of its existence, they showed no inclination to join.[57]

Chicago club women and employers manipulated themselves into positions of control within the union. Perhaps they were able to achieve their infiltration because of internal differences in the organization. Possibly they feared that the union might actually be successful. In any case local newspapers put great emphasis on this element and very little on the servant role. Very likely the newspapers were deceived by reform elements speaking of what they wished to see accomplished for the Chicago domestic worker. But far more distressing than the increasing influence of reformers was the infiltration by employers. Their presence became very apparent at the organization's first open meeting of August 23, 1901.[58]

The August gathering was particularly significant not only because it was the union's first public forum, but because there was an impressive array of prominent labor leaders, women's club leaders, and nationally known social

reformers in attendance. These individuals included H. J.
Sheffington of the Boot and Shoe Workers' Union, J. H.
Bowman of the AFL, Ellen Lindstrom and Emma Lamphere,
general organizers of the retail clerks, W. A. Campbell,
grand marshall of the Labor Day parade, Jane Addams,
and prominent club woman Mrs. Charles Henrotin. All delivered speeches favoring the objectives of the union and
lauding the goal of upgrading the standing of service occupations.[59]

A surprising blow came when Mrs. Henrotin, while
supporting the union's demand for reform, also proposed
the creation of an employer's association. This was necessary in order "to meet and talk over the problems with the
girls, discuss their needs, and the housewives' needs."[60]
Most certainly, this was not what the domestics had hoped
would come out of their meeting, especially from a woman
who, they believed, supported their endeavor. The pro-
posal may have contributed to a significant decline in membership, which was noticeable at the next meeting.

In September two important mass circulation periodicals ran featured articles on Chicago's Workingwomen of
America. Although conceding the issues raised by the
union merited serious consideration, the Nation held that
"only one speaker showed insight into the real difficulties
by suggesting that the new movement would 'force the employers to organize'!"[61]

In a more protracted discussion the Independent discussed how the union would have far-reaching effects. In-
dicating its support for the organization's objectives to establish hours of labor, relaxation, and standards for compensation, the writer went on to mock the value of the
other union goals. Still the general tone of the magazine
was favorable to the movement. Despite the tone, the author maintained that organization details could never be
successfully applied to country life, and it was doubtful
if they were applicable to the city. According to the Independent:

> [The final upshot of] this aggressive action
> of the serving woman of America will lead
> to a rational union of their employers.
> What we need is some basis of contract that
> will bond both maid and mistress and be
> just to all concerned. It seems quite prob-
> able that there will come about, through

> this movement, a more rational grading of
> prices, so that the raw, untrained woman
> cannot secure or demand wages equal to
> those demanded by the better educated.
> It will be well if the whole servant girl
> question can be stirred up to the very
> bottom.[62]

Actually, positive or negative attitudes such as
these mattered far less than the membership's diminishing
enthusiasm. This development seems to have occurred because of internal division and the fact that the domestics
were losing control of their union. Fewer and fewer members attended meetings and no new members joined. The
constitution was never ratified, and by October of 1901 the
treasury was empty. These crucial issues were shoved
aside to discuss the proposed Christmas dance. But after
the October 24 meeting the Workingwomen of America went
the way of its earlier counterparts.[63]

Restiveness was even found among southern black
servants at the turn of the twentieth century. Walter
Fleming concluded that blacks reached a point where they
felt their situation was impossible. They discussed an organized strike or in their words a general "quitten." To
this end the women set up a society or a club. All members paid regular dues, and when the women determined
their financial situation was sound enough, they planned
to go on strike. They intended to show their southern mistresses how dependent the latter were on their help.[64]

The women planned to proceed with their idea by
hiring out at the beginning of the college term because
the town population would be at its peak. After one day's
work, with no rate of pay established, the servant women
would demand $12 a month as a general pay standard.
The going rate was $4 to $5 a month. If their demand
was not met, they planned to strike. No record indicates
whether these southern black servant women ever carried
their plans to fruition.[65]

A flurry of collective attempts occurred during the
first two decades of the twentieth century. Thus on December 3, 1912 a Mrs. Krentzer of Cleveland, Ohio, asked
for endorsement of a maid's union.[66] No further mention
was made of Krentzer, but by 1913 Rose Charvat had organized a Housemaid's Union in the city. The organization
was reportedly growing in strength and preparing to pre-

sent a wage scale and to demand a ten-hour work day on July 27, 1913. The members proposed to blacklist all housewives who hired nonunion domestics.[67]

In 1918 domestic workers in Kansas City and Norfolk, Virginia, met in small groups and agreed to demand a two-dollar a day salary from their employers. By 1919 household laborers had collectivized in Mobile, Alabama; Tulsa and Lawton, Oklahoma; and Fort Worth, Texas. They hoped to better both their wages and working conditions.[68]

From what little evidence can be ascertained about these various attempts at collective action, all were short-lived. Yet these organizations attest to the rather persistent effort of domestic workers to better their lot. Excluding the ten locals in the urban South, all of which were affiliated with the Hotel and Restaurant Employees Union of the AFL, the single successful independent domestic union formed during the conservative 1920s appears to have been established by Miss I. of Detroit, Michigan. Her efforts centered on bringing maids and mistresses together to discuss their differences. "This is not a one-sided task. Domestic workers must want better conditions and greater respect themselves, but they must make their position clear to employers. By our working together, an impression can be made on the community."[69]

Like other independent collective actions, Miss I. proposed a long and somewhat elaborate list of organizational objectives. But Miss I.'s objectives were couched in the form of worker responsibilities. Possibly she hoped to make them more palatable in an otherwise conservative and antiunion era. In any case the responsibilities allotted free time for the maid and were intended to set a model for household laborers everywhere. Collectively the following objectives directed domestics to "fight, if necessary, for good conditions"[70]:

Responsibilities of the Domestic Worker

1. Toward the employer—to do her best; to take an interest in the work; to use care; to be economical; to help train the employer in up-to-date methods.
2. Toward the other workers in the same house (difficult to remember and fulfill)—to see that all get right amount and kind of food; right treatment; keep clear of jealousy.

Methods (a) Make your own financial
              bargain for your own kind
              and amount of work and let
              the others do likewise.
          (b) Keep outside interests.
  3. To herself--keep a high standard of--
          (a) Health
          (b) Morals
          (c) Cheerfulness and sense of
              humor
          (d) Mental alertness.[71]

Time and circumstances seem to have been no more
or no less kind to Miss I. She, too, vanished from the
written page and no further trace of her is to be found.
Perhaps as historian Daniel E. Sutherland noted, the failure of Miss I. and other collective attempts was predictable.
In numerous instances the domestics were divided among
themselves and consequently could not concur on what program to adopt. In other cases, once unionization lost its
novelty, and once the women learned that change would be
evolutionary rather than revolutionary, they lost interest.
This was particularly evident after reformers and community leaders infiltrated and took over the movements, and
established a more moderate tone.[72]

In the end domestic unions resembled the proverbial
ephemeral ship in the night. Very possibly the women understood this and thus never truly took much stock in organization. Possibly they found individualized resistance
more productive in their dealings with employers. Perhaps
the effectiveness of individualized efforts helped to mitigate
the chance for successful large-scale unionization. Whatever the answer, there was a rather strong tradition for
domestics to work out their own limits of respect and obligation within the highly charged personal context of the
home. When employers crossed over these bounds, they
were met by employee resistance. From the employer's
perspective this resistance was an act of defiance. One
ultimate expression of defiance was quitting. A very dramatic example of this occurred in the summer of 1891. In
this instance, the entire staff of servants walked out en
masse from the John Jacob Glessner household located in
Chicago.[73]

Far less dramatic but far more common was the individual practice of quitting. In other words high job

turnover was a fundamental characteristic of domestic service and a way the worker sought to find improved working
conditions.   The high degree of domestic worker turnover
may well have been a reflection of the many difficulties
inherent in unionization.   A much simpler and seemingly
more successful tactic was simply to quit.   The significance of high turnover rates can hardly be overemphasized.
They stand as a clear expression of worker discontent.
Nor was this practice endemic to service occupations.   For
example, turnover rates reached unbelievable proportions
in Ford plants prior to World War II.   During the conservative 1920s leaving a job was a basic way for a laborer to
react to oppressive working conditions, particularly given
the absence of collective options.[74]

Studies and reports analyzing high turnover rates
for domestic servants found them to be a historical constant.   Lucy Maynard Salmon, the pioneer scholar of domestic work, undertook a national sample of turnover rates in
1889 and 1890.   She found the average length of service
was less than a year and one half.   In her famous study
of Philadelphia's Seventh Ward, Isabel Eaton found the
longest average term of service was four years and five
months.   An early twentieth-century study found the average tenure of service in cities less than one and one half
years, and in towns "where the desire to go to the cities
is strong it is still shorter."[75]   One later investigation
done in Baltimore, Maryland, revealed similar patterns.
This particular tabulation, done in 1925, was based on a
sample of 810 women.   The report found 18.9 percent of the
workers stayed on a job under three months; 17.9 percent
between three and six months; 15.4 percent between six
months and one year; 34.4 percent between one year and
five years; 7.7 percent between five and ten years; and
only 5.7 percent ten years and over.   Nor was there much
variance in Baltimore between the rates of turnover for
white and black domestics.   Specifically, 48.7 percent of
white women as compared to 53.4 percent of black women
remained less than a year in one place.[76]   Table 7.1 further illustrates the propensity for servants to move from
one position to another.

In some instances turnover rates were facilitated by
employers who lured away well-trained and competent domestics.   Although this practice was considered underhanded,
it was used—the most common inducements being higher
wages and greater privileges.   When such inducements were

Table 7.1

Length of Service for Female Domestic Servants
in Selected Cities, Percent Distribution

Length of Service	New York City 1906-9 (blacks)	Gainesville, GA 1919 (blacks)	Baltimore 1923 (whites)	Baltimore 1923 (blacks)
Under 3 months	20	38	18	19
3 months to under 6 months	22	16	16	19
6 months to under 1 year	25	13	16	15
1 year to under 2 years	18	7	16	14
2 years to under 5 years	12	13	19	20
5 years to under 10 years	2	4	9	7
10 years and over	1	9	6	5
	100	100	100	100
Under 1 year	67	67	50	43
	n=761	n=69	n=231	n=552

Sources: New York City: George Edmond Haynes, The Negro At Work in New York City (Original, 1912; reprint, New York, 1968), pp. 84-85. Gainesville: Ruth Reed, "The Negro Woman of Gainesville, Georgia," Bulletin of the University of Georgia 22 (December 1921):25; Baltimore: Mary V. Robinson, Domestic Workers and Their Employment Relation, U.S. Department of Labor, Women's Bureau, Bulletin No. 39 (Washington D.C., 1920), pp. 72-73.

made and accepted, the worker tended to give her former employer no notice. Despite these instances, the propensity to change positions was part of a much larger issue; it was an aspect of the constant search for better living and working conditions. As long as demand exceeded supply, household laborers could, and did, feel free to move as frequently as their personal circumstances allowed. However, few could remain out of work for long. Changing jobs was the one great power the domestic possessed. But this power was an individual, not a collective one.[77]

If changing positions was the one great power the domestic worker possessed, it was not her only power. For example, southern black domestics were known to work out their own common understanding. When one of their own was wrongfully discharged by an employer, no others would fill the position.   One black domestic, discharged under the rubric of general worthlessness by an unwise employer, told everyone she had not been fired, but was taking a rest.   Consequently for six weeks the mistress in question was forced to perform her own housework.[78]

Unable to undermine white power and white control, blacks could exert some influence over their individual work tasks.   A commonly used device was the so-called incipient strike.   One author argued that incipient strikes occurred all the time with the exception of the winter season when black food supplies ran short.   Because Negro domestics in the South had few privileges, because holidays were rare, and because domestics were expected to labor seven days a week, blacks simply declared their own holidays.   They failed to show up for work.   Thus the incipient strike was seldom for higher wages; it was for greater privileges and less work.[79]

Work stoppages and work slowdowns were additional ways to cut down on the number of employer demands. Blacks, once again, deployed these techniques most effectively.   They played on commonly held racial stereotypes and used them to their own advantage.   Slow-paced work poorly performed was often attributed to the nature of black people.   White employers were prone to interpret visits home during the workday and the desire to return home at night as examples of Negro laziness.   They also saw these trips as a major way for black servants to steal from white kitchens; this was the well-known practice of toting.   The reality of these practices was generally at variance with white perceptions.   Extra time at home gave married black women more opportunity to care for their homes and families.   Extra food often meant the difference in an otherwise marginal diet.   Since time and food were "given freely," black women seized it.[80]

Not all domestic worker resistance occurred within the confines of the slower paced rural South.   Nor was it always this genteel.   Although associated most with the unionization of mass production industries, the sit-down strike, first used by the IWW, was deployed by one Long Island domestic named Johanna O'Reilly.   O'Reilly used the technique in her employer's home and in the process manhandled two police officers after they were summoned to deal with the situation.   Eventually she was driven from the home, tried, found guilty, and sentenced to twenty-five days in the Riverhead jail on the charge of disorderly conduct.[81]

However dramatic and colorful the escapades of O'Reilly were, domestics were more notorious for engaging in various forms of sabotage, theft, and willful destruction of private property. All these forms of resistance were designed to bring employers to terms. Imagine the master of the house dressing in his favorite soft shirt only to find it had been "sabotaged" with heavy starch. Consider the angry domestic who, when washing the dishes, let a cup fall on purpose. Gaining an angry rise out of her mistress, she proceeded to break a plate. Many employers, probably without ever understanding the motivation behind a certain behavior, believed that servants who destroyed cooking utensils, wasted fuel, used unnecessarily large quantities of supplies when cooking, and wasted good food were shiftless. So widespread was thievery among black domestics that there was virtually no attempt to stop it. When attempts were made to establish "Caucasian honesty" among blacks, the results led to an "abiding disgust on the part of the reformer, and her unpopularity among the negroes."[82]

Although individual acts of rebellion may have given the domestic a personal sense of satisfaction--a sense of revenge well-deserved--few tangible gains were actually achieved. In the end, whatever course of action was undertaken, disparity between the mistress and her maid remained as great as ever. The odds against the domestic remained insurmountable. Essentially the economic conditions of the nation were not much affected by domestic service. As one author concluded, "The whole body of domestic employees might strike and industry would not be stagnated, transportation would go on just the same, trade would not be interfered with, and manufacturers would know no difference."[83]

NOTES

1. "The Maid's Defiance," written for the Denver Housemaid's Union, Solidarity, 6 May 1916.
2. Gerda Lerner, ed., Black Women in White America: A Documentary History (New York: Vintage Books, 1973), pp. 231-32.
3. Although the domestic worker was not a slave, the excessive control exercised by the mistress offers some interesting analogies when analyzing methods of individual-

ized resistance. See David M. Katzman's comments on this in Seven Days a Week: Women and Domestic Service in Industrializing America (New York: Oxford University Press, 1978), pp. 195, 197.

4. Alice Henry, The Trade Union Women (New York: D. Appleton, 1915), pp. 94–95; "Plans for Improvement of Domestic Service," Monthly Labor Review 10 (May 1920): 1190; and Lerner, ed., Black Women in White America, pp. 231–32.

5. Philip S. Foner, Women and the American Labor Movement: From Colonial Times to the Eve of World War I (New York: Free Press, 1979), p. 188; Katzman, Seven Days a Week, pp. 195–96; Philip S. Foner, Organized Labor and the Black Worker: 1619–1973 (New York: International Publishers, 1976), p. 48; Sidney H. Kessler, "The Organization of Negroes in the Knights of Labor," Journal of Negro History 37 (July 1952):258–59, 272–73. The most thorough account of domestics in the Knights can be found in U.S. Congress, Senate, Report on Condition of Women and Child Wage Earners in the United States, 19 vols., Doc. 645, 61st Cong., 2nd sess., 1911, History of Women in Trade Unions, by John B. Andrews and W. D. P. Bliss, vol. 10 (Washington, D.C.: Government Printing Office, 1911), pp. 129–31.

6. Philip S. Foner, History of the Labor Movement in the United States, vol. 4: The Industrial Workers of the World, 1905–1917 (New York: International Publishers, 1965), pp. 128–29.

7. "House Maids Form Union in Denver," Solidarity, 1 April 1916, pp. 1, 4.

8. Ibid., p. 1.

9. Ibid.

10. Ibid.

11. Foner, Women and the American Labor Movement, p. 402.

12. Daniel T. Hobby, "We Have Got Results: 'A Document in the Organization of Domestics in the Progressive Era,'" Labor History 17 (Winter 1976):104. Also see "Denver Housemaids Join I.W.W.," Solidarity, 22 April 1916, p. 1.

13. Hobby, "We Have Got Results," p. 104.

14. "House Maids Form Union in Denver," Solidarity, 1 April 1916, p. 1; "Denver House Maids Join I.W.W.," Solidarity, 22 April 1916, p. 1; and Hobby, "We Have Got Results," p. 105.

15.   Ibid.; Solidarity, 6 May 1916, p. 1; "House Maids Form Union in Denver," Solidarity, 1 April 1916, p. 1.

16.   Hobby, "We Have Got Results," pp. 104–5.

17.   Success had its pitfalls because it caused dissension and the eventual theft of the union's card file. Consult Foner, Women and the American Labor Movement, pp. 410–11; and C. W. Sellers, "Denver Housemaid's List Stolen," Solidarity, 11 November 1916, p. 1.

18.   See Frank Jakel, "Wanted Women Organizers on Pacific Coast," Solidarity, 9 December 1916, p. 2; "Seattle House Workers Organize," Solidarity, 28 October 1916, p. 1. Also consult Mort E. Washawsky, "The Domestic's Industrial Union," Solidarity, 2 November 1916, p. 2; and "Where Do You Belong?" Solidarity, 28 October 1916, p. 2.

19.   Foner, Women and the American Labor Movement, p. 411.   Also see Hobby, "We Have Got Results," p. 103.

20.   Bertha H. Smith, "A Club for Maids," Ladies Home Journal, February 1916, p. 64; and "A Servant's Union," Harper's Bazaar, June 2, 1900, p. 319.   Also see Ida Tarbell, "What Shall We Do for Maids?" Good Housekeeping, November 1917, p. 106.

21.   Spectator, July 16, 1892, p. 92.   Also consult Dolores Hayden, The Grand Domestic Revolution: A History of Feminist Designs for American Homes, Neighborhoods, and Cities (Cambridge, Mass.:   MIT Press, 1981), pp. 170–71.

22.   Helen Campbell, Women Wage-Earners: Their Past, Their Present, and Their Future (Boston: Roberts Brothers, 1893), pp. 244–45.

23.   Support for this assertion can be found in Tarbell, "What Shall We Do for Maids?," pp. 22–23; Henry, Trade Union Women, pp. 166–67; and Jane Edna Hunter, A Nickel and a Prayer (Cleveland: Elli Kani, 1940), pp. 97, 101.

24.   Flora Thompson McDonald, "The Servant Question," Cosmopolitan: A Monthly Illustrated Magazine, March 1900, p. 528.

25.   Simeon Strunsky, "Help Wanted Female," Harper's Monthly, February 1919, pp. 405–6; Lillian Pettengill, Toilers of the Home: A Record of a College Woman's Experience as a Domestic Servant (New York: Doubleday, Page, 1903), p. 393; and Rheta Childe Dorr, "The Prodigal Daughter," Hampton's Magazine, May 1910, p. 682.

26.   I. M. Rubinow, "Household Service as a Labor Problem," Journal of Home Economics 3 (April 1911):135–37.

27. Ibid., pp. 137, 139–40.

28. Robin Miller Jacoby, "The Women's Trade Union League and American Feminism," in Class, Sex, and the Woman Worker, Milton Cantor and Bruce Laurie, eds. (Westport, Conn.: Greenwood Press, 1979; Contributions in Labor History, Number 1), pp. 202–4.

29. "Want Women in Unions," New York Times, 29 June 1915, p. 9.

30. Alice Kessler-Harris, Out to Work: A History of Wage-earning Women in the United States (New York: Oxford University Press, 1982), pp. 165–66.

31. Foner, Women and the American Labor Movement, p. 319.

32. Ibid. In fact, serious tensions would develop when the league attempted to go contrary to the wishes of Gompers and his associates.

33. Izola Forrester, "The Girl Problem," Good Housekeeping, September 1912, p. 382; and Henry, Trade Union Women, p. 239.

34. Jacoby, "The Women's Trade Union League," pp. 203, 205–6.

35. Tarbell, "The Woman and Democracy," p. 218; Henry, Trade Union Women, pp. 238–39; and Foner, Women and the American Labor Movement, pp. 316–17.

36. Stanley Lebergott, Manpower in Economic Growth: The American Record Since 1800 (New York: McGraw-Hill, 1964), pp. 282–83; U.S. Congress, Senate, Report on Condition of Women and Child Wage-Earners in the United States, 19 vols., Doc. 645, 61st Cong. 2d sess., 1911, History of Women in Industry in the United States by Helen L. Sumner, vol. 9 (Washington, D.C.: Government Printing Office, 1911), p. 184.

37. Foner, Women and the American Labor Movement, pp. 120–21; and Daniel E. Sutherland, Americans and Their Servants: Domestic Service in the United States from 1800 to 1920 (Baton Rouge, La.: Louisiana State University Press, 1981), p. 134.

38. U.S. Congress, Senate, Report--History of Women in Trade Unions, pp. 16–17.

39. Sutherland, Americans and Their Servants, p. 134; Helen C. Callahan, "Upstairs-Downstairs in Chicago, 1870–1907: The Glessner Household," Chicago History, vol. 6 (1977–78), p. 208; "United Labor," Weekly Pelican of New Orleans, 18 December 1886, p. 3; and Katzman, Seven Days a Week, pp. 195–96.

40. Ibid., p. 196. Also see Howard N. Rabinowitz, "The Search for Social Control: Race Relations in the Urban South, 1865-1890" (Ph.D. dissertation, University of Chicago, 1973).

41. Walter L. Fleming, "The Servant Problem in a Black Belt Village," Sewanee Review 13 (January 1905):16; and Katzman, Seven Days a Week, pp. 196-97.

42. "Servant Girls Organizing," New York Times, 10 May 1897, p. 2.

43. Ibid.

44. Ibid.

45. Ibid.

46. Ibid.

47. Ibid.

48. "Servant Girls May Strike," New York Times, 5 December 1900, p. 16.

49. "Grievances of Servant Girls," New York Times, 6 December 1900, p. 5; and "Servant Girls Union," New York Times, 13 December 1900, p. 2. Also consult "Servant Girls May Strike," New York Times, 5 December 1900, p. 16.

50. Reference to Mother Jones and the International Socialist Review can be found in Foner, Women and the American Labor Movement, p. 283. "Union Maid the Kitchen Queen," Chicago Tribune, 28 July 1901, p. 1.

51. "Union Maid in the Kitchen," Chicago Tribune, 28 July 1901, p. 1.

52. Ibid. Also see "Servant Girls Make Rules," New York Times, 29 July 1901, p. 1.

53. "Housemaids and Their Work," Chicago Tribune, 25 August 1901, p. 8.

54. Ibid.

55. Ibid.

56. Chicago Tribune, 27 July 1901, p. 1; "Union Maid in the Kitchen," Chicago Tribune, 28 July 1901, p. 1; and "Housemaids and Their Work," Chicago Tribune, 25 August 1901, p. 8.

57. Ibid.

58. "Club Women Meet Maids," Chicago Tribune, 23 August 1901, p. 7.

59. Ibid.

60. Ibid.

61. "Union in the Kitchen," Nation, September 5, 1901, p. 182.

62. "The Servant Girl Problem," Independent, September 12, 1901, pp. 2194-95.

63. Foner, Women and the American Labor Movement, pp. 242-43; and Sutherland, Americans and Their Servants, p. 137.

64. Fleming, "The Servant Problem in a Black Belt," pp. 15-16.

65. Ibid.

66. I am grateful to my friend and colleague Marian J. Morton of John Carroll University for calling my attention to this organizer. See the Florence Crittenden Papers, Western Reserve Historical Society, Cleveland, Ohio.

67. William Ganson Rose, Cleveland: The Making of a City (New York: World Publishing Company, 1950), p. 716.

68. Elizabeth Ross Haynes, "Negroes in Domestic Service in the United States," Journal of Negro History 8 (October 1923):435-36; and Maurine Weiner Greenwald, Women, War, and Work: The Impact of World War I on Women Workers in the United States (Westport, Conn.: Greenwood Press, 1980; Contributions in Women's Studies, Number 12), pp. 40-41.

69. Jessie L. Welch, "Help Wanted," Survey, January 15, 1927, p. 520.

70. Ibid., p. 522.

71. Ibid.

72. Sutherland, Americans and Their Servants, p. 137.

73. Callahan, "Upstairs-Downstairs in Chicago," pp. 208-9.

74. Katzman, Seven Days a Week, p. 138; and James R. Green, The World of the Worker: Labor in Twentieth-Century America (New York: Hill & Wang; American Century Series, 1980), p. 103.

75. Bertha M. Terrill, Household Management (Chicago: American School of Home Economics, 1914), p. 83.

76. "Domestic Workers in Baltimore," Monthly Labor Review 20 (February 1925):236; Lucy Maynard Salmon, Domestic Service (New York: Macmillan, 1897; repr. ed., New York: Arno Press, 1972), pp. 109-10; Isabel Eaton, "Special Report on Negro Domestic Service in the Seventh Ward, Philadelphia," in W. E. B. DuBois, The Philadelphia Negro: A Social Study (Philadelphia: University of Pennsylvania), repr. ed., with an Introduction by E. Digby Baltzell, New York: Schocken Books, 1967), pp. 497-80.

77. Fleming, "The Servant Problem in a Black Belt," p. 14; and Katzman, Seven Days a Week, pp. 139-40.

78. Fleming, "The Servant Problem in a Black Belt," p. 15.

79. Katzman, Seven Days a Week, p. 197; and Fleming, "The Servant Problem in a Black Belt," p. 15.

80. Katzman, Seven Days a Week, p. 197; and A Negro Nurse, "More Slavery at the South," Independent, January 25, 1912, p. 200.

81. "'Sit-Down' Strike Lands Maid in Jail," New York Times, 13 February 1937, p. 15.

82. Fleming, "The Servant Problem in a Black Belt," p. 11; "Housemaids' Union Plots Revenge," Solidarity, 1 April 1916, p. 1; Annie Marion MacLean, "The Diary of a Domestic Drudge," World Today: A Monthly Record of Human Progress, June 1906, pp. 602-3; and Frances A. Kellor, Out of Work: A Study of Employment Agencies, Their Treatment of the Unemployed and Their Influence Upon Homes and Business (New York: G. P. Putnam's Sons, 1905), p. 125.

83. George Gorham Groat, An Introduction to the Study of Organized Labor (New York: Macmillan, 1926), pp. 148-59.

8

From Collapse to Promise to Hope—to No Change

"Weep no more, my lady
Weep no more today"[1]

If the years between World War I and World War II provided the American steelworker the first opportunities to
challenge and eventually organize their industry, has
there ever been a comparable period for the household
laborer? This seems a particularly appropriate question
considering the fact that between 1930 and 1940 the tide
finally shifted to labor's side.[2]

The salience of this fact is particularly striking
when some rudimentary statistics are observed. Prior to
the collapse of the American economy in 1929, the labor
movement in the United States had under 3 million members.
As a group, they constituted no more than one tenth of
the nonagricultural work force. Totally excluded from this
number were the mass production workers of the nation.
By the mid-1930s the situation had changed considerably.
For example, 10.2 percent of production workers in metal
manufacturing were unionized and by 1939 the percentage
had risen to 51. In addition, by that same year the other
mass production industries were well on their way toward
unionization. At the conclusion of the Second World War,
over 14 million American workers, or 21 percent, were
union members.[3]

Perhaps greatly facilitating the union-organizing
energy of the nation was the sudden stock market crash in
1929 and the New Deal of Franklin Delano Roosevelt. The
crash brought unprecedented misery to millions of Americans and constituted the most severe economic disaster in
the history of the nation. So profound was the Depression's

impact and so intense was the fear it engendered that many
worried that the entire capitalist system would crumble.
Following the presidential election of 1932, the administration of Franklin Roosevelt attempted to cope with the problems through a wide and ambitious array of reform programs. Thus the Congress of the United States passed
legislation covering male and female workers; the federal
government created jobs; a combination of administrative
and legislative regulations corrected some of the worst
abuses of the sweatshop system and prohibited homework in
many industries where it still continued to exist. Workmen's disability compensation, unemployment compensation,
and social security were offered.[4]

Very possibly the most significant and long-lasting
impact of the New Deal on the American work force was its
endorsement of unionism.[5] Section 7a of the National Labor
Relations Act guaranteed laborers in certain industries the
right to organize, even to have government-supervised
elections, and to engage in collective bargaining. Although invalidated by the Supreme Court decision of 1935
declaring the National Industry Recovery Act unconstitutional, the right to organize and engage in collective bargaining was reembodied in the Wagner Act of 1935. After
the Supreme Court validation of the act in 1937, unionization became a matter of free choice for many American
workers.[6]

The likelihood of unionization seemed all the greater
after a new federation--the Congress of Industrial Organization (CIO)--severed ties with the conservative, if not
reactionary, American Federation of Labor. Even during
the depths of the Great Depression, the AFL failed to combat wage cuts and layoffs. Equally significant, it continued its opposition to organizing the unskilled, and proceeded to defend the privileges of a minority of skilled
workers who comprised the craft unions of the country.
Once in existence, the CIO undertook organizing drives on
an industrial basis. Millions of workers in mass production industries like steel, electricity, automobiles, packing
houses, and rubber became part of the labor movement.
Consequently, from 1936 to 1940 organized labor tripled its
numbers.[7]

Within the cataclysms of war, paralyzing depression,
and what one historian has termed the "Third American
Revolution,"[8] what benefits accrued to the domestic worker?
While other segments of the work force collectivized and

struggled through the 1930s to gain for themselves what was left of the American pie, did conditions and circumstances provide similar opportunity to those who labored in the homes of others? Did the housemaid catch up with other members of the work force? Did her position remain the same, or did she fall further behind the times?

Although approximately a million and one half to 2 million women were employed as domestics between 1920 and 1930, serious problems continued to plague the occupation.[9] Essentially these were the very issues that had troubled domestic labor ten, twenty, thirty, and sixty years earlier. Although one of the oldest labors performed for another, household work was the last to be modernized with respect to conditions of labor, hours, and skill of the worker. While other occupations had begun to feel the impact of labor laws, codes, limited hours, and unionization, domestic workers remained untouched. Feudalism still reigned in the home. It was difficult for the domestic to think of herself as much other than a serf. How could she when after ten years of service in Chicago one maid recalled, "The treatment is terrible and you feel housework is about the lowest work there is to do. We are cooks, dishwashers, washwomen, ironers, scrub women, waitresses, housekeepers, and nurse maids, but are we people?"[10]

Approximately one year before the stock market crashed, an important conference was held at the U.S. Bureau of Home Economics. In attendance were representatives from various social welfare organizations, delegates from the American Home Economics Association, housewives, employment bureaus, and government agencies. The conference was called into session by Lucy P. Carner, industrial secretary for the National Young Women's Christian Association, Dr. Louise Stanley, chief of the Bureau of Home Economics, Mary Anderson, director of the Women's Bureau of the U.S. Department of Labor, and Amy Watson of the Philadelphia Committee on Household Occupations. From a constructive perspective they hoped to deal head-on with the problems in domestic service. Specifically the women wanted to bring about a "better adjustment of relationships between the homemaker and her employee."[11]

One of the conference results was the creation of the National Committee on Employer-Employee Relationships in the Home, an organization that would continue to function throughout the following decade of the Depression. The initial days of the first conference were important because a list of recommendations was drawn up. The recommendations were an attempt to improve the current unsatisfactory conditions in the home, taking into consideration the needs of employer and employee. The recommendations included the following points: (1) employees and employers would form a joint organization and agree on working contracts which would establish basic standards; (2) the basic standards would include weekly hours with extra pay for overtime (a forty-eight-hour week was the ultimate objective); (3) in the future an employer-employee relationship would replace the mistress-maid relationship (the new term for the worker was "household employee")[12]; (4) all contracts would be made on an individual basis, but could not undercut the general minimum standards of the committee; and (5) ten representatives from various concerned bureaus and organizations would continue to study the field and find out what was being done with respect to the problems of education, standards of employment, legislation, organization, placement, and follow-up.[13]

At a second conference, held a short time later in New York City, the emphasis was placed on lifting service occupations out of the menial and into the professional class. To foster this objective, the idea of definite working hours and not "time off" was stressed. Those in attendance also supported the concepts of having the worker "tak[e] her meals out and . . . live out." The call for improved education was a final important theme.[14]

One of the most remarkable and obvious observations about the conferences and their recommendations was their all but total lack of ingenuity. There was scarcely an idea that had not been advocated and tried repeatedly in the past. Equally if not more important was the fact that these would be the very women charged with implementing New Deal policy as it affected the service occupations. This was of singular importance in the case of Mary Anderson, director of the Women's Bureau in the U.S. Department of Labor.

Consequently, when the Depression came, the service occupations were not prepared to meet the needs of those women who had to fall back on such work as a means of livelihood. Decade-old problems remained. There were no standards for either worker qualifications or working conditions. Furthermore, neither the employer nor the employee was willing to develop the standards necessary to improve the occupation. Still significant was the social

stigma attached to domestic service, a stigma commonly expressed in the belief that "in a pinch any one can do
housework."[15]   In fact, so powerful was this stigma that
in the early days of the Depression service vacancies went
unfilled.   Unemployed women were so reluctant to adopt the
stigma that went along with domestic work that they sometimes preferred to remain unemployed.[16]

          Like other women, and of course men, some house-
hold workers did go hungry.   Some estimates maintained
that during the first three years of the Depression unemployment rates for women were higher than for men.[17]   In
a 1933 Women's Bureau report, unemployment fluctuations
and declines were found to have affected women to a greater degree than men.   The cause of this difference was attributed to occupational segmentation.[18]   Those female-
employment sectors which experienced the most serious
fluctuations were manufacturing, and personal and domestic
service.[19]

          These fluctuations were caused by at least two major
factors directly related to the Depression.   In the first
place, the supply of workers frequently exceeded demand.
Many households reduced the number of employees and
others could no longer afford to employ help.   In the second place, many women previously employed in other occupations were seeking domestic positions.   The following
might be taken as something of a typical pattern: before
1930 Mary Smith had made dashboard equipment in an auto-
mobile shop.   When the Depression came, she was laid off
and then spent several months seeking other employment.
Finally, she gave up and returned home to her family,
which lived on a farm.   When the financial crunch worsened
at home because enough crops were not sold, Mary in des-
peration accepted a job as a domestic.[20]

          The unemployed Mary Smiths had the general effect
of lowering wages in the service occupations.   Desperate,
unskilled, and inexperienced, they found that any wage
was better than no wage at all.   Employers were aware of
this fact and took advantage of those women less fortunate
than themselves.   The pattern was repeated across the
country.   Reemployment headquarters in Yonkers, New York,
reported 50 to 55 percent of their requests were for domestics.   Many of these jobs were rated substandard by the
bureau because the housewives expected too much work for
too little pay.   According to Dorothy Wells of the national
YWCA employment service, employers in a midwestern city

were attempting to hire domestics for fifty cents a day.
Other calls were asking for full-time work in exchange for
room and board. Life and Labor Bulletin, the official publication of the Women's Trade Union League, reported wages
for household workers had fallen more than for any other
group. In New York City live-in service wages, which had
ranged from $40 to $70 a month, dropped to $15 to $55 a
month. The average salary paid per month was $40. Live-
out domestics had averaged from $12 to $16 a week, but
now the best they could hope to make was $9 to $12 per
week.[21]

When the National Committee on Employer-Employee
Relations in the Home sent out questionnaires, they found
similar trends. For example, wages of $8 to $12 had
dropped to $3 and $5 per week in the city of Muskegon,
Michigan. In Indianapolis, Indiana, those who had previously been paid $10 and $12 were now offered $7 or $8.
In San Antonio, Texas, although room and board was included, wages ran as low as $3 to $5 a week. One writer
related an incident about employers who were not suffering
in any way from the Depression: "The hostess . . . tri-
umphantly explained that she had fired her $60-a-month
maid and gotten another 'who gave her perfect service for
$25 a month.' The general idea among the ladies seemed
to be that they should all club together to keep wages
down now that they had servants 'where they wanted
them.'"[22]

If there was a propensity for employers to reduce
wages, there was also a move to retain or increase working hours. In part, this was due to the fact that some
employers were able to hire household assistance for the
first time. Unable to afford help before the Depression,
they felt the unemployed could be "worked" for next to
nothing. Not only could they be "worked," they would do
so at substandard pay in poor working and living conditions. An extensive study of service in Philadelphia
seemed to substantiate these kinds of complaints by domestics. For example, three fifths of the almost 3,000 household employees sampled worked at least a twelve-hour day.
For one tenth of the domestics the workday was less than
eight hours, but for less than one third it was from eight
to twelve hours per day.[23] Workers who lived in reported
that they, too, worked as many as twelve hours per day.
Two fifths of the sample said they went on duty between 7
and 8 A.M. Almost one half of the reporting sample stated
that their quitting time was between 7 and 8 P.M.[24]

Nor were the conditions under which domestics sought employment optimal. One writer reported that the large metropolitan employment agency strongly resembled the old slave markets:

> Having paid the usual $10 fee to manage-
> ment, the employer is free to interview the
> employee to try her luck. The employer
> looks over the day's selection, points her
> finger, says "That one," and the interview
> has begun. Madam questions—questions
> ranging from "Do you cook?" to "Do you
> bite your fingernails?" and "Have you any
> callers?" Anna answers as best she can,
> asks some questions herself.[25]

With no group was the "slave market" more obvious than the black domestic. On various urban street corners every morning of every week, black women stood and waited for potential employers. Prices varied and were subject only to the skill of the individual bargainers. Rates ranged from a "high" of thirty cents an hour to a "low" of ten cents an hour. As the Daily Worker reported in 1940:

> Every morning, rain or shine, groups of
> women with brown paper bags or cheap
> suitcases stand on street corners in the
> Bronx and Brooklyn waiting for a chance
> to get some work. Sometimes there are 15,
> sometimes 30, some are old, many are young
> and most of them are Negro women waiting
> for employers to come to the street corner
> auction blocks to bargain for their labor.
>   They come as early as 7 in the morn-
> ing, wait as late as four in the afternoon
> with the hope that they will make enough
> to buy supper when they go home. Some
> have spent their last nickel to get to the
> corner and are in desperate need. . . .
> In the afternoon their labor is worth only
> half as much as in the morning. If they
> are lucky, they get about 30 cents an
> hour scrubbing, cleaning, laundering,
> washing windows, waxing floors and wood-

work all day long; in the afternoon, when
most have already been employed, they are
worth the degrading sum of 20 cents an
hour.
     Once hired on the "slave market," the
women often find after a day's backbreak-
ing toil, that they worked longer than was
arranged, got less than was promised,
were forced to accept clothing instead of
cash and were exploited beyond human en-
durance. Only the urgent need for money
makes them submit to this daily routine.[26]

As this particular passage implies, the situation of
the black domestic tended to be worse than that of her
white counterpart. The basic and traditional discriminatory practices in employment remained. Not surprising is
the fact that in 1940 of the 2 million women employed as
domestics, half were Hispanic or black. A 1938 Women's
Bureau study revealed that 10 percent of all working black
women were gainfully employed in manufacturing. This
represented a very meager 7 percent gain since 1890.
Furthermore, other occupations such as clerical and office
work were closed to Negro females. Ellen Terry, a social
worker, recalled that in Harlem in 1930 all the sales
clerks in the stores on 125th Street, the black mercantile
center, were white.[27]
     When the Depression struck the nation, perhaps the
single mitigating factor for these women was their familiarity with deprivation. In fact, white employers seem to
have recognized this fact and used it to their own advantage. Employers took undue liberties. Officials of the
Urban League argued that the position of the Negro household worker was particularly unfavorable. They were regarded as marginal workers now being replaced by desperate white women seeking employment.[28]
     If black women had difficulty finding positions as
domestics during the Depression, those who could do so
often found a smaller paycheck. In Philadelphia, for example, the median wage for white domestics was $15.35 per
month, but for black domestics it was $14.50. Low wages
were a constant thorn in the side of the Employment Department of the Phillis Wheatley Association in Cleveland,
Ohio. At one point the organization was even considering
spending some of its all too meager financial resources to

run an ad in one of the city's papers. Administrators
thought this might be a way of securing better jobs for
their members. The necessity of this is reflected in the
downward spiraling of wages: 1930, $7 to $8 per week;
1931, $3 to $4 per week and no carfare. Further reduc-
tions were reported by early December of 1933. In February of 1934, day workers were unable to increase their
wages from $1.50 to $2.00. Near the end of the decade,
the Phillis Wheatley Employment Department could report
wages no higher than $5, $6, or $7 per week.[29]
    The situation for black domestics was equally bleak
elsewhere. In New York City one black woman related the
following incident to a reporter:

> The other day I didn't have a cent in my
> pocket and I just had to find work in or-
> der to get back home and so I took the
> first thing that turned up. I went to
> work about 11 o'clock and I stayed until
> 5:00--washing windows, scrubbing floors
> and washing out stinking baby things. I
> was surprised when she gave me lunch.
> You know, some of 'em don't even do that.
> When I got through she gave me thirty-five
> cents. Figure it out for yourself. Ten
> cents an hour.[30]

    To this and the mass sufferings of a deeply wounded
nation, Franklin Roosevelt promised a New Deal. The New
Deal was a promise to restore the good life to Americans.
In order to do that, the President would have to find ways
to put people back to work. In the plethora of activity
and legislation that issued forth, some working women and
men benefited from protective legislation, legislation whose
historical origins dated back to the Muller v. Oregon land-
mark decision of 1908. They also benefited from a massive
unionizing drive. The creation of the Congress of Industrial Organization (CIO) began to include workers never
embraced before by organized labor. Still and all, the
New Deal was never new enough to alter significantly the
second-class economic status of the American woman. As
one historian has written, "The New Deal was willing to
give women an old deal when the Friday paychecks came
around."[31] In no single instance does this appear more
correct than with those women who constituted the forces of

the newly designated household employee. After World War II, 57 percent of all working women were black and foreign-born. These women were either garment workers or domestics. In the case of the latter, their salaries had decreased from $731 per year in 1929 to $554 per year in 1940![32]

The significance of these generalizations is well illustrated in an examination of the first sweeping program to bring about economic recovery, the National Industrial Recovery Act (NIRA). Passed by Congress in May of 1933, the NIRA consisted of two totally distinct programs. The first section dealt directly with economic recovery by suspending government antitrust activities and by promoting the establishment of voluntary industrial codes. The codes were agreements on distribution, price, and production policies. Profoundly significant was the establishment of labor standards. Included here were the provisions of Section 7a, which sanctioned collective bargaining and labor organization. The second part of the bill established the Public Works Administration (PWA), which was granted an appropriation of $3.3 billion.

Little discussion of the PWA is necessary because it ignored women. Administered by Secretary of the Interior Harold Ickes, PWA programs were primarily concerned with construction projects. PWA appropriations helped build city halls, schools, bridges, and hospitals. They stood as a permanent testimony to the New Deal and provided work for construction laborers and architects. Obviously women, and particularly domestic workers, were not included in such projects. In fact, the absence of women was pointed out by Congresswoman Edith Rodgers.[33]

Women were included under NIRA Title I codes. But not long after the first of these were written, it became apparent that many of the wage provisions discriminated against females. In short, the codes permitted industries to pay women less than men even though women performed similar jobs. Although the established minimum wages did tend to increase women's pay, fully one quarter of all the NIRA codes contained some degree of salary discrimination.[34] This was particularly true in industries that employed large numbers of women workers. Perhaps most noteworthy and most notorious was the garment industry code. It read: "Jacket, Coat, Reefer, and Dress Operations, Male, $1.00 an hour. Jacket, Coat, Reefer, and Dress Operations, Female, 90¢ an hour. Shirt Operators,

Male, 90¢ an hour. Shirt Operators, Female, 80¢ an hour."35

If such was the treatment accorded women workers in general, what about the domestic worker? The answer is simple--she was excluded. She was excluded because the codes were limited to industries engaged in interstate commerce. Ellen S. Woodward, at one time director of women's projects for the Federal Emergency Relief Administration (FERA), the Civilian Works Administration (CWA), and the Works Progress Administration (WPA), attempted to explain this exclusion in an important article in the Journal of Home Economics. Woodward claimed domestics could not be considered for a code because there was neither an organized group of workers nor employers to speak for the occupation. Without organizations no code could be drawn up. Consequently, when working hours and pay rates were formulated by other industries, the domestic worker was left unprotected just as she had been throughout American history.36

Even the appeals of Eleanor Roosevelt could not bring the household worker under NIRA codes. Nor could the studies and reports done by local employment agencies and the YWCA. All indicated the serious problems that continued to exist in this occupation. Wages continued to be low; time-off remained an uncertain commodity; hours ranged anywhere from 60 to 90 a week; and living accommodations often bordered on the horrendous. In the Carolinas wages ranged from $2 to $2.50 a week, and this was at the end of the decade. A weekly wage of one dollar was not atypical in Texas. The average weekly salary in the North was approximately $5 per week. Women's Press, reporting on the conditions of California domestics, revealed workers who slept on cots or sofas hurriedly assembled at night. Others were forced to sleep on back porches next to the washtubs and garbage cans. Still others had to sleep with children. Some employers were still refusing their help access to the bathtub.37

The black domestic was sometimes worse off. She had to withstand the pressure of economic competition now exacerbated by the Depression. But the black woman also had to confront American racism made all the worse by a constricted labor market.38 For the female black domestic exclusion from the NIRA codes was a particularly sad disappointment. The sense and depth of this disappointment, as well as faith in the benevolence of the President, is reflected in the following letter of protest:

My dear Mr. President,

When you delivered your message to
Congress in January, I was eager to hear
you and under almost unsurmountable difficulties I did, but was sadly disappointed
to find that the large and unprotected
class of Domestics were not thought of. I
keenly felt for my kind who you spoke of
the robbery of the Banker but never men-
tioned the robbery of the Housewives.

Today as never before we are being
robbed, for now it is in three ways,
through our stomachs, our strength and
health through long hours and last our
pocketbooks, which we are called upon to
do three and sometimes four Domestics work
by one person for less than half of what
they formly paid one. And it is a case of
try and do it or starve.

When you mention a code for Domestics,
they arrogantly tell you it will and can
never be done.

I wonder why it is that the same God
made us made the rest of mankind and yet
when it comes to hours and wages there is
such a difference.

Now, Mr. President, as you are the top
of this Great American Body and possess
more authority than any other President
ever has, will you use some of it for our
cause and see that these intolerable conditions are changed.[39]

Roosevelt never did see that the conditions were
changed. The only steps taken about wage standards,
hours, and working conditions for domestics were those set
up by some placement agencies, local organizations, and a
suggested code forwarded to Washington, D.C., by the YWCA.
Sensitive to the plight of these otherwise neglected women,
the Y code recommended a six-day week, a ten-hour day, a
nine-dollar minimum for live-in help, and hourly plus
overtime pay for day labor. All of these efforts were entirely informal and advisory. The Women's Bureau lauded
such attempts but at the same time pointed out that most
of the formulated standards could not adequately protect
the domestic worker.[40]

One month prior to the passage of the NIRA, Congress allocated funds for emergency relief. Administered by Harry Hopkins, the Federal Emergency Relief Administration was a program that combined work relief and cash. The FERA clearly put the federal government in charge of unemployment relief, but also used grants-in-aid to the states. Much like the PWA, the great bulk of FERA projects were in construction and consequently excluded women. Still the Worker's Education Section of the program indicated a possible entry for household workers. In fact, Ellen S. Woodward proposed a domestic worker project in a memorandum. She suggested that a preliminary canvass of local domestic demand and supply be undertaken. She also recommended that a suitable training center be established. The center would be equipped much like the homes in which the women would work. Potential employees and employers were to agree on the types of work to be included in the training and the conditions under which it would be performed. Nothing appears to have come out of Woodward's memorandum because it was not included in FERA programs.[41]

NIRA exclusion and FERA neglect were not repeated in the New Deal's Works Projects Administration programs. Roosevelt's request for 5 billion dollars in January of 1935 launched the so-called Second New Deal and gave birth to a massive program of work relief known as the WPA. The program's goal was the employment of 3.5 million workers. Some of these 3.5 million were to be domestic workers because part of a 5 billion dollar appropriation was to pay for a special training program. Begun in February of 1936, the program had the objective of training women on relief rolls and preparing them for domestic employment in private homes. In the first phase of the program, 137 training schools were established throughout the United States. By 1940 the program was operational in twenty states and the District of Columbia. Sixty-five schools were functional in 1940; fifteen of them were for white women, twenty for black women, and thirty for black and white. All projects were supervised by trained home economists and thus the centers provided a source of employment for about ninety of the approximate 900 trained home economists in the nation.[42]

Although the program was intended to set up training programs primarily for women on relief rolls (they were to have first priority), selection criteria and other program objectives were included. Enrollment was open to women referred by public agencies or the U.S. Employment Service. Women officially entered the program if they met certain personal qualifications and had an aptitude for the work. Therefore, trainees on relief rolls who were between the ages of seventeen and thirty-five were preferred. This also included young women who were not interested in other more academic programs, who had a liking for child care or housework, or who were financially unable to continue in school. Trainees who were not economic heads of families were preferred, especially if the prospective employer desired live-in help. However, female breadwinners could enter the program if their home responsibilities permitted their acceptance of household employment. At the time of their acceptance and entrance into the program, the trainee had to agree to accept domestic work when her studies were completed. Of course, this acceptance was predicated on a reasonable offer of employment.[43]

There were also reasons for disqualification from the program. These included the obvious ones of age, appearance, physical and mental handicaps, undesirable personal qualifications, lack of recent experience, inability to take a live-in position because of home responsibilities, and inefficiency. Race was often a disqualifier. For example, in certain northern cities black women were not in demand, and shortages, should they exist, pertained to white workers. Finally, "Many of the workers reported as having had domestic experience have done a type of work wholly different from that of a general maid. Many formerly worked in hotels and institutions where they acquired 'rough and ready' ways unacceptable in private households."[44]

First and foremost, the primary objectives of the program were to provide a thorough training and a satisfactory job placement. Others hoped the program would educate employers about their duties toward workers and result in the employers' willingness to accept and perform those duties. In total, the program represented "the most systematic attempt yet made in the United States to raise the status of household employment."[45]

To achieve these ends, various types of training courses and basic employment standards were worked out by the Women's Division of the WPA. For example, courses in cooking and food serving, general housekeeping, and child care were put in operation in training centers around

the country. In addition, second maid and nursemaid instruction was available. Every student admitted to the
program could choose one of the courses or opt to take all
of the courses offered. Instruction was designed so each
trainee could progress at whatever speed her capabilities
allowed. A basic period of eight weeks was allotted for
course completion, but it was estimated the program could
be finished in four to six weeks. All program activities
were supervised in close cooperation with other interested
agencies and organized groups. These included not only
WPA employees but also representatives from women's clubs,
home economics associations, community groups, and the
U.S. Employment Service.[46]

Of all these functions and activities, Ellen Woodward considered the establishment of wage standards, living conditions, and hours the most important. To this end
program administrators recommended that employers and
employees come to a definite understanding regarding
wages, hours, and the work to be performed. Free hours
were times when the worker had no responsibility either to
her employer or her job. Most recommended that the workweek not exceed sixty hours, and that all employees be
required to submit evidence of satisfactorily passing a
physical exam. This generally meant a Wassermann test.[47]
Other important program recommendations included the following suggestions:

> Two half days off a week, beginning not
> later than 2 P.M. on the weekday and 3
> P.M. on Sunday, or one whole day a week
> should be scheduled.
>
> One week's vacation with pay after
> the first years [sic] service should be
> granted.
>
> The minimum wage for the full-time
> general worker living in the home of the
> employer should be determined by deducting
> from the cost of living of independent women
> at a healthy and efficiency level, the cost
> of board and room.
>
> The wage of the skilled worker should
> be determined by an efficiency rating.
>
> Workers who live outside the home of
> the employer should receive carfare in ad-
> dition to the wage.

Payment should be made preferably
weekly or by-weekly [sic], and if paid
monthly 4 1/3 weeks be calculated to the
month. Wages should be paid on the day
due.

Overtime should be compensated for by
extra time off within one month . . . or
by extras basis of 20 cents per hour.
Overtime should not exceed 12 hours in any
one week.

Comfortable living conditions should
include (a) adequate food; (b) private bedroom, possibly shared with another employee; (c) access to bath; (d) space for
personal possessions; and (d) adequate
heat.

Employer shall give one week's notice
or a week's pay for termination of employee's services after the trial period is
passed. Trial period should be two weeks.
Employer should give one week's notice
after the trial period.[48]

In July of 1937, a slightly different program was
inaugurated by the WPA. Called the Household Service
Demonstration Project, its purpose was to provide training
and employment for women on the relief rolls, but in centers where the American public could observe demonstra-
tions on the proper methods of child care, cooking, housework, and other household functions. But by October of
1938, since it was obvious to all concerned that the Household Service Demonstration Project was less than successful,
it was abandoned. The WPA revised its procedures so as
to permit a complete return to the original type of program.[49]

By January of 1938, Woodward was claiming that
some 15,000 women had received training under the WPA
household service program. In December of that same year,
there were training centers in twenty-six states of the
Union and the District of Columbia. There was some indication that trainees who had received certificates of efficiency and who had been placed in positions were receiving
higher compensation. For example, trainees with certificates were paid $8.79 a week while those without certifi-
cates received only $5.61 a week.[50]

But in sum, the basic operating assumption of the program—that training in housekeeping skills would prepare women for domestic work and upgrade the esteem of domestic work—was naive. Indicative of this is the fact that almost half of the women who met program eligibility requirements had already worked in personal service and domestic occupations. A May 1934 study of sixty American cities revealed that 52.8 percent (one half million women) fell into this category. Furthermore, in 1935, 47.6 percent of all women on relief in the country had worked in domestic and personal service occupations. None could find work. The program, therefore, trained women who did not need such training; it trained them in employment areas severely contracted by the Depression; and it trained them in an occupation that had been losing occupational status and prestige for over a century![51]

Minority relief recipients in the WPA household training programs suffered even more tangible discriminations and hardships than their white counterparts. Donald S. Howard revealed that they were frequently paid half the average rate received by other unskilled workers in their localities. Furthermore, black women represented a very high proportion of those eligible for the program. Most tended to have little experience in gainful employment except as domestics. Consequently, the household training programs came to be a very effective way to discriminate against women on racial grounds. In the South these women were placed on a lower wage scale and in projects that offered virtually no prospect for future employment opportunities. Officials were known to place them so they could work for part of their regularly scheduled hours. This practice tended to reduce their relief payments even further.[52]

Despite the neglect of the National Recovery Act and the Federal Emergency Relief Administration, despite the discriminatory policies of the Works Progress Administration in its dealings with minority relief recipients, and despite the occasional harm and waste of resources under the WPA household service program, permanent legislation could have rectified the situation. None of it did! Thus the Social Security Act of 1935 created an old age insurance plan that covered all workers under the age of sixty-five who were engaged in industry or commerce. People were fully insured if they had $2,000 cumulative wage credits and had been gainfully employed for five years. Along with agricultural laborers, employees in nonprofit religious, scientific, charitable, educational, and governmental institutions, domestic workers were excluded.[53]

Much the same was true of another tremendously significant piece of legislation passed the same year, the National Labor Relations Act. Better known as the Wagner Act, it granted workers the right to vote for the union they wished, outlawed various unfair practices used by employers against unions, and created the National Labor Relations Board (NLRB) with the authority to enforce the act. Even early appeals by Eleanor Roosevelt and popular public personalities like Heywood Hale Broun could not persuade officials to include domestic workers under the protective umbrella of the new labor legislation. Certainly their inclusion was necessary, and it might well have been a subtle way of altering the work relationship in the home for the better. It would have given "the household worker a sense of being upon the same footing as other employees. It [would have] mark[ed] the limitations of the job."[54]

With or without domestic workers, the unionization of American workers rushed forward. From the time of the fifty-fifth AFL convention came the organized thrust for industrial unionism and the organization of the heretofore unorganized. Composed of the United Mine Workers, the Amalgamated Clothing Workers Union, the International Union of Mine, Mill & Smelter Workers, the International Typographical Union, the International Ladies' Garment Workers' Union, the Oil Field, Gas, Well & Refinery Workers, the United Textile Workers of America, and the United Halters, Cap & Millinery Workers, the Congress of Industrial Organization (CIO) was founded on November 9, 1935. Led by John L. Lewis, the new labor organization was committed to building industrial unions in the mass production industries of the nation. As yet the craft–oriented AFL had made virtually no impact in these areas of American industry.[55]

There were no specific references to women in the statements that launched the CIO. However, logic dictated that unionization along industrial lines would require both the participation and active cooperation of women and other minorities. Historically many workers--black, female--had been excluded from craft unions. In the case of these two groups, organizational gains were achieved. Thus, beginning in 1936 the CIO conducted massive organizing drives. All workers gained substantially. For example, before the founding of the CIO, there were scarcely 100,000 Negroes in American trade unions. By 1940 their number had risen to approximately 500,000. Before the establishment of the CIO, black union officials were a rarity, but after 1939–1940 they were somewhat more visible.[56]

Women also gained in the wake of the CIO. Reports on AFL membership figures revealed that as late as 1924 only a little more than 200,000 women belonged. This represented about .07 percent of the total AFL membership. Over half of these 200,000 were concentrated in the various garment industries of the country. By 1938 the number of female union members had risen to approximately 800,000. Unionization had occurred in the following industries: confectionery manufacturing, restaurants and laundries, cigar manufacturing, and the paper and paper products industries. Nonaffiliated organizations such as the International Ladies' Garment Workers' Union also made sizable gains.[57]

Still and all, the major thrust of the CIO organizing drives were in the heavy industries of the country, where relatively few women were employed. Although the CIO can be given credit for breaking down the lines of discrimination in industries where blacks were employed, thus permitting advancement to better jobs, it cannot be credited with any strong feminist sentiment. For example, few women or blacks reached leadership ranks of the CIO. Despite the numerical gains, union organization among women was not especially extensive. No domestic worker chapter appeared before 1942.[58] As late as 1973 there was only one third as many women as men in organized labor. Among this one third, domestic workers were blatantly absent.[59]

Ignored by labor unions, discriminated against, neglected, and at best patronized by their government, domestic workers once again attempted to form independent unions. "What we need," said one domestic, "is a Domestic Union with a hostel and agency."[60] The pleas were heeded by some and supported by others: the national and local branches of the YWCA and the Communist party. Historically the YWCAs had shown the most consistent concern and interest in the plight of this most neglected female worker. This concern continued in the 1930s. In fact, the Cleveland, Ohio, branch of the Y was accused of being a Communist-front organization because it supported domestic worker unionization, included the old IWW song "Solidarity" in its songbook, and allowed the CIO to meet in YWCA buildings.[61]

In a more serious vein the National Negro Congress sponsored a Domestic Workers' Association in New York City in 1937, but the most ambitious organizing effort was supported by the Trade Union Unity League. A Communist organization, the TUUL was eventually dissolved in March of 1935. The decision to dissolve was in keeping with the party's decision to work within the existing trade union structure of the nation. After 1935 TUUL militants began to infiltrate into and play an important role in the CIO. Prior to this decision to infiltrate, the Domestic Workers' Union headed by a black woman, Dora Jones, was established in 1934. The domestics were affiliated with Local 149 of the Building Service Union in New York City. Although this union was reported to have 500 members five years later, it--like all other previous individual attempts at collective action--was at best locally effective and short-lived.[62]

The last significant piece of New Deal legislation, the Fair Labor Standards Act, was passed in 1938. New Deal administrators hoped this legislation would maintain reasonable hour and wage standards for workers who had lost protection under the unconstitutional NIRA codes. They also hoped to establish protection in the unorganized industries. However, the finished piece of legislation exempted numerous workers. Among those excluded, and thus ineligible for the forty cents an hour pay minimum and the forty-hour workweek, were domestic workers. By 1940 only one state, Washington, had established a maximum workweek for household employees. But even here there were inadequate provisions for enforcement. Official rationale for the exclusion of domestic workers was the objective of forcing marginal work out of existence. This was a somewhat ironic turn of events since, under the WPA programs, the official rationale for training was upgrading the status of domestic work.[63]

Surely few events in the history of the United States shook the forces of economic, social, and political stability as profoundly as did the Great Depression. Yet despite this fact, the most numerically significant category of women workers--those engaged in personal service occupations--were still the most neglected, abused, and forgotten members of the work force. Many concerned and knowledgeable persons recognized this fact. Mary Anderson, chief of the Women's Bureau of the Department of Labor, conceded this as late as 1939 when she admitted, "Domestic service is one of the least standardized fields of employment in regard to hours, wages, and working conditions for women wage earners in the United States."[64]

Her statement was abundantly substantiated by an extensive study done on household employment in New York State in 1940 and another similar study done in Kentucky in 1939. In both states working hours were still inordinately long. In New York the shortest work week was sixty hours, while in Kentucky it was forty-two. Some employers in New York offered two dollars a week for seventy-two hours of labor. The lowest weekly salary in Kentucky was $3.50, with an average of $7 per week. Workers still complained about unsatisfactory working and living conditions, and too much work was still being demanded from a single person. Heavy laborious tasks such as laundry, window washing, and woodwork washing were still combined with child care responsibilities. Domestics were still forced to share their quarters with family members, sometimes small infants. Nor were they protected by modern trends in hygiene or preventive medicine. None were covered by minimum wage laws, workmen's compensation, or Social Security.[65]

In a summary of domestic service that could have been entitled "Situations Unwanted," one author provided a description of domestic service that could have been written seventy years earlier.[66] The conclusion read, "Domestic work is not an attractive occupation, not only because of the unfavorable hours, wages and working conditions, but also because of the social stigma attached to it, [and] the difficulty of maintaining family and social relaltionships."[67]

Thus for the American domestic the New Deal and Great Depression brought neither a "Third American Revolution"[68] nor "Benefits of Labor Segregation in an Age of Depression."[69] She was doing just as she had been doing from time immemorial, cleaning someone else's house; and she was unprotected by legislation and excluded from the ranks of organized labor.

NOTES

1. Jane Edna Hunter, A Nickel and a Prayer (Cleveland: Elli Kani, 1940), p. 48.
2. David Brody, Steelworkers in America: The Non-Union Era (Cambridge, Mass.: Harvard University

Press), Chapters 10–11; and ibid., Workers in Industrial America: Essays on the 20th Century Struggle (New York: Oxford University Press, 1980), pp. 138–39.

3. Ibid., p. 139.

4. Rosalyn Baxandall, Linda Gordon, and Susan Reverby, eds., America's Working Women: A Documentary History––1600 to the Present (New York: Vintage Books, 1976), p. 220.

5. Considerable controversy centers around this statement. See, for example, Brody, Workers in Industrial America, pp. 123–24; and Selig Perlman, "Labor and the New Deal in Historical Perspective," in Labor and the New Deal, Milton Derber and Edwin Young, eds. (Madison, Wis.: University of Wisconsin Press, 1961), pp. 363–70.

6. Brody, Workers in Industrial America, p. 139; and Baxandall, Gordon, and Reverby, eds., America's Working Women, p. 221.

7. Ibid.

8. Carl N. Degler, Out of Our Past: The Forces That Shaped Modern America (New York and Evanston, Ill.: Harper & Row; Harper Colophon Books, 1959), Chapter 13.

9. U.S. Department of Labor, Bureau of Labor Statistics, Women in Domestic Work: Yesterday and Today by Allyson Sherman Grossman, Special Labor Force Report 242 (Washington, D.C.: Government Printing Office, 1981), p. 18.

10. Dorothy Dunbar Bromley, "Are Servants People?" Scribner's Magazine, February 1933, p. 379; and Benjamin R. Andrews, "Household Employment: Its Background and Prospects," from Woman's Press, July 1931, quoted in Industrial Committee of the Cleveland YWCA, "Suggestions for a Better Household," May 1937, in the Phillis Wheatley Association Papers, Container 8, Folder 20, pamphlet, Western Reserve Historical Society, Cleveland, Ohio. Hereafter referred to as the PWA Papers.

11. "Getting the Home Work Done," Life and Labor Bulletin, November 1928, p. 3; and Mathilde C. Hader, "Conference on Employer–Employee Relationship in the Home, Journal of Home Economics 23 (July 1931):640.

12. "Getting the Home Work Done," p. 3.

13. Ibid.; and Hader, "Conference," p. 640.

14. "Employer–Employee Relations in the Home," Good Housekeeping, February 1929, p. 104.

15. "Household Workers," New York Times, 19 January 1932, p. 20.

16. "Household Employment—A Symposium," Journal of Home Economics 31 (February 1939):86; and "Factory vs. Kitchen," Commonweal, December 10, 1930, p. 144.

17. Early unemployment rates for domestics averaged approximately 30 percent. See Alice Kessler-Harris, Out to Work: A History of Wage-Earning Women in the United States (New York: Oxford University Press, 1982), p. 270.

18. Recent discussions of this phenomenon can be found in Marianne A. Ferber and Helen M. Lowry, "Women: The New Reserve Army of the Unemployed," Signs: Journal of Women in Culture and Society 1 (Spring 1972, Part 2), p. 227 fn.; and Francine D. Blau and Carol L. Jusenius, "Economists' Approaches to Sex Segregation in the Labor Market: An Appraisal," Signs: Journal of Women in Culture and Society 1 (Spring 1976):181-99.

19. Mary Elizabeth Pidgeon, Employment Fluctuations and Unemployment of Women: Certain Indications from Various Sources, 1928-31, Women's Bureau Bulletin 113 (Washington, D.C.: Government Printing Office, 1933), pp. 4, 6; and "Employment Conditions and Unemployment Relief," Monthly Labor Review 38 (April 1934):791.

20. Hader, "Conference," p. 641; Ellen S. Woodward, "Household Employment and the W.P.A.," Journal of Home Economics 28 (September 1936):439; "Household Workers," New York Times, 19 January 1932, p. 20; Lois W. Banner, Women in Modern America: A Brief History (New York: Harcourt, Brace, Jovanovich, 1974), p. 187.

21. Hader, "Conference," p. 641; Woodward, "Household Employment and the W.P.A.," p. 439; Judith Alden, "Help!" Literary Digest, September 11, 1937, p. 18; "Unionizing the Hired Girl," Literary Digest, May 9, 1931, p. 23; and "Biggest Drop for Household Workers," Life and Labor Bulletin, June 1931, p. 2.

22. Ibid.; and Bromley, "Are Servants People?" p. 94.

23. "Domestic Service in Philadelphia Homes," Monthly Labor Review 35 (July 1932):33.

24. Ibid., pp. 34-35; and Woodward, "Household Employment in the W.P.A.," p. 439.

25. "Below Stairs: Master's Problems," Literary Digest, July 10, 1937, p. 22; and Alden, "Help!" p. 19.

26. Louise Mitchell, "Slave Markets Typify Exploitation of Domestics," Daily Worker, 5 May 1940, cited in Gerda Lerner, ed., Black Women in White America: A Documentary History (New York: Vintage Books, 1973), pp. 229-

30; Ella Baker and Marvel Cooke, "The Bronx Slave Market," Crisis 42 (November 1935):330–32; C. Offord, "Slave Markets in the Bronx," Nation, June 29, 1940, pp. 780–81; and August 3, 1940, p. 100.

27. Banner, Women in Modern America, pp. 188–89; Kessler-Harris, Out to Work, p. 270; Ellen Terry, The Third Door: An Autobiography of an American Negro Woman (New York: David McKay, 1955), p. 88.

28. Banner, Women in Modern America, pp. 188–89; Hader, "Conference," p. 641; Hunter, A Nickel and a Prayer, p. 146; and PWA Papers, Container 8, Folder 20, March 1, 1932.

29. "Domestic Service in Philadelphia Homes," p. 35; PWA Papers, Container 8, Folder 20, October 1, 1929; January 21, 1931; November 3, 1931; December 5, 1933; February 6, 1934; and February 2, 1938.

30. Baker and Cooke, "Bronx Slave Market," p. 331.

31. Carol Ruth Berkin, "Not Separate, Not Equal," in Women of America: A History, Carol Ruth Berkin and Mary Beth Norton, eds. (Boston: Houghton Mifflin, 1979), p. 278.

32. Ibid., p. 276; Carol Hymowitz and Michaele Weisman, A History of Women in America (New York: Bantam Books, 1978), pp. 307–9; Banner, Women in Modern America, pp. 155–61; William Chafe, The American Woman: Her Changing Social, Economic and Political Role, 1920–1970 (New York: Oxford University Press, 1972), pp. 48–65; and Stanley Lebergott, Manpower in Economic Growth: The American Record Since 1800 (New York: McGraw-Hill, 1964), p. 526.

33. William E. Leuchtenberg, Franklin D. Roosevelt and the New Deal, 1932–1940 (New York: Harper & Row; Harper Torch Books, 1963), pp. 120–21; and Helena Hill Weed, "The New Deal That Women Want," Current History 41 (November 1934):181–82.

34. This was not disputed by the NRA assistant council, which conceded that one fourth of 465 codes included lower pay rates for women. They varied anywhere from 14 to 30 percent lower for women than for men. See Lois Scharf, To Work and to Wed: Female Employment, Feminism, and the Great Depression (Westport, Conn.: Greenwood Press, 1980; Contributions in Women's Studies, Number 15), p. 112.

35. Mary Anderson, "Report" (delivered at the Annual Meeting of the International Association of Government

Labor Officials, September 27, 1934), cited in Kessler-Harris, Out to Work, p. 262; Banner, Women in Modern America, p. 185. The most thorough discussion is provided in Scharf, To Work and to Wed, pp. 111-14.

36. Woodward, "Household Employment and the WPA," p. 439; Banner, Women in Modern America, p. 185; Kessler-Harris, Out to Work, p. 270.

37. Bromley, "Are Servants People?" pp. 377-79; Woodward, "Household Employment and the W.P.A.," p. 439; Evelyn Seeley, "Our Feudal Housewives," Nation, May 28, 1938, pp. 613-14; Margaret T. Applegate, "Is the Lady of the House at Home?" Woman's Press 27 (November 1933):472-74; and Jean Collier Brown, "Labor Relationships in the Home," Woman's Press 34 (October 1940):417-18.

38. Scharf, To Work and to Wed, pp. 115-16. Also consult Ira De A. Reid, "The Negro Woman Worker," Woman's Press 26 (April 1932):204-6; and "The Negro Woman Worker," Woman's Press 24 (June 1930):405.

39. Serena Ashford to President Roosevelt, 9 March 1934, NRA Files, Library of Congress, Washington, D.C., in Baxandall, Gordon, and Reverby, eds., America's Working Women, pp. 248-49.

40. "Concerning Codes," Woman's Press 27 (September 1933):395; 27 (October 1933):331; "Labor Standards for Domestic Employees," Monthly Labor Review 39 (November 1934):1110, 1112; and "Cooks and Maids Have Codes Too," Literary Digest, April 28, 1934, p. 10. The interest and concern of the Cleveland, Ohio YWCA is reflected in the activities of the Industrial Committee and recorded in the Minutes and Records of the Board of Trustees. See Industrial Committee of the Cleveland YWCA, pamphlet, May 1937; and YWCA, Cleveland, Ohio, Minutes and Records, Board Minutes 1936 through 1938 Inclusive, Container 4, Western Reserve Historical Society, Cleveland, Ohio. Hereafter referred to as the Cleveland Y Papers.

41. "Training for Household Employment," p. 230.

42. Florence Kerr, "Training for Household Employment," Journal of Home Economics 32 (September 1940):437-38; Alden, "Help!" p. 18; Ellen S. Woodward, "W.P.A.'s Programs of Training for Housework," Journal of Home Economics 31 (February 1939):86; and Amy E. Watson, "The Responsibility of the Home Economist for Improving Employer-Employee Relationships in the Home," Journal of Home Economics 28 (September 1936):90.

43. Kerr, "Training for Household Employment," p. 438; Woodward, "Household Employment and the W.P.A.," p. 440; and ibid., "W.P.A.'s Program of Training," p. 86.

44. Ibid., p. 87.

45. Woodward, "Household Employment and the W.P.A.," pp. 440-41; Kerr, "Training for Household Employment," p. 438; and "Household Employment--A Symposium," p. 86.

46. Woodward, "Household Employment and the W.P.A.," p. 440; and ibid., "W.P.A.'s Program of Training," p. 88. In Cleveland, Ohio, the YWCA was one of those interested community groups. See Cleveland Y Papers, Board Minutes 1936-1938 Inclusive, Container 4, March 17, and April 21, 1936.

47. A discussion of this test and domestics is provided in Charles V. Craster, "Medical Examination of Domestic Servants," American Journal of Public Health 23 (May 1933):433-36.

48. Woodward, "Household Employment and the W.P.A.," pp. 441-42.

49. Woodward, "W.P.A.'s Program of Training," pp. 86-87.

50. Ibid., p. 88; and Kerr, "Training for Household Employment," p. 439.

51. Ellen S. Woodward, "Making Housework a Skilled Occupation," Journal of the American Association of University Women 30 (October 1936):23-25; "Women's and Professional Work in the W.P.A.," Journal of Home Economics 28 (November 1936):618; "W.P.A. Puts Women to Work," Labor Information Bulletin 3 (July 1936):3-5; and FERA Division of Research, Statistics and Finance, "Occupations and Sex Distribution of Gainful Workers on Urban Relief Rolls," May 1934, cited in Lois Scharf, "'The Forgotten Woman': Women Workers, the New Deal and Feminism," typescript, n.p.

52. Donald S. Howard, The W.P.A. and Federal Relief Policy (New York: Russell Sage Foundation, 1943), pp. 165, 284, 294.

53. Leila Doman, "Legislation in the Field of Household Employment," Journal of Home Economics 28 (September 1936):90-95; Watson, "The Responsibility," p. 90; Joseph A. Peckman et al., Social Security: Perspectives for Reform (Washington, D.C.: Brookings Institute, 1968), p. 255.

54. Heywood Broun, "Like One of the Family," Nation, May 29, 1935; Philip S. Foner, Organized Labor and

the Black Worker: 1619–1973 (New York: International Publishers, 1976), p. 215; "Servant Union Urged by Mrs. Roosevelt," New York Times, 23 May 1930, p. 15.

55. Foner, Organized Labor and the Black Worker, pp. 212–13; ibid., Women and the American Labor Movement: From World War I to the Present (New York: Free Press, 1980), Chapter 16.

56. Foner, Organized Labor and the Black Worker, pp. 216, 231; Sumner N. Rosen, "The CIO Era, 1935–55," in The Negro and the American Labor Movement, Julius Jacobson, ed. (Garden City, N.Y.: Anchor Books, 1968), p. 188; and Jacobson, "Union Conservatism: A Barrier to Racial Equality," in ibid., pp. 5–6.

57. Consult Theresa Wolfson, The Woman Worker and the Trade Unions (New York: International Publishers, 1926), pp. 213–14; Alfred G. Trembly, The Distinct Problem of Women Employees, Industrial Commentaries, vol. 1 (Chicago: n.p., 1940), pp. 20–21; and Scharf, To Work and to Wed, p. 130.

58. See Caroline Ware, "Labor and Democracy in the Home," typescript in File 43, Hilda W. Smith Collection, Schlesinger Library, Radcliffe College, cited in Kessler-Harris, Out to Work, fn, pp. 72, 379.

59. Foner, Organized Labor and the Black Worker, pp. 233, 237; and Banner, Women in Modern America, p. 191.

60. "Needed--A Domestic Union," Life and Labor Bulletin, December 1931, p. 3.

61. Gerda Lerner, ed., Black Women in White America, p. 232; and the Cleveland Y Papers, Minutes and Records, Board Minutes 1936–1938 Inclusive, Container 4, October 9, 1937; December 21, 1937; January 1, 1938; and December 20, 1938.

62. Lerner, ed., Black Women in White America, pp. 232–33; and Foner, Women and the American Labor Movement: From World War I to the Present, pp. 297–301.

63. Kerr, "Training for Household Employment," p. 437; Banner, Women in Modern America, p. 185; Leuchtenberg, Franklin D. Roosevelt, p. 263; Trembly, Problem of Women Employees, p. 42; and Scharf, To Work and to Wed, p. 133.

64. "Standards for Women as Household Employees: Women's Bureau Investigation," Journal of Home Economics 31 (April 1939):350; and Benjamin R. Andrews, "New York Symposium on Household Employment," Journal of Home Economics 32 (February 1940):98–99.

65. "Household Employment in New York State, 1938–39," Monthly Labor Review 50 (October 1940):907–10; Virginia Harrison Marrs and Harriet Walton Williams, "No Yard-Stick for Household Employment," Journal of Home Economics 31 (May 1939):316.

66. This was a title given to a sketch performed at the New York Symposium on Household Employment. See Andrews, "New York Symposium," p. 99.

67. "Household Employment in New York State," pp. 907–8.

68. Degler, Out of Our Past, title to Chapter 13.

69. Kessler-Harris, Out to Work, title to Chapter 9.

9

Change within Continuity

"The thery's plain enough
It's jest the human natur side that's tough."[1]

It would be incorrect to characterize the history of domestic service as a homogenous entity.[2] The four periods delineated in this study—early colonization to the American Revolution, the Revolution to 1850, the 1850s to the turn of the twentieth century, and the early twentieth century to the 1930s—belie such an interpretation. Each of these periods marked important changes in some dimension of the occupation.

During the first phase of its existence, service changed from an unfree to a free labor system. Of course, this was not true of blacks in the South. The second period in the history of domestic work began with a relatively egalitarian mistress-servant relationship at a time when American life was organized around handicraft production, agriculture, and rural customs. This period ended with an increasing number of immigrant domestics, especially Irish, German, Scandinavian, and (in the Far West) Chinese. In addition, this phase was characterized by significant socioeconomic and ideological transformations as urban, industrial, and capitalistic social relations transformed American society. The nation experienced rather significant alterations in relations between home and production, as well as between marketplace and worker. Thus came about, as one historian has characterized it, the shift from the "help" or "hired girl" to the "domestic."[3]

This transformation witnessed a significant devaluation of domestic work at the same time as greater economic and social options were available for the women who em-

ployed servants. The mistress was to reside in her special
sphere, the home, and achieve fulfillment in the elabora-
tion of female domesticity. In running her home, the mistress would supervise work performed by servants and thus
avoid tasks no longer considered very valuable by society.
Furthermore, supervising servants accorded rather powerless women access to authority in an otherwise male-
dominated world. Such supervision was sometimes construed as an act of benevolence since the mistress could
fill the role of mother, teacher, and perhaps even entre-
preneurial benefactor.

The third period in the history of domestic service
also brought important changes. Urbanization increased,
creating new employment opportunities for white women.
At the same time influxes of immigrants from central,
southern, and eastern European countries flooded the country. These women were less likely to work as domestics,
and thus the cry that the servant girl was vanishing began
to be heard. For example, in the last three decades of
the nineteenth century the demand for servants doubled
but the supply increased by only half.[4]

The shortage of servants was also created by a reduction of young women in the work force. Until 1880
nearly 10 percent of all female domestics were between the
ages of ten and fifteen years. They constituted 9.4 percent of all female domestics in the country. Thereafter,
their numbers began to decline. Thus by 1920 only 31,000
young white females were servants. These changes were
the direct result of increased family prosperity, child labor
legislation, and compulsory education requirements. The
withdrawal of these females helped contribute to a servant
shortage that was soon to be filled by black women migrating northward.[5]

Continued urbanization and World War I altered the
nature of female employment patterns and thus inaugurated
the final period in domestic service. As more and more
white women worked in professions, especially nursing and
teaching, as well as in clerical, sales, and manufacturing
jobs, the number of domestics continued to decline. But
black women who had been concentrated in the South began
migrating in force to the North. Because the war virtually
ended immigration and because native-born white women
were leaving domestic service for other occupations or marriage, black women, having practically no other employment options, became domestics in the North.[6]

By 1920 black domestics were no longer an exclusive fixture of the South. In fact, between 1910 and 1920 the proportion of Negroes in the servant population doubled. Nationwide they comprised more than 39 percent of all domestics in cities with populations of one hundred thousand or more. Equally significant, regardless of their marital status, these women worked outside the home to a much greater degree than did white women. Live-out positions allowed black women to work and still raise their families. Thus they helped transform domestic service from a live-in to a live-out occupation.[7]

Despite the important changes that took place in each of these four periods of domestic service, none served to advance the cause of unionization. In fact, they sometimes did just the opposite. For example, as the maturation and growth of modern manufacturing and industry progressed, nontechnical, menial tasks, particularly those performed by women in the home, would continue to lose status. Occupations like domestic service would fall further behind the times. The reality of this was captured in expressions such as a "belated industry," or "feudalism in the home."[8]

As domestic service continued to lose status, fewer and fewer women wished to perform it. When they did become domestic workers, they tended to view the work as a temporary option--something to tide them over until they married or found a better opportunity. Interested basically in leaving service, and divided by race, religion, and ethnicity, these women would have little interest in unionizing to improve domestic work. Once abandoning this occupation, they would have little, if any, desire to ever return to it. Speaking to this point, one nineteenth-century woman wrote, "I saw in the Tribune of Sunday morning that 'Pater familias' suggested the propriety of us sewing girls giving up our trade and becoming house servants. Now in all humility, may I ask what encouragement there is for us to do so. . . ."[9]

If domestics expressed reservations about the value of their occupation, thus diminishing their propensity to remain in it and organize unions, employers were equally if not more circumspect. They expressed their dislike of domestic work in a variety of ways. For example, they refused to perform it whenever possible; they refused to consider it a serious occupation; and sometimes they characterized it as monotonous, degrading, menial, demeaning, uninteresting, and a drudgery.[10]

Profound as their reservations about domestic labor were, mistresses realized the occupation was riddled with serious problems. They knew hours were long, that living and working conditions were not always optimal, that personal freedoms were lacking, and that general working standards were absent. [11] But employers also recognized how dependent they were on their domestics. [12] In short, they knew that reforms were necessary and they wanted to be in charge of all change. Reform should occur, but it should come from the top down. At all costs collective action should be prevented. Thus employers endeavored to make their servants one of the family. They tried to structure household labor on modern business principles. They even introduced the concept of welfare capitalism into their homes. In the end they seldom fostered a spirit of self-reliance, independence, or self-respect in their employees. To that degree mistresses never lost control and thus contributed to the prevention of unionization.

If employers were concerned about retaining control over their employees, organized labor was not interested in the domestic worker at all. The servant was preponderantly unskilled, female, and often a member of an ethnic or racial minority. Few labor organizations, especially the most powerful one, the American Federation of Labor, were willing to include such workers. Thus by 1940 the domestic woman remained a worker excluded from the ranks of organized labor. [13]

Despite the obstacles from within their own forces, from their employers, and from much of the American labor movement, domestic workers did form collective organizations, and they did engage in individualized acts of rebellion. Whenever possible, they joined mainstream unions such as the Knights of Labor, the American Federation of Labor, the International Workers of the World, and the Congress of Industrial Organization. If these options were unavailable or unlikely, domestics established their own independent unions. Some of their organizations were reported to have as many as three hundred members, while others had as few as six. [14] Despite the fact that none of these organizations survived, domestics did attempt to improve their working conditions by going against the forces of the status quo.

Surely few events in the history of the United States threatened the forces of social, economic, and political stability as profoundly as did the Great Depression and

the New Deal. Despite the hypothesis of David Brody--that
the varied elements of worker, employer, and labor should
act together to establish a situation of labor stability--that
stability was certainly disrupted during the years from
1929 to 1940. But unlike the steelworker in 1919 and then
again in 1939, the American domestic worker saw few
changes. For her, there has never really been any time
but the nonunion era.[15]

Women, and domestic workers in particular, were
never really prime candidates for labor organization.
Those groups that have historically possessed the greatest
potential for organizing were permanent wage earners in
skilled occupations. Furthermore, they tended to hold key
positions in industries that themselves occupied strategic
positions within the entire industrial system. Equally essential has been the use of the right organizational methods
for the industry in question. Little of these essentials
apply to the domestic. Too long and too often was she a
temporary worker in a low-skill occupation. Essentially
she has been judged a marginal, nonessential member of
the work force.[16]

Perhaps this judgment--a marginal, nonessential
member of the work force--helps account for the neglect of
the domestic worker in the histories of the American worker.
But this neglect ignores what ought to be a very important
concern--the changing work experiences of ordinary Americans. Philosopher Jean-Paul Sartre explained the significance of this when he observed, "The essential is not what
'one' has done to man, but what man does with what 'one'
has done to him."[17]

What such individuals have experienced retains
great interest and importance, but how they understood
and dealt with their situation becomes another concern.
As resistance to dependence and inequality has been an
irregular but constant theme in American history, so, too,
has it been in the history of domestic workers. Their resistance would rekindle again when inner-city black women
would have their awareness and sensitivity heightened by
the increasing tempo of the Civil Rights Movement of the
1960s. Such was the case of Geraldine Roberts, the founder
of the Domestic Workers of America, which was located in
Cleveland, Ohio.[18]

One powerful dimension of the Sartre question (as
stated above) and the value of confronting the history of
the American worker--the constant if ever shifting tension

inside and outside the workplace between individualist and collective ways of achieving autonomy--can be understood through Roberts's words:

> I became quite knowledgeable of many
> things that I had never known or under-
> stood before, by bein' involved in the
> civil rights struggle. I sorta, you might
> say grew up, mentally being involved . . .
> and I felt quite healthy. . . . I felt
> great to sit down with people, black people,
> white people, all kinds of people who were
> talking about justice. . . .[19]

The final word on domestic workers has yet to be heard.

NOTES

1.   Mary Hinman Abel, "The Eight Hour Day in Housekeeping: Why It Is Not Practicable," American Kitchen Magazine, February 1902, p. 178.

2.   This is the basic theme presented by Daniel E. Sutherland up to 1920. Consult Americans and Their Servants: Domestic Service in the United States from 1800 to 1920 (Baton Rouge, La.: Louisiana State University Press, 1981).

3.   Faye E. Dudden, Serving Women: Household Service in Nineteenth-Century America (Middletown, Conn.: Wesleyan University Press, 1983), p. 5.

4.   I. M. Rubinow and Daniel Durant, "The Depth and Breadth of the Servant Problem," McClure's Magazine, March 1910, p. 586.

5.   David M. Katzman, Seven Days a Week: Women and Domestic Service in Industrializing America (New York: Oxford University Press, 1978), pp. 71-76.

6.   U.S. Department of Labor, Bureau of Labor Statistics, Women in Domestic Work: Yesterday and Today by Allyson Sherman Grossman, Special Labor Force Report 242 (Washington, D.C.: Government Printing Office, 1981), p. 18.

7.   Katzman, Seven Days a Week, pp. 72-73, 75-76, 79-80; and U.S. Department of Labor, Bureau of Labor Statistics, Women in Domestic Work, p. 18.

8. See Jane Addams, "A Belated Industry," American Journal of Sociology 1 (March 1896):536-50; and I. M. Rubinow, "Household Service as a Labor Problem," Journal of Home Economics 3 (April 1911):131-40. Feudalism was an expression still used in the 1930s. For examples, consult Dorothy Dunbar Bromley, "Are Servants People?" Scribner's Magazine, February 1933, pp. 377-79; Ellen S. Woodward, "Household Employment and the W.P.A.," Journal of Home Economics 28 (September 1936):439-42; and Benjamin R. Andrews, "Household Employment: Its Background and Prospects," from Woman's Press, July 1931, quoted in Industrial Committee of the Cleveland YWCA, "Suggestions for a Better Household," May 1937, in the Phillis Wheatley Association Papers, Container 7, Folder 20, pamphlet, Western Reserve Historical Society, Cleveland, Ohio.

9. "Sewing vs. House-Service," Chicago Tribune, 17 September 1873, p. 2.

10. "Below Stairs: Master's Problems," Literary Digest, July 10, 1937, p. 22; Frank Crane, "How Do You Get Along with Your Hired Girl?" American Magazine, October 1924, p. 61; Mary Roberts Smith, "Domestic Service: The Responsibility of Employers," Forum, August 1899, pp. 688-89; A Mere Man, "The Servant Question," Woman's Home Companion, October 1911; and Annie Nathan Meyer, ed., Woman's Work in America (New York: Henry Holt, 1891), p. iv.

11. U.S. Industrial Commission Report, 18 vols., "Domestic Service" by Gail Laughlin, vol. 14 (Washington, D.C.: Government Printing Office, 1900-1902); and "Household Employment in New York State, 1938-39," Monthly Labor Review 50 (October 1940):907-10.

12. One touching acknowledgement of this dependence was made by Elizabeth Cady Stanton. See Elizabeth Cady Stanton, Eighty Years and More: Reminiscences, 1815-1897 (1898; repr. ed., New York: Schocken Books, 1971), pp. 115-21, cited in Dudden, Serving Women, p. 241.

13. Philip S. Foner, Organized Labor and the Black Worker: 1619-1973 (New York: International Publishers, 1976), p. 174.

14. "Union Maid in the Kitchen," Chicago Tribune, 28 July 1901, p. 1; and "Grievances of Servant Girls," New York Times, 6 December 1900, p. 5.

15. David Brody, Steelworkers in America: The Non-Union Era (Cambridge, Mass.: Harvard University Press, 1960), p. ix, and Chapters 10-11; and ibid., Workers in

Industrial America: Essays on the 20th Century Struggle (New York: Oxford University Press, 1980), pp. 138-39.

16.   Edith H. Altbach, Women in America (Lexington, Mass.: D. C. Heath, 1974), p. 77.

17.   Quoted in Herbert Gutman, "Labor History and the 'Sartre Question,'" Humanities, September/October 1980, p. 1.

18.   Donna L. Van Raaphorst, "I Won't Give Up, I Can't Give Up, I'll Never Give Up: The Motto of Geraldine Roberts, Founder of the Domestic Workers of America," typescript, n.p.

19.   Interview with Geraldine Roberts, founder of the Domestic Workers of America, Cleveland, Ohio, 25 February 1975.

Appendix: Knights of Labor Composed Entirely of Women, 1882-1887

Date of Organization	Local Assembly No.	Locality	Trade	Lapsed or Suspended[1]
Sept. 1881	1684	Phila., PA	Shoeworkers	Oct. 1890
Sept. 1881	1789	Chicago, IL	....	July 1888
April 1882	1843	Camden, NJ	Shoeworkers	
April 1882	1845	Brockport, NY	Various	
April 1882	1848	Rochester, NY	Sewing	
Feb. 1883	2508	Chicago, IL	Bohemian women	___. 1884
		Utica, NY		
Feb. 1883	2585	Utica, NY	....	
Aug. 1883	2825	Toledo, OH	Dress & cloakmakers	
Aug. 1883	2827	Marblehead, MA	Various	
Oct. 1883	2948	Saginaw, MI	Various	
Dec. 1883	2994	Saginaw, MI	Sewing	
Dec. 1883	3016	Lynn, MA	Shoeworkers	
Dec. 1883	3062	Brockton, MA	Various	
Dec. 1883	3080	Manistee, MI	Various	Dec. 1887
March 1884	3090	Troy, NY	Collar & shirt-Ironers	
March 1884	3102	Detroit, MI	Various	June 1892
March 1884	3117	Haverhill, MA	Shoeworkers	Oct. 1888
March 1884	3142	Salem, MA	Shoeworkers	Dec. 1887
March 1884	3150	Port Huron, MI	Housekeepers	
May 1884	3213	Minneapolis, MN	Various	
May 1884	3214	Baltimore, MD	Mill operatives	
June 1884	3250	New Haven, CT	Rubber-shoeworkers	
July 1884	3314	Denver, CO	Various	
Sept. 1884	3427	Phila., PA	Patent ironers	Oct. 1892
Oct. 1884	3474	Nashville, TN	Patent ironers	
Dec. 1884	3502	London, Ontario	Various	
Dec. 1884	3525	Taunton, MA	Mill operatives	March 1887
Jan. 1885	3568	Richmond, VA	Various	
Feb. 1885	3582	Burlington, IA	Various	
Feb. 1885	3598	New York, NY	Dressmakers	July 1888
Feb. 1885	3600	Brooklyn, NY	Shoeworkers	Sept. 1889
March 1885	3621	St. Louis, MO	Stocking knitters	
March 1885	3636	Amsterdam, NY	Mill operatives	April 1889
March 1885	3649	Brantford, ONT	Factory & sewing girls	

Date of Organi- zation	Local Assem- bly No.	Locality	Trade	Lapsed or Suspended
March 1885	3672	St. Paul, MN	Various	Feb. 1892
March 1885	3681	Marlboro, MA	Shoeworkers	
May 1885	3805	New York, NY	Shoeworkers	Nov. 1890
June 1885	3929	Richmond, VA	Various	
June 1885	3952	New York, NY	Shirt operatives	Sept. 1889
June 1885	3991	Washington, DC	Government employees	
July 1885	3998	New Britain, CT	Various	
July 1885	4027	Phila., PA	Leather sewers	
Aug. 1885	4071	Johnstown, NY	Various	Jan. 1890
Aug. 1885	4077	Providence, RI	Burlers and sewers	
Aug. 1885	4082	Orange, NJ	Hatters	
Aug. 1885	4096	Richmond, VA	Various (colored)	
Aug. 1885	4120	Amsterdam, NY	Carpetmakers	
Sept. 1885	4167	Parsons, KS	Various	
Sept. 1885	4237	Schenectady, NY	Various	Dec. 1887
Sept. 1885	4277	Beverly, MA	Buttonhole (shoe) operators	Jan. 1887
Oct. 1885	4349	Williamsport, PA	Various	
Oct. 1885	4400	Fort Worth, TX	Labourers	
Oct. 1885	4427	Belleville, Ont.	Various	
Nov. 1885	4468	Petersbury, VA	Various	
Nov. 1885	4474	Richmond, VA	Various	
Nov. 1885	4515	Milford, MA	Various	July 1891
Nov. 1885	4548	Natick, MA	Shoeworkers	
Dec. 1885	4610	Gardiner, ME	Shoeworkers	
Dec. 1885	4633	Jackson City, MI	Housewives	
Dec. 1885	4645	Indianapolis, IN	Various	
Dec. 1885	4648	Lynn, MA	Paper-box makers	
Dec. 1885	4650	St. Thomas, Ont.	Various	
Dec. 1885	4661	North Adams, MA	Shoeworkers	
Dec. 1885	4677	Troy, NY	Various	Oct. 1888
Dec. 1885	4681	Amsterdam, NY	Loopers	June 1887
Dec. 1885	4684	Richmond, VA	Various	
Dec. 1885	4695	Knoxville, TN	Various	
Dec. 1885	4726	North Adams, MA	Factory employees	Aug. 1889
Dec. 1885	4755	Petersbury, VA	Various	

Date of Organization	Local Assembly No.	Locality	Trade	Lapsed or Suspended
Dec. 1885	4757	Petersbury, VA	Various	
Dec. 1885	4784	Little Rock, AK	Various (colored)	
Dec. 1885	4785	Argenta, AK	Various	
Jan. 1886	4880	Biddleford, ME	Cotton-mill operatives	
Jan. 1886	4902	Cohoes, NY	Various	Feb. 1888
Jan. 1886	5069	Richmond, VA	Various	
Jan. 1886	5142	Galveston, TX	Various	
Feb. 1886	5193	Petersbury, VA	Various	
Feb. 1886	5199	Dayton, OH	Various	
Feb. 1886	5226	Phila., PA	Various	May 1887
Feb. 1886	5258	Danville, VA	Various (colored)	
Feb. 1886	5261	Minneapolis, MN	Various	Feb. 1894
Feb. 1886	5268	Danville, VA	Various (colored)	
Feb. 1886	5273	Manchester, VA	Various	
Feb. 1886	5302	Lynn, MA	Heelsheeters	March 1888
Feb. 1886	5305	Jacksonville, VA	Various (colored)	
Feb. 1886	5325	Cohoes, NY	Rubbermakers	Dec. 1888
Feb. 1886	5334	Wabash, IN	Housekeepers	
Feb. 1886	5347	Newark, NJ	Tailoresses	
Feb. 1886	5542	Stratford, Ont.	Various	
Feb. 1886	5607	Richmond, VA	Various	
Feb. 1886	5611	Little Rock, AK	Various	
March 1886	5731	South Boston Heights, MA	Various	
March 1886	5803	Cohoes, NY	Paper-box makers	
March 1886	5804	North Cohoes, NY	Woolen operatives	Feb. 1888
March 1886	5848	Cincinnati, OH	Shoeworkers	
March 1886	5855	San Francisco, CA	White-ware workers	
March 1886	5911	Bellaire, OH	Various	
March 1886	5947	Raleigh, NC	Various (colored)	
March 1886	5953	Petersburgh, VA	Various	
March 1886	5962	Waterford, NY	Various	
March 1886	6043	Hoosick Falls, NY	Various	July 1888
April 1886	6300	Melville, NJ	Various	Sept. 1888

Date of Organization	Local Assembly No.	Locality	Trade	Lapsed or Suspended
April 1886	6338	Mantaoca, VA	Cotton-factory employees	
April 1886	6346	Brooklyn, NY	Laundry workers	Aug. 1887
April 1886	6357	Hallowell, ME	Cotton-mill operatives	
April 1886	6437	Indianapolis, IN	Sewing and housekeepers	
April 1886	6461	Petersbury, VA	Various	
April 1886	6471	Norfolk, VA	Various (colored)	
April 1886	6481	Phila., PA	Shirt operators	Oct. 1892
April 1886	6491	New York, NY	Gold cutters	June 1890
April 1886	6590	Henderson, KY	Cotton-mill employees	
April 1886	6591	Evansville, IN	Cotton-mill employees	
April 1886	6675	Lynchburg, VA	Cotton-mill employees	
April 1886	6711	Hartford, CT	Various	
April 1886	6714	Waterbury, CT	Various	
April 1886	6753	Norfolk, VA	Housekeepers and laundresses (colored)	
May 1886	6821	Fort Plain, NY	Various	Sept. 1887
May 1886	6843	North Danville, VA	Housekeepers and laundresses	
May 1886	6882	Brooklyn, NY	Various	
May 1886	6950	Indianapolis, IN	Housekeepers and sewing	
May 1886	6964	Cohoes, NY	Finisher on knit goods	May 1893
May 1886	6965	Cohoes, NY	Trimmers, neckers, and folders	Feb. 1888
May 1886	7019	Milwaukee, WI	Tailoresses	
May 1886	7075	Albany, NY	Laundresses	Dec. 1887
May 1886	7095	Lynchburg, VA	Washers and cooks	
May 1886	7120	Baltimore, MD	Sewing-machine operatives	

Date of Organi- zation	Local Assem- bly No.	Locality	Trade	Lapsed or Suspended
May 1886	7137	Altantic City, VA	Cotton-mill knit- ting operatives	
May 1886	7170	Chicago, IL	Cloakmakers	
May 1886	7179	Pensacola, FL	Chambermaids and laundresses (colored)	
May 1886	7195	New York, NY	Lead-pencil workers etc.	July 1887
May 1886	7211	New York, NY	Feathercurlers	Feb. 1889
May 1886	7228	Pittsburg, PA	Various	
May 1886	7280	Waterville, ME	Cigar makers	
May 1886	7295	Boston, MA	Cloak and suit makers	
May 1886	7297	Biddleford, ME	Millhands	
May 1886	7332	Norfolk, VA	Various (colored)	
May 1886	7383	Richmond, VA	Various	
May 1886	7384	Saccarappa, ME	Cotton-mill opera- tives	
May 1886	7466	Detroit, MI	Shoeworkers	
May 1886	7590	Lynchburg, VA	Housekeepers, gen- erally	
May 1886	7591	Lynchburg, VA	General housekeepers	
May 1886	7608	West Troy, NY	Various	March 1887
May 1886	7629	Toronto, Ontario	Various	
June 1886	7707	Chicago, IL	Tailoresses	July 1889
June 1886	7740	Memphis, TN	Various	
June 1886	7754	Chesterfield, VA	Servants and washer women	
June 1886	7793	Berkley, VA	Housekeepers and cooks	
June 1886	7830	Ettricks, VA	Cotton-mill opera- tives	
June 1886	7933	Norfolk, VA	Various	
June 1886	7934	Bloomington, IL	Various	Jan. 1890
June 1886	7991	Newark, NJ	Various	Aug. 1887
June 1886	8007	Argenta, AK	Farmers	

Date of Organization	Local Assembly No.	Locality	Trade	Lapsed or Suspended
June 1886	8021	Brooklyn, NY	Hatters	
July 1886	8103	Worcester, MA	Various	
July 1886	8113	South Bend, IN	Various	
July 1886	8117	Danville, VA	Various	
July 1886	8156	Watertown, NY	Various	June 1890
July 1886	8166	Portsmouth, VA	Housekeepers	
July 1886	8168	Detroit, MI	Cabinetmakers	Feb. 1888
July 1886	8179	Cleveland, OH	Various	
July 1886	8218	Chicago, IL	Shoeworkers	March 1891
July 1886	8228	Seneca Falls, NY	Shoeworkers	
July 1886	8257	Troy, NY	Collar ironers	Oct. 1888
July 1886	8288	Richmond, VA	Various	
July 1886	8298	Lasalle, IL	Housekeepers	Nov. 1888
Aug. 1886	8328	Willowdale, AK	Various	
Aug. 1886	8380	Galloway, AK	Various	
Aug. 1886	8388	Newhope, VA	Various	
Aug. 1886	8411	Streator, IL	Various	April 1889
Aug. 1886	8516	Newport News, VA	Various	
Sept. 1886	8565	Wilmington, NC	Various	
Sept. 1886	8625	Thorold, Ontario	Various	
Sept. 1886	8626	West Gardner, MA	Various	
Sept. 1886	8664	Petersbury, VA	Various	
Sept. 1886	8665	Petersbury, VA	Various	
Sept. 1886	8683	Peoria, IL	Various	Dec. 1889
Sept. 1886	8736	Peterson, NY	Flax operatives	Dec. 1887
Sept. 1886	8761	Abingdon, VA	Various	
Sept. 1886	8774	Duquoin, IL	Housekeepers	July 1889
Sept. 1886	8781	Natick, MA	Shoeworkers (stitchers)	Sept. 1889
Oct. 1886	8804	Boston, MA	Tailoresses	June 1889
Nov. 1886	9011	Lima, OH		
Nov. 1886	9064	Rackensack, AK	Various	
Nov. 1886	9066	Rackensack, AK	Various	
Nov. 1886	9111	New York, NY	Bookbinders	Dec. 1888
a	9245	New York, NY	Shoeworkers	Aug. 1888
a	9361	North Adams, MA	Weavers	Oct. 1888

Date of Organization	Local Assembly No.	Locality	Trade	Lapsed or Suspended
a	9459	Chicago, IL		Sept. 1887
a	9605	St. Louis, MO	Tailoresses	July 1887
a	9736	Auburn, NY	Various	May 1889
a	9794	Chicago, IL	Various	April 1889
a	9837	Fall River, MA	Factory operatives	Sept. 1890

[a]Not reported.

Source: U.S. Congress, Senate, Report on the Condition of Woman and Child Wage-Earners in the United States, 19 vols., Doc. 645, 61st Congress, 2nd sess., 1911; History of Women in Trade Unions by John B. Andrews and W. D. P. Bliss, vol. 10 (Washington, D.C.: Government Printing Office, 1911), pp. 129-131.

[1]This table was taken directly from the U.S. Congress, Senate, Report cited above. Information relative to lapsed or suspended chapter was frequently not available.

Selected Bibliography

BOOKS

Abbott, Edith, ed. Historical Aspects of the Immigration Problem: Select Documents. Chicago: University of Chicago Press, 1926.

_____. Women in Industry: A Study in American Economic History. New York: D. Appleton, 1910.

Abbott, Grace. The Immigrant and the Community. New York: Century Company, 1921.

Addams, Jane. Democracy and Social Ethics. Edited by Anne Frior Scott. Cambridge, Mass.: Belknap Press of Harvard University Press, 1964.

Alta. The Shameless Hussy: Selected Stories, Essays, and Poetry. Trumansburg, N.Y.: Crossing Press, 1980.

Altbach, Edith H. Women in America. Lexington, Mass.: D. C. Heath, 1974.

Baker, Elizabeth F. Technology and Women's Work. New York: Columbia University Press, 1964.

Banner, Lois W. Women in Modern America: A Brief History. New York: Harcourt, Brace, Jovanovich, 1974.

Barker, Clara Helene. Wanted, A Young Woman to Do Housework. New York: Moffat, Yard, 1915.

Baxandall, Rosalyn; Gordon, Linda; and Reverby, Susan, eds. America's Working Women: A Documentary History--1600 to the Present. New York: Vintage Books, 1976.

Beard, Mary Ritter, ed. America through Women's Eyes. New York: Macmillan Company, 1933; repr. ed., Westport, Conn.: Greenwood Press, 1961.

_____. Woman's Work in Municipalities. New York: D. Appleton, 1915.

Beecher, Catherine. A Treatise on Domestic Economy. New York: Marsh, Capen, Lyon, and Webb, 1841; repr. ed., New York: Schocken Books, 1977.

Berg, Barbara J. The Remembered Gate: Origins of American Feminism. New York: Oxford University Press, 1978.

Berkin, Carol Ruth, and Norton, Mary Beth, eds. Women of America: A History. Boston: Houghton Mifflin, 1979.

Bernstein, Irving. The Lean Years: A History of the American Worker 1920-1930. Baltimore: Penguin Books, 1960.

_____. Turbulent Years: A History of the American Worker, 1933-1941. Boston: Houghton Mifflin, 1970.

Bimba, Anthony. The History of the American Working Class. New York: International Publishers, 1927.

Blassingame, John W. The Slave Community: Plantation Life in the Ante-Bellum South. New York: Oxford University Press, 1972.

Bogardus, Emory S. Immigration and Race Attitudes. New York: D. C. Heath, 1928.

Bosworth, Louise Marion. The Living Wage of Women Workers: A Study of Incomes and Expenditures of Four Hundred and Fifty Women Workers in the City of Boston. Philadelphia: American Academy of Political and Social Sciences, 1911.

Brissenden, Paul F. The I.W.W.: A Study of American Syndicalism. New York: Columbia University Press, 1919.

Brody, David. Steelworkers in America: The Non-Union Era. Cambridge, Mass.: Harvard University Press, 1960.

_____. Workers in Industrial America: Essays on the
20th Century Struggle. New York: Oxford University
Press, 1980.

Brooks, John Graham. American Syndicalism, The I.W.W.
New York: Macmillan Company, 1913.

Brooks, Thomas R. Toil and Trouble: A History of American Labor. 2d ed., New York: Delacorte Press, 1971.

Brown, Louise Fargo. Apostle of Democracy: The Life of
Lucy Maynard Salmon. New York: Harper & Brothers,
1943.

Brown, Richard D. Modernization: The Transformation of
American Life, 1600–1865. New York: Hill & Wang,
1976.

Brownlee, W. Elliot, and Brownlee, Mary M., eds.
Women in the American Economy: A Documentary History
1675–1929. New Haven: Yale University Press, 1976.

Burns, James MacGregor. Roosevelt: The Lion and the
Fox. New York: Harcourt, Brace & World, 1956.

Campbell, Helen. Prisoners of Poverty: Women Wage-
Workers, Their Trades and Their Lives. Boston:
Roberts Brothers, 1887; repr. ed., Westport, Conn.:
Greenwood Press, 1970.

Cantor, Milton, ed. American Working-Class Culture: Ex-
plorations in American Labor and Social History.
Westport, Conn.: Greenwood Press, 1979; Contributions
in Labor History, Number 7.

Cantor, Milton, and Laurie, Bruce, eds. Class, Sex, and
the Woman Worker. Westport, Conn.: Greenwood Press,
1977; Contributions in Labor History, Number 1.

Chafe, William H. The American Woman: Her Changing
Social, Economic, and Political Roles, 1920–1970. New
York: Oxford University Press, 1972.

Child, Lydia Maria. The American Frugal Housewife. 20th
ed. Boston: American Stationer's Company, 1836; repr.
ed., New York: Harper & Row, 1972.

Clark, Alice. Working Life of Women in the Seventeenth Century. New York: Harcourt, Brace & Howe, 1920; repr. ed., New York: Augustus M. Kelly, 1968.

Commons, John R. and Associates. History of Labour in the United States. 4 vols. New York: Macmillan Company, 1918; 1935.

_____. Races and Immigrants in America. New York: Macmillan Company, 1915.

_____, ed. Trade Unionism and Labor Problems, 2d series. Augustus M. Kelly, 1967.

Conklin, Paul. The New Deal. New York: Thomas Y. Crowell, 1967.

Cott, Nancy F. The Bonds of Womanhood: "Woman's Sphere" In New England, 1780–1835. New Haven: Yale University Press, 1977.

_____, ed. Roots of Bitterness: Documents of the Social History of American Women. New York: E. P. Dutton, 1972.

Cott, Nancy F., and Pleck, Elizabeth H., eds. A Heritage of Her Own: Toward a New Social History of American Women. New York: Simon & Schuster, 1979; A Touchstone Book.

David, Paul A.; Gutman, Herbert G.; Sutch, Richard; Temin, Peter; and Wright, Gavin. Reckoning with Slavery: A Critical Study in the Quantitative History of American Negro Slavery. New York: Oxford University Press, 1976.

Davis, Jerome. The Russian Immigrant. New York: Macmillan Company, 1922; repr. ed., New York: Arno Press and the New York Times, 1969.

Degler, Carl N. At Odds: Women and the Family from the Revolution to the Present. New York: Oxford University Press, 1980.

_____. Out of Our Past: The Forces That Shaped Modern America. New York: Harper & Row; Harper Colophon Books, 1959.

Derber, Milton, and Young, Edwin, eds. Labor and the New Deal. Madison, Wisc.: University of Wisconsin Press, 1961.

Dinnerstein, Leonard, and Reimers, David M. Ethnic Americans: A History of Immigration and Assimilation. New York: Dodd, Mead, 1975.

Dorr, Rheta Childe. What Eight Million Women Want. Boston: Small, Maynard & Company, 1910; repr. ed., New York: Kraus Reprint, 1971.

Douglas, Ann. The Feminization of American Culture. New York: Alfred A. Knopf, 1977; Avon Books, 1978.

Dublin, Thomas. Women at Work: The Transformation of Work and Community in Lowell, Massachusetts, 1826-1860. New York: Columbia University Press, 1979.

Dubofsky, Melvyn. We Shall Be All: A History of the Industrial Workers of the World. Chicago: Quadrangle Books, 1969.

Dubois, Ellen C. Feminism and Suffrage, The Emergence of an Independent Women's Movement in America 1848-1869. New York: Oxford University Press, 1978.

Dubois, W. E. B. The Philadelphia Negro: A Social Study. Philadelphia: University of Pennsylvania, 1899; repr. ed. With an introduction by E. Digby Baltzell; New York: Schocken Books, 1967.

Dudden, Faye E. Serving Women: Household Service in Nineteenth-Century America. Middletown, Conn.: Wesleyan University Press, 1983.

Dulles, Foster Rhea. Labor in America: A History. 3rd ed. New York: Thomas Y. Crowell, 1966.

Eaves, Lucille. A History of California Labor Legislation. University of California Publications in Economics II. Berkeley, Calif.: University of California, 1910.

Ellis, Ann. *The Life of an Ordinary Woman*. Boston: Houghton Mifflin, 1929.

Ely, Richard T. *The Labor Movement in America*. Rev. ed. New York: Macmillan Company, 1905.

Epstein, Melech. *Jewish Labor in the U.S.A.: An Industrial, Political and Cultural History of the Jewish Labor Movement, 1822-1914*. 2 vols. New York: Trade Union Sponsoring Committee, 1950.

Erickson, E. H. *Childhood and Society*. New York: W. W. Norton, 1950.

Ernst, Robert. *Immigrant Life in New York City 1825-1863*. New York: Kings Crown Press, Columbia University, 1949.

Feldman, Herman. *Racial Factors in American Industry*. New York: Harper & Brothers, 1931.

Filene, Peter Gabriel. *Him/Her/Self Sex Roles in Modern America*. New York: Harcourt, Brace, Jovanovich, 1974; Mentor Books, 1976.

Flexner, Eleanor. *Century of Struggle*. New York: Atheneum, 1968.

Flynn, Elizabeth Gurley. *I Speak My Own Piece*. New York: Masses & Mainstream, 1955.

Foner, Philip S. *History of the Labor Movement in the United States*. Vol. 1: *From Colonial Times to the Founding of the American Federation of Labor*. New York: International Publishers, 1947.

_____. *History of the Labor Movement in the United States*. Vol. 2: *From the Founding of the American Federation of Labor to the Emergence of American Imperialism*. New York: International Publishers, 1955.

_____. *History of the Labor Movement in the United States*. Vol. 3: *The Policies and Practices of the American Federation of Labor 1900-1909*. New York: International Publishers, 1964.

_____. History of the Labor Movement in the United States. Vol. 4: The Industrial Workers of the World, 1905–1917. New York: International Publishers, 1965.

_____. Organized Labor and the Black Worker: 1619–1973. New York: International Publishers, 1976.

_____. Women and the American Labor Movement: From Colonial Times to the Eve of World War I. New York: Free Press, 1979.

_____. Women and the American Labor Movement: From World War I to the Present. New York: Free Press, 1980.

Freidel, Frank. Franklin D. Roosevelt, Launching the New Deal. Boston: Little, Brown, 1973.

Galenson, Marjorie. Women and Work. Ithaca, N.Y.: New York School for Industrial Relations, 1973.

Galenson, Walter. The CIO Challenge to the AFL: A History of the American Labor Movement 1935–1941. Cambridge, Mass.: Harvard University Press, 1960.

Gilman, Charlotte Perkins. The Home: Its Work and Influence. New York: McClure, Phillips, 1903.

_____. Women and Economics: The Economic Factor Between Men and Women as a Factor in Social Evolution. Boston: Small, Maynard, 1896; repr. ed., edited by Carl Degler, New York: Harper & Row; Harper Torch Book, 1966.

Gompers, Samuel. Seventy Years of Life and Labour: An Autobiography. 2 vols. New York: E. P. Dutton, 1925; repr. ed., New York: Augustus M. Kelly, 1967.

Green, James R. The World of the Worker: Labor in Twentieth-Century America. New York: Hill & Wang; American Century Series, 1980.

Greene, Lorenzo J., and Woodson, Carter G. The Negro Wage Earner. Washington, D.C.: Association for the Study of Negro Life and History, 1930; repr. ed., New York: Russell & Russell, 1969.

Greenwald, Maurine Weiner. Women, War and Work: The Impact of World War I on Women Workers in the United States. Westport, Conn.: Greenwood Press, 1980; Contributions in Women's Studies, Number 12.

Groat, George Gorham. An Introduction to the Study of Organized Labor. New York: Macmillan Company, 1926.

Grund, Francis Joseph. Aristocracy in America: From a Sketch Book of a German Nobleman. London: Richard Bentley, 1839; repr. ed., with a Foreword by George E. Probst; New York and Evanston, Ill.: Harper & Row; Harper Torch Book, 1959.

Gutman, Herbert G. The Black Family in Slavery & Freedom, 1750-1925. New York: Pantheon Books, 1976.

_____. Work, Culture & Society in Industrializing America: Essays in American Working Class and Social History. New York: Random House, 1966; Vintage Books, 1977.

Handlin, Oscar. Boston's Immigrants: A Study in Acculturation. Rev. ed. Cambridge, Mass.: Harvard University Press, 1941; repr. ed., New York: Atheneum, 1969.

Harland, Marion. Common Sense in the Household: A Manual of Practical Housewifery. New York: Charles Scribner's Sons, 1890.

Hartman, Mary, and Banner, Lois, eds. Clio's Consciousness Raised: New Perspectives on the History of Women. New York: Harper & Row; Harper Torch Book, 1974.

Hayden, Dolores. The Grand Domestic Revolution: A History of Feminist Designs for American Homes, Neighborhoods, and Cities. Cambridge, Mass.: MIT Press, 1981.

Hecht, Marie B.; Berbrich, Joan D.; Healey, Salley A.; and Cooper, Clare M., eds. The Women, Yes! New York: Holt, Rinehart & Winston, 1973.

Henry, Alice. The Trade Union Women. New York: D. Appleton, 1915.

_____. Women and the Labor Movement. New York: George H. Doran, 1923.

Herron, Belva M. Progress of Labor Organization Among Women. University of Illinois Studies, vol. 1. Urbana, Ill.: University of Illinois Press, 1908.

Hollander, Jacob H. and Barnett, George E., eds. Studies in American Trade Unionism. New York: Henry Holt, 1907.

Hourwich, Isaac A. Immigration and Labor: The Economic Aspects of European Immigration to the United States. New York: G. P. Putnam's Sons, 1912; repr. ed., New York: Arno Press and the New York Times, 1969.

Howard, Donald S. The W.P.A. and Federal Relief Policy. New York: Russell Sage Foundation, 1943.

Hoxie, Robert Franklin. Trade Unionism in the United States. New York: D. Appleton, 1917.

Hunter, Jane Edna. A Nickel and a Prayer. Cleveland: Elli Kani, 1940.

Hunter, Robert. Poverty: Social Consciousness in the Progressive Era. New York: Macmillan Company, 1904; repr. ed., edited by Peter d'A. Jones, New York: Harper & Row, 1965.

Hymovitz, Carol, and Weisman, Michaele. A History of Women in America. New York: Bantam Books, 1978.

Jacobson, Julius, ed. The Negro and the American Labor Movement. Garden City, N.Y.: Anchor Books, 1968.

Johnson, Charles S. Shadow of the Plantation. Chicago: University of Chicago Press, 1934; Phoenix Books, 1966.

Johnson, Paul E. A Shopkeeper's Millennium: Society and Revivals in Rochester, New York, 1815-1837. New York: Hill & Wang, 1978.

Jones, Mary Harris. Autobiography of Mother Jones. Edited by Mary Field Parton. Chicago: Charles H. Kerr, 1925.

Kammen, Michael, ed. The Past before Us: Contemporary Historical Writing in the United States. Ithaca, N.Y.: Cornell University Press, 1980.

Katzman, David M. Seven Days a Week: Women and Domestic Service in Industrializing America. New York: Oxford University Press, 1978.

Kellor, Frances A. Out of Work: A Study of Employment Agencies: Their Treatment of the Unemployed, and Their Influence Upon Homes and Business. New York: G. P. Putnam's Sons, 1905.

Kennedy, Louise Venable. The Negro Peasant Turns Cityward: Effects of Recent Migrations to Northern Centers. New York: Columbia University Press, 1930.

Kennedy, Susan Estabrook. If All We Did Was to Weep at Home: A History of White Working-Class Women in America. Bloomington, Ind.: Indiana University Press, 1979.

Kessler-Harris, Alice. Out to Work: A History of Wage-Earning Women in the United States. New York: Oxford University Press, 1982.

Kett, Joseph. Rites of Passage: Adolescence in America, 1790 to the Present. New York: Basic Books, 1977.

Kiser, Clyde Vernon. Sea Island to City: A Study of St. Helena Islanders in Harlem and Other Urban Centers. New York: Columbia University Press; repr. ed., Studies in American Negro Life. New York: Atheneum, 1969.

Kornbluh, Joyce L., ed. Rebel Voices, an IWW Anthology. Ann Arbor, Mich.: University of Michigan Press, 1968.

Kraditor, Aileen S., ed. Up from the Pedestal: Selected Writings in the History of American Feminism. Chicago: Quadrangle Books, 1968.

Krohn, Alan. Hysteria: The Elusive Neurosis. New York: International Universities Press, 1978.

Kusmer, Kenneth. A Ghetto Takes Shape: Black Cleveland, 1870–1930. Urbana, Ill.: University of Illinois Press, 1976.

Lebergott, Stanley. Manpower in Economic Growth: The American Record Since 1800. New York: McGraw-Hill, 1964.

Leiserman, William M. Adjusting Immigrant and Industry. New York: Harper & Brothers, 1924.

Lerner, Gerda, ed. Black Women in White America: A Documentary History. New York: Vintage Books, 1973.

Leuchtenberg, William E. Franklin D. Roosevelt and the New Deal, 1932–1940. New York: Harper & Row; Harper Torch Book, 1963.

Litwack, Leon F. North of Slavery: The Negro in the Free States, 1790–1860. Chicago: University of Chicago Press, 1961.

Lobsenz, Johanna. The Older Woman in Industry. New York: Charles Scribner's Sons, 1929.

McBride, Theresa M. The Domestic Revolution: The Modernisation of Household Service in England and France 1820–1920. New York: Holmes & Meier, 1976.

McLaurin, Melton Alonza. The Kinghts of Labor in the South. Westport, Conn.: Greenwood Press, 1978; Contributions in Labor History, Number 4.

MacLean, Annie Marion. Modern Immigration: A View of the Situation in Immigrant Receiving Countries. Philadelphia: J. B. Lippincott, 1925.

_____. Women Workers and Society. New York: A. C. McClurg, 1916.

Mandel, Bernard. Samuel Gompers: A Biography. Yellow Springs, Ohio: Antioch Press, 1963.

Marot, Helen. American Labor Unions. New York: Henry Holt, 1914.

Matthews, Lillian R. Women in Trade Unions in San Francisco. University of California Publications in Economics, No. 3. Berkeley, Calif.: University of California, 1913.

Merton, Robert K. and Nisbet, Robert A., eds. Contemporary Social Problems. 2d ed. New York: Harcourt, Brace & World, 1966.

Meyer, Annie Nathan, ed. Woman's Work in America. New York: Henry Holt, 1891.

Northrup, Herbert R. Organized Labor and the Negro. New York: Harper & Brothers, 1944.

Oakley, Ann. Woman's Work: The Housewife, Past and Present. New York: Vintage Books, 1974.

Odencrantz, Louise. Italian Women in Industry: A Study of Conditions in New York City. New York: Russell Sage Foundation, 1919.

O'Neill, William L. Everyone Was Brave: A History of Feminism in America. Chicago: Quadrangle Books, 1969.

Oppenheimer, Valerie Kincade. The Female Labor Force in the United States. Institute of International Studies. Berkeley, Calif.: University of California, 1970.

Osofsky, Gilbert. Harlem: The Making of a Ghetto 1890-1930. New York: Harper & Row, 1963; Harper Torch Book, 1968.

O'Toole, James, ed. Work and the Quality of Life. Cambridge, Mass.: MIT Press, 1974.

Ovington, Mary White. Half a Man: The Status of the Negro in New York. New York: Longmans, Green, 1911.

Owen, Catherine. Progressive Housekeeping: Keeping House without Knowing How, and Knowing How to Keep House Well. Boston: Houghton Mifflin, 1889.

Park, Robert E., and Miller, Herbert A. <u>Old World Traits Transplanted</u>. New York: Harper & Brothers, 1921; repr. ed., New York: Arno Press and the <u>New York Times</u>, 1969.

Parker, Carleton H. <u>The Casual Laborer and Other Essays</u>. New York: Harcourt, Brace, 1920.

Peckham, Joseph A. et al. <u>Social Security: Perspectives for Reform</u>. Washington, D.C.: Brookings Institute, 1968.

Pettengill, Lillian. <u>Toilers of the Home: The Record of a College Woman's Experience as a Domestic Servant</u>. New York: Doubleday, Page, 1903.

Putman, Emily James. <u>The Lady: Studies of Certain Phases of Her History</u>. New York: G. P. Putnam's Sons, 1921.

Raper, Arthur F. <u>Preface to Peasantry: A Tale of Two Black Belt Countries</u>. Chapel Hill, N.C.: University of North Carolina Press, 1936, repr. ed., Studies in American Negro Life, New York: Atheneum, 1968.

Rayback, Joseph G. <u>A History of American Labor</u>. New York: Free Press, 1966.

Rees, Albert. <u>The Economics of Trade Unions</u>. Cambridge Economics Handbooks. Chicago: University of Chicago Press, 1962.

Rischin, Moses. <u>The Promised City</u>. 2 vols. Cambridge, Mass.: Harvard University Press, 1962.

Roberts, Peter. <u>Immigrant Races in North America</u>. New York: YMCA Press, 1912.

_____. <u>The New Immigration: A Study of the Industrial and Social Life of Southeastern Europeans in America</u>. New York: Macmillan, 1912.

Rodgers, Daniel T. <u>The Work Ethic in Industrial America 1850-1920</u>. Chicago: University of Chicago Press, 1974.

Rose, William Ganson. Cleveland: The Making of a City. New York: World Publishing Company, 1950.

Rothman, Sheila M. Woman's Proper Place: A History of Changing Ideals and Practices, 1870 to the Present. New York: Basic Books, 1978.

Ryan, Mary P. Cradle of the Middle Class: The Family in Oneida County, New York, 1790-1865. Cambridge: Cambridge University Press, 1981.

Salmon, Lucy Maynard. Domestic Service. New York: Macmillan, 1897; repr. ed., New York: Arno Press, 1972.

_____. Progress in the Household. Boston: Houghton Mifflin, 1906.

Savage, Marion Dutton. Industrial Unionism in America. New York: Ronald Press, 1922.

Scharf, Lois. To Work and to Wed: Female Employment, Feminism, and the Great Depression. Westport, Conn.: Greenwood Press, 1980; Contributions in Women's Studies, Number 15.

Schlesinger, Arthur Meier. The Rise of the City 1878-1898. A History of American Life. Vol. 10. New York: Macmillan, 1933.

Schob, David. Hired Hands and Plowboys: Farm Labor in the Midwest, 1815-1860. Urbana, Ill.: University of Illinois Press, 1975.

Silverberg, W. V. Childhood Experience and Personal Destiny. New York: Springer Publishing, 1952.

Sklar, Kathryn Kish. Catherine Beecher: A Study in American Domesticity. New Haven: Yale University Press, 1973; repr. ed., New York: W. W. Norton, 1976.

Smith, Abbott Emerson. Colonists in Bondage: White Servitude and Convict Labor in America 1607-1776. Chapel Hill, N.C.: University of North Carolina Press, 1947; repr. ed., New York: W. W. Norton, 1971.

Smuts, Robert W. Women and Work in America. New York: Columbia University Press, 1959; repr. ed., New York: Schocken Books, 1971.

Spear, Allan H. Black Chicago: The Making of a Negro Ghetto, 1890–1920. Chicago: University of Chicago Press, 1967.

Spero, Sterling D., and Harris, Abram L. The Black Worker: The Negro and the Labor Movement. New York: Columbia University Press, 1931; repr. ed., Studies in American Negro Life, New York: Atheneum, 1968.

Spruill, Julia Cherry. Women's Life and Work in the Southern Colonies. Chapel Hill, N.C.: University of North Carolina Press, 1938; repr. ed., New York: W. W. Norton, 1972.

Stolberg, Benjamin. The Story of the CIO. New York: Viking Press, 1938; repr. ed., New York: Arno Press and the New York Times, 1971.

Sutherland, Daniel E. Americans and Their Servants: Domestic Service in the United States from 1800–1920. Baton Rouge, La.: Louisiana State University Press, 1981.

Taft, Phillip. The A.F. of L. in the Time of Gompers. New York: Harper & Row, 1957.

Tentler, Leslie Woodcock. Wage-Earning Women: Industrial Work and Family Life in the United States, 1900–1930. New York: Oxford University Press, 1979.

Terrill, Bertha M. Household Management. Chicago: American School of Home Economics, 1914.

Terry, Ellen. The Third Door: An Autobiography of an American Negro Woman. New York: David McKay, 1955.

Thernstrom, Stephen. Poverty and Progress: Social Mobility in a Nineteenth Century City. Cambridge, Mass.: Harvard University Press, 1964; repr. ed., New York: Atheneum, 1969.

Thomas, William I., and Znaniecki, Florian. The Polish Peasant in Europe and America. 2 vols. New York: Alfred A. Knopf, 1927.

Thompson, E. P. The Making of the English Working Class. New York: Random House, 1964.

de Tocqueville, Alexis. Democracy in America. Rev. ed. Translated by Henry Reeve. New York: Colonial Press, 1899.

Trembley, Alfred G. The Distinct Problem of Women Employees. Industrial Commentaries, vol. 1. Chicago: n.p., 1940.

Wandersee, Winifred. Women's Work and Family Values, 1920–1940. Cambridge, Mass.: Harvard University Press, 1980.

Ware, Norman J. The Industrial Worker, 1840–1860. Boston: Houghton Mifflin, 1924.

_____. The Labor Movement in the United States 1860–1895: A Study in Democracy. New York: D. Appleton, 1929.

Warner, Sam Bass, Jr. The Private City: Philadelphia in Three Periods of Its Growth. Philadelphia: University of Pennsylvania Press, 1968.

Wertheimer, Barbara Mayer. We Were There: The Story of Working Women in America. New York: Pantheon Books, 1977.

Wesley, Charles H. Negro Labor in the United States: 1850–1925. New York: Russell & Russell, 1927.

White, Robert W. The Abnormal Personality. 3rd ed. New York: Ronald Press, 1904.

Wolfson, Theresa. The Woman Worker and the Trade Unions. New York: International Publishers, 1926.

Woods, Robert A., ed. Americans in Process: A Settlement Study. Boston: Houghton Mifflin, 1903.

Woods, Robert A., and Kennedy, Albert J. Young Working
    Girls: A Summary of Evidence from Two Thousand
    Social Workers. Boston: Houghton Mifflin, 1913.

Woody, Thomas. A History of Women's Education in the
    United States. 2 vols. New York: Octagon Books,
    1966.

Zinn, Howard, ed. New Deal Thought. Indianapolis, Ind.:
    Bobbs-Merrill, 1966.

ARTICLES IN BOOKS

Beale, Jessie Fremont, and Withington, Anne. "Life's
    Amenities." In Americans in Process: A Settlement
    Study, pp. 224-53. Edited by Robert A. Woods.
    Boston: Houghton Mifflin, 1903.

Brody, David. "Labor History in the 1970s: Toward a
    History of the American Worker." In The Past before
    Us: Contemporary Historical Writing in the United
    States, pp. 252-69. Edited by Michael Kammen.
    Ithaca, N.Y.: Cornell University Press, 1980.

Bushee, Frederick A. "The Invading Host." In Americans
    in Process: A Settlement Study, pp. 40-70. Edited by
    Robert A. Woods. Boston: Houghton Mifflin, 1903.

_____. "Population." In The City Wilderness: A Settle-
    ment Study, pp. 33-57. Edited by Robert A. Woods.
    Boston: Houghton Mifflin, 1898.

Cole, William I. "The Church and the People." In The
    City Wilderness: A Settlement Study, pp. 201-30.
    Edited by Robert A. Woods. Boston: Houghton Mifflin,
    1898.

Cole, William I., and Miles, Rufus E. "Community of In-
    terest." In Americans in Process: A Settlement Study,
    pp. 321-55. Edited by Robert A. Woods. Boston:
    Houghton Mifflin, 1903.

Cowan, Ruth Schwartz. "A Case Study of Technological and
    Social Change: The Washing Machine and the Working

Wife." In Clio's Consciousness Raised: New Perspec-
tives on the History of Women, pp. 245–53. Edited by
Mary Hartman and Lois W. Banner. New York: Harper
& Row; Harper Torch Book, 1974.

Furstenberg, Frank F., Jr. "Work Experience and Family
Life." In Work and the Quality of Life, pp. 341–60.
Edited by James O'Toole. Cambridge, Mass.: MIT
Press, 1974.

Gilman, Charlotte Perkins. "Economic Basis of the Woman
Question." In The Women, Yes!, pp. 85–87. Edited
by Marie B. Hecht, Joan D. Berbrich, Salley A. Healey,
and Clare M. Cooper. New York: Holt, Rinehart &
Winston, 1973.

Glasco, Lawrence A. "The Life Cycles and Household Structure of American Ethnic Groups: Irish, Germans, and
Native-Born Whites in Buffalo, New York, 1855." In
A Heritage of Her Own: Toward a New Social History of
American Women, pp. 268–97. Edited by Nancy F. Cott
and Elizabeth H. Pleck. New York: Simon & Schuster,
1979; A Touchstone Book.

Jacobson, Julius. "Union Conservatism: A Barrier to
Racial Equality." In The Negro and the American
Labor Movement, pp. 1–26. Edited by Julius Jacobson.
New York: Anchor Books, 1968.

Jacoby, Robin Miller. "The Women's Trade Union League
and American Feminism." In Class, Sex, and the
Woman Worker, pp. 203–24. Edited by Milton Cantor
and Bruce Laurie. Westport, Conn.: Greenwood Press,
1977; Contributions in Labor History, Number 1.

Karson, Marc, and Radosh, Ronald. "The American Federation of Labor and the Negro Worker, 1894–1949." In
The Negro and the American Labor Movement, pp. 155–
87. Edited by Julius Jacobson. New York: Anchor
Books, 1968.

Kessler-Harris, Alice. "Where Are the Organized Women
Workers?" In A Heritage of Her Own: Toward a New
Social History of American Women, pp. 343–66. Edited
by Nancy F. Cott and Elizabeth H. Pleck. New York:
Simon & Schuster, 1979; A Touchstone Book.

Kirk, William. "The Knights of Labor and the American Federation of Labor." In Studies in American Trade Unionism, pp. 353-80. Edited by Jacob H. Hollander and George E. Barnett. New York: Henry Holt, 1912; repr. ed., New York: Arno Press and the New York Times, 1969.

Marshall, Ray. "The Negro in Southern Unions." In The Negro and the American Labor Movement, pp. 128-54. Edited by Julius Jacobson. New York: Anchor Books, 1968.

Meier, August, and Rudwick, Elliot. "Attitudes of Negro Leaders toward the American Labor Movement from the Civil War to World War I." In The Negro and the American Labor Movement, pp. 27-48. Edited by Julius Jacobson. New York: Anchor Books, 1968.

Perlman, Selig. "Labor and the New Deal in Historical Perspective." In Labor and the New Deal, pp. 363-70. Edited by Milton Derber and Edwin Young. Madison, Wis.: University of Wisconsin Press, 1961.

Pleck, Elizabeth H. "A Mother's Wages: Income Earning among Married Italian and Black Women, 1896-1911." In A Heritage of Her Own: Toward a New Social History of American Women, pp. 367-92. Edited by Nancy F. Cott and Elizabeth H. Pleck. New York: Simon & Schuster, 1979; A Touchstone Book.

Rhine, Alice Hyneman. "Women in Industry." In Woman's Work in America, pp. 276-322. Edited by Annie Nathan Meyer. New York: Henry Holt, 1891.

Rosen, Sumner M. "The CIO Era, 1935-55." In The Negro and the American Labor Movement, pp. 188-208. Edited by Julius Jacobson. New York: Anchor Books, 1968.

Stearns, Peter N. "Toward a Wider Vision: Trends in Social History." In The Past before Us: Contemporary Historical Writing in the United States, pp. 205-30. Edited by Michael Kammen. Ithaca, N.Y.: Cornell University Press, 1980.

Woods, Robert A. "Assimilation: A Two-Edged Sword." In Americans in Process: A Settlement Study, pp. 356-83. Edited by Robert A. Woods. Boston: Houghton Mifflin, 1903.

_____. "Livelihood." In Americans in Process: A Settlement Study, pp. 104-46. Edited by Robert A. Woods. Boston: Houghton Mifflin, 1903.

_____. "Social Recovery." In The City Wilderness: A Settlement Study, pp. 245-87. Edited by Robert A. Woods. Boston: Houghton Mifflin, 1898.

_____. "The Total Drift." In The City Wilderness: A Settlement Study, pp. 288-311. Edited by Robert A. Woods. Boston: Houghton Mifflin, 1898.

_____. "Work and Wages." In The City Wilderness: A Settlement Study, pp. 82-113. Edited by Robert A. Woods. Boston: Houghton Mifflin, 1898.

Yans-McLaughlin, Virginia. "Italian Women and Work: Experience and Perception." In Class, Sex, and the Woman Worker, pp. 101-19. Edited by Milton Cantor and Bruce Laurie. Westport, Conn.: Greenwood Press, 1977; Contributions in Labor History, Number 1.

MAGAZINES AND JOURNALS

"A Maid in the House." Atlantic Monthly, May 1920, pp. 714-15.

A Mere Man. "The Servant Question." Woman's Home Companion, October 1911, p. 74.

A Negro Nurse. "More Slavery at the South." Independent, January 25, 1912, pp. 196-200.

"A St. Louis Study of Household Employment." Journal of Home Economics 28 (September 1936):463-64.

"A Servant on the Servant Problem." American Magazine, September 1909, pp. 502-4.

"A Servant's Union." Harper's Bazaar. June 2, 1900, p. 319.

A Thankful Husband. "How My Wife Keeps Her Maids." Harper's Bazaar, December 1909, p. 1231.

"A Vanishing Relation." Independent, August 23, 1906, pp. 466–67.

Abbott, Edith, and Breckinridge, Sophonisba P. "Employ-ment of Women in Industries—Twelfth Census Statistics." Journal of Political Economy 14 (January 1906):14-40.

Abbott, Frances M. "How to Solve the Housekeeping Prob-lem." Forum and Century, February 1893, pp. 778–88.

Abbott, Grace. "The Chicago Employment Agency and the Immigrant Worker," American Journal of Sociology 14 (November 1908):289-305.

Abel, Mary Hinman. "Another View of the Eight Hour Day." American Kitchen Magazine, December 1901, pp. 88–90.

_____. "The Eight Hour Day in Housekeeping: Why It Is Not Practicable." American Kitchen Magazine, Feb-ruary 1902, pp. 177–80.

_____. "A Training-School for Servants." Outlook, Octo-ber 28, 1899, pp. 501-3.

Addams, Jane. "A Belated Industry." American Journal of Sociology 1 (March 1896):536-50.

_____. "The Problem of Domestic Service Viewed Scien-tifically." Review of Reviews, May 1896, pp. 604-5.

Alden, Judith. "Help!" Literary Digest, September 11, 1937, pp. 18-20.

Allen, Annie Winsor. "Both Sides of the Servant Question." Atlantic Monthly, April 1913, pp. 496-506.

"American Women and Housework: The Problem Presented by the Prophesied Decline in Immigration." Craftsman, October 1914, pp. 53-58.

"An Unsettled Question." Outlook: A Family Paper, July 7, 1894, pp. 59-60.

Anderson, Hattie E. "Adult Training in Domestic Service." Journal of Home Economics 25 (February 1933):124-26.

Anderson, Mary. "Domestic Apprenticeship--Different Forms of Realizing in the United States." Journal of Home Economics 27 (January 1935):7-30.

_____. "Domestic Service in the United States." Journal of Home Economics 20 (January 1928):7-12.

Andrews, Benjamin R. "New York Symposium on Household Employment." Journal of Home Economics 32 (February 1940):98-99.

Andrews, William D., and Andrews, Deborah C. "Technology and the Housewife in Nineteenth Century America." Women's Studies 2 (1974):309-28.

A. O. C. "A Letter and Reply on the Servant Question." Colliers: The National Weekly, April 26, 1911, p. 36.

"Appeal to Woman." Harper's Weekly, October 18, 1902, pp. 1506-7.

Applegate, Margaret T. "Is the Lady of the House at Home?" Woman's Press 27 (November 1933):472-74.

Bacon, Josephine Daskam. "We and Our Servants." American Magazine, February 1907, pp. 349-60.

Baker, Ella, and Cooke, Marvel. "The Bronx Slave Market." Crisis 42 (November 1935):330-32, 340.

Barbara--The Commuter's Wife. "Why Domestic Service Is a Problem." New Outlook, October 1, 1904, pp. 299-303.

Barnum, Gertrude. "Fall River Mill Girls in Domestic Service: A Strike Time Experiment." Charities, February 11, 1905, pp. 550-51.

Baron, Harold M. "The Demand for Black Labor: Historical Notes on the Political Economy of Racism." Radical America 5 (March-April 1971):1-46.

Barr, Amelia E. "The Servant-Girls' Point of View."
North American Review 154 (June 1892):729-32.

"Below Stairs: Master's Problems." Literary Digest, July
10, 1937, pp. 21-22.

Bentley, Mildred Maddocks. "The Psychology of Servants."
Ladies Home Journal, December 1925, pp. 161-62, 165.

Bernard, Jessie. "Historical and Structural Barriers to
Occupational Desegregation." Signs: Journal of Women
in Culture and Society 1, Part 2 (Spring 1976):87-94.

Bernard, Richard M., and Vinovskis, Marie A. "The Female
School Teacher in Antebellum Massachusetts." Journal
of Social History 10 (March 1977):332-45.

"Biggest Drop for Household Workers." Life and Labor
Bulletin, June 1931, p. 2.

Blau, Francine D., and Jusenius, Carol L. "Economists'
Approaches to Sex Segregation in the Labor Market:
An Appraisal." Signs: Journal of Women in Culture
and Society 1, Part 2 (Spring 1976):181-99.

Bodner, John; Weber, Michael; and Simon, Roger. "Migration, Kinship and Urban Adjustment: Blacks and Poles
in Pittsburg, 1900-1930." Journal of American History
66 (December 1979):548-65.

"Body-Servants." Scribner's Magazine, August 1907, pp.
251-52.

Bolin, Winifred. "The Economics of Middle Income Family
Life: Working Women during the Depression." Journal
of American History 65 (June 1979):60-74.

Bornet, Vaughn Davis. "The New Labor History: A Challenge for American Historians." The Historian 18
(Autumn 1955):1-24.

Bowles, Eva D. "The Colored Girl in Our Midst." Association Monthly 11 (December 1917):491-493.

Branca, Patricia. "A New Perspective on Women's Work: A Comparative Typology." Journal of Social History 9 (Winter 1975):121–53.

Breckenridge, Sophonisba P. "Legislative Control of Women's Work." Journal of Political Economy 14 (January 1906): 107–9.

Brody, David. "Radical Labor History and Rank-and-File Militancy." Labor History 16 (Winter 1975):117–26.

Bromley, Dorothy Dunbar. "Are Servants People?" Scribner's Magazine, February 1933, pp. 377–79.

Broun, Heywood. "Housekeepers of the World Unite!" New Republic, July 6, 1938, pp. 248–49.

_____. "Like One of the Family." Nation, May 29, 1935, p. 631.

Brown, Jean Collier. "Labor Relations in the Home." Woman's Press 34 (October 1940):417–18.

Brown, Richard D. "Modernization and the Modern Personality in Early America, 1600–1865: A Sketch of a Synthesis." Journal of Interdisciplinary History 2 (Winter 1972):1220–28.

Brueré, Martha Bensley. "The New Home-Making." Outlook, March 16, 1912, pp. 591–95.

Bularzik, Mary. "Sexual Harassment at the Workplace." Radical America 12 (July–August 1978):25–42.

Butler, James D. "British Convicts Shipped to American Colonies." American Historical Review 2 (October 1896):12–33.

Call, Annie Payson. "The Spoiling of Servants." Century Magazine, April 1913, pp. 915–16.

Callahan, Helen C. "Upstairs-Downstairs in Chicago." Chicago History 6 (1977–78):195–209.

Cole, Arthur. "The Tempo of Mercantile Life in Colonial America." Business History Review 33 (Autumn 1959): 277–99.

Collins, James H. "Woman's Mishandling of Labor." Ladies Home Journal, October 1920, pp. 34, 141–42.

Comstock, Sarah. "Mistress Problem: Is the Difficulty Really with the Servant?" Colliers: The National Weekly, February 1, 1913, pp. 15–16.

"Concerning Codes." Woman's Press 27 (September 1933): 395, (October 1933):441.

"Concerning Mother's Hinderers." New Outlook, January 15, 1919, pp. 92–93.

"Cooking and Dusting Raised to a Profession." Literary Digest, June 25, 1927, pp. 56–59.

"Cooks and Maids Have Codes Too." Literary Digest, April 28, 1934, p. 10.

Cowan, Ruth Schwartz. "The Industrial Revolution in the Home: Household Technology and Social Change in the Twentieth Century." Technology and Culture 17 (January 1976):1–23.

_____. "Two Washes in the Morning and a Bridge Party at Night: The American Housewife between the Wars." Women's Studies 3 (1976):147–72.

Crane, Frank. "How Do You Get Along with Your Hired Girl?" American Magazine, October 1924, pp. 61, 166–68.

Craster, Charles V. "Medical Examination of Domestic Servants." American Journal of Public Health 23 (May 1933):433–36.

Curran, Henry H. "The Cooks Are Coming." Ladies Home Journal, November 1925, pp. 33, 101, 174.

Davis, Allen F. "The Women's Trade Union League: Origins and Organization." Labor History 5 (Winter 1964): 3–17.

Davis, Rebecca Harding. "The Recovery of Family Life." Independent, September 21, 1905, pp. 673–75.

Dickson, Harris. "Help! Help! Help!: The Bogy That Darkens the Sun of Southern Domesticity." Delineator, July 1912, pp. 7, 66–67.

Doman, Leila. "Legislation in the Field of Household Employment." Journal of Home Economics 28 (September 1936):90–95.

"Domestic Service in Philadelphia Homes." Monthly Labor Review 35 (July 1932):33–35.

"Domestic Workers in Baltimore." Monthly Labor Review 20 (February 1925):235–37.

Dorr, Rheta Childe. "The Prodigal Daughter." Hampton's Magazine, April 1910, pp. 526–38; May 1910, pp. 679–88.

DuBois, W. E. B. "The Negroes of Farmville, Virginia: A Social Study." Bulletin of the Department of Labor 3 (January 1898):1–38.

Dunne, Peter Finley. "Mr. Dooley on the Servant Problem." Harper's Weekly, February 17, 1900, p. 160.

Dynock, James. "The High Cost of Livery." Saturday Evening Post, July 27, 1935, pp. 23, 55, 58–59.

Earle, Mrs. C. W. "Mistresses and Servants." Cornhill Magazine, February 1898, pp. 155–64.

Eliot, George Fielding. "Where Do We Go from Here?" New Republic, July 20, 1938, p. 310.

"Employees of the Household." Outlook, August 20, 1910, pp. 857–58.

"Employer-Employee Relations in the Home." Good Housekeeping, February 1929, p. 104.

"Employer-Employee Relations in the Home." Journal of Home Economics 21 (February 1929):120–22.

"Employment Conditions and Unemployment Relief." Monthly Labor Review 38 (April 1934):791.

Evanshon, John; Foner, Laura; Naison, Mark; Meyerowitz, Ruth; and Brumbach, Will. "Literature on the American Working Class." Radical America 3 (March–April 1969):32–33, 36–55.

"Factory vs. Kitchen." Commonweal, December 10, 1930, p. 144.

Faler, Paul. "Working Class Historiography." Radical America 3 (March–April 1969):56–68.

Farragher, Johnny, and Stansell, Christine. "Women and Their Families on the Overland Trail to California and Oregon, 1842–1867." Feminist Studies 2 (Winter 1975): 150–66.

Ferber, Marianne A., and Lowry, Helen M. "Women: The New Reserve of the Unemployed." Signs: Journal of Women in Culture and Society 1, Part 2 (Spring 1976): 213–32.

Fleming, Walter L. "The Servant Problem in the Black Belt." Sewanee Review 13 (January 1905):1–17.

de Ford, Miriam Allen. "The Hired Girl." New Republic, March 4, 1931, pp. 68–71.

Forrester, Izola. "The Girl Problem." Good Housekeeping, September 1912, pp. 375–82.

Fowler, Grace A. "The Servant Question at Harbor Hill." Harper's Bazaar, September 1904, pp. 857–65.

Frazer, Elizabeth. "The Servant Problem." Saturday Evening Post, February 25, 1928, pp. 10–11, 36, 38, 40.

Frederick, Christine. "The New Housekeeping." Ladies Home Journal, December 1912, pp. 16, 79.

_____. "Suppose Our Servants Didn't Live with Us." Ladies Home Journal, October 1914, p. 102.

_____. "Will the Eight Hour Home-Assistant Plan Work out?" Ladies Home Journal, September 1919, p. 47.

_____. "Why Should Our Servants Live with Us?" Ladies Home Journal, October 1915, pp. 47, 98.

Furstenberg, Frank F., Jr.; Hershberg, Theodore; and Modell, John. "The Origins of the Female-Headed Black Family: The Impact of the Urban Experience." Journal of Interdisciplinary History 6 (Autumn 1975): 211-33.

Gale, Zona. "The Eight-Hour Home Assistant." Ladies Home Journal, April 1919, pp. 35, 86.

Gerould, Katharine Fullerton. "The New Simplicity." Harper's Monthly Magazine, December 1918, pp. 14-24.

"Getting the Home Work Done." Life and Labor Bulletin, November 1928, p. 3.

Glass, Montague. "Couple Trouble." Saturday Evening Post, July 18, 1931, pp. 23, 90, 93.

Godman, Inez A. "A Nine-Hour Day for Domestic Servants." Independent, February 13, 1902, pp. 397-400.

_____. "A Professional Servant." Independent, February 6, 1913, pp. 309-12.

_____. "Ten Weeks in a Kitchen." Independent, October 17, 1901, pp. 2459-64.

Goldmark, Josephine C. "Working Women and Laws: A Record of Neglect." Annals of the American Academy of Political and Social Science 28 (September 1906): 70-85.

Gompers, Samuel. "Should the Wife Help Support the Family?" American Federationist 12 (January 1906):36.

Greenbaum, Fred. "The Social Ideas of Samuel Gompers." Labor History 7 (Winter 1966):35-61.

Greene, Dorothea Pearson. "My Experiences with Servants." Ladies Home Journal, April 1914, p. 28.

Grove, Lady. "Hotels as Homes." Critic: An Illustrated Monthly Review of Literature, Art and Life 41 (October 1902):353–57.

Guernsey, John B. "Scientific Management in the Home." Outlook, April 13, 1912, pp. 821–25.

Gutman, Herbert. "Labor History and the 'Sartre Question.'" Humanities, September/October 1980, pp. 1–2.

Hader, Mathilde C. "Conference on Employer-Employee Relationships in the Home." Journal of Home Economics 23 (July 1931):640–42.

Hall, Bolton. "The Servant Class on the Farm and in the Slums." Arena, September 1898, pp. 373–77.

Hanson, Alice, and Douglas, Paul H. "Wages of Domestic Labor in Chicago." Journal of the American Statistical Association 25 (March 1930):47–50.

Harland, Marion. "One Housewife's Protest." Independent, March 6, 1902, pp. 564–65.

Harrison, E. B. "Mistress and Maid." Nineteenth Century and After, February 1903, pp. 284–89.

Hartman, Heidi. "Capitalism, Patriarchy, and Job Segregation by Sex." Signs: Journal of Women in Culture and Society 1 (Spring 1976):137–69.

Hartsock, Nancy. "Staying Alive." Quest: A Feminist Quarterly 3 (Winter 1976–77):2–14.

Haynes, Elizabeth Ross. "Negroes in Domestic Service in the United States." Journal of Negro History 8 (October 1923):384–442.

Herrick, Christine Terhune. "Duties of the Maid-of-All Work." Harper's Bazaar, November 1904, pp. 1116–17.

_____. "The Household of Two Servants." Harper's Bazaar, March 1906, pp. 274–77.

_____. "The Other Side of the Shield." North American Review 164 (April 1897):507–12.

Hobby, Daniel T. "'We Have Got Results': A Document in the Organization of Domestics in the Progressive Era." Labor History 17 (Winter 1976):103-8.

"'Home Assistants' as a Solution to the Servant Problem." Literary Digest, June 19, 1920, pp. 82-83.

Hopkins, Mary Alden. "A Letter and Reply on the Servant Question." Colliers: The National Weekly, April 22, 1911, p. 36.

Hotchkiss, T. W. "Advice to Employers." Good Housekeeping, September 1909, p. 244.

"Household Employment." Journal of Home Economics 23 (July 1930):649-53.

"Household Employment—A Symposium." Journal of Home Economics 23 (July 1931):649-53.

"Household Employment in New York State, 1938-39." Monthly Labor Review 51 (October 1940):907-10.

Howe, Frederick C. "The Vanishing Servant Girl." Ladies Home Journal, May 1918, p. 48.

Howells, William Dean. "Editor's Easy Chair." Harper's Magazine, January 1908, pp. 309-12.

Huebner, Grover G. "The Americanization of the Immigrant." Annals of the American Academy of Political and Social Science 27 (May 1906):192-213.

Hunt, Caroline L. "More Life for the Household Employee." Chautauquan, January 1903, pp. 392-96.

Isaacs, Edith J. R. "My Servants and Yours." Delineator, November 1911, p. 380.

Jackson, Ida. "The Factory Girl and Domestic Service." Harper's Bazaar, October 1903, pp. 953-57.

Johnson, B. Eleanor. "A Study of Household Employment in Chicago." Journal of Home Economics 25 (February 1933):115-21.

Kann, Kenneth. "Knights of Labor." Labor History 18 (Winter 1977):49–70.

Katz, Michael B. "Social Class in North American Urban History." Journal of Interdisciplinary History 11 (Spring 1981):579–605.

Kellor, Frances A. Immigrants in America Review 1 and 2 (March 1915–March 1916; April 1916–July 1916).

_____. "Immigration and Household Labor: A Study of Sinister Social Conditions." Charities: A Weekly Review of Local and General Philanthropy, February 6, 1904, pp. 151–52.

_____. "Intelligence Offices." Atlantic Monthly, October 1904, pp. 458–64.

_____. "The Housewife and Her Helper." Ladies Home Journal, October–December 1905; January–June 1906; February–October 1907.

Kelly, Florence. "From Field to Factory: The Industrial Significance of the Recent Negro Migration." Association Monthly 12 (March 1918):80–81.

Kennelly, A. E. "Electricity in the Household." Scribner's Magazine, January 1890, pp. 102–15.

Kerr, Florence. "Training for Household Employment." Journal of Home Economics 32 (September 1940):437–42.

Kessler, Sidney H. "The Organization of Negroes in the Knights of Labor." Journal of Negro History 37 (July 1952):248–75.

Kingsley, Florence Morse. "The Maid and the Mistress." New Outlook, October 1, 1904, pp. 295–97.

Kirtland, J. C., Mrs. "Servants and Labor-Saving Devices." Good Housekeeping, December 1912, pp. 859–60.

Klaczynska, Barbara. "Why Women Work?: A Theory for Comparison of Ethnic Groups." Labor History 17 (Winter 1976):73–87.

Kleinberg, Susan J. "The Systematic Study of Urban Women." Historical Methods Newsletter 9 (December 1975):14–25.

Klink, Jane Seymour. "Put Yourself in Her Place." Atlantic Monthly, February 1905, pp. 169–77.

_____. "The Housekeeper's Responsibility." Atlantic Monthly, March 1905, pp. 372–81.

Kortrecht, Augusta. "Put Yourself in Her Place." Good Housekeeping, November 1910, pp. 588–89.

"Labor Standards for Domestic Employees." Monthly Labor Review 39 (November 1934):1110–11.

Laws, Judith Long. "Work Aspirations of Women: False Leads and New Starts." Signs: Journal of Women in Culture and Society 1 (Spring 1976):33–49.

Leach, Anna. "Science in the Model Kitchen." Cosmopolitan: A Monthly Illustrated Magazine, May 1899, pp. 95–104.

Leonard, Priscilla. "Boston's Housework Experiment." Harper's Bazaar, March 1905, pp. 225–27.

Lerner, Gerda. "The Lady and the Mill Girl: Changes in the Status of Women in the Age of Jackson." Midcontinent American Studies Journal 10 (1969):5–15.

Life and Labor, 1903–1925.

Life and Labor Bulletin, 1925–1940.

Lindel, Ethel Mae. "A Business Woman's Attitude Toward Legislation." Woman's Press, September 1923, pp. 577–78.

Lipman-Blumen, Jean. "Toward a Homosocial Theory of Sex Roles: An Explanation of Sex Segregation of Social Institutions." Signs: Journal of Women in Culture and Society 1 (Spring 1976):577–78.

McCardell, Roy L. "Help! Help! Help!" Everybody's Magazine, October 1906, pp. 477–84.

McCracken, Elizabeth. "The Problem of Domestic Service: From the Standpoint of the Employer." Outlook, February 15, 1908, pp. 368–73.

McCullock, William. "The Logic of the Servant Problem." Harper's Bazaar, November 1908, pp. 1146–47.

McLaurin, Melton A. "The Racial Policies of the Knights of Labor and the Organization of Southern Black Workers." Labor History 17 (Fall 1976):568–85.

MacLean, Annie Marion. "The Diary of a Domestic Drudge." World Today: A Monthly Record of Human Progress, June 1906, pp. 601–5.

_____. "The Problem of Domestic Service: From the Standpoint of the Employee." Outlook, February 29, 1908, pp. 493–99.

Major, Martha. "The Domestic Problem." Living Age, September 8, 1900, pp. 642–45.

Mandel, Bernard. "Samuel Gompers and the Negro Workers, 1886–1914." Journal of Negro History 40 (January 1955):34–60.

Marrs, Virginia Harrison, and Williams, Harriet Walton. "No Yard-Stick for Household Employment." Journal of Home Economics 31 (May 1939):315–17.

Marsh, Helen Ester. "A School for Housemaids." Journal of Home Economics 7 (October 1915):435–37.

"Martyrdom of the Housewife." Nation, October 22, 1903, p. 317.

Mason, Walt. "The Dearth of Damsels." Colliers: The National Weekly, August 7, 1915, p. 26.

Mead, S. W., Mrs. "Home Life, Not Business." Outlook, September 14, 1912, pp. 71–72.

Miller, Annette Jaynes. "Why I Never Have Trouble with My Servants." Ladies Home Journal, March 1905, pp. 4, 52.

"Mistress and Servant." Living Age, January 15, 1898, pp. 213–14.

Moody, Helen Watterson. "The Unquiet Sex—Fourth Paper—The Case of Maria." Scribner's Magazine, August 1898, pp. 234–42.

Murphy, Ida Garrett. "The Unmarried Mother at Work." Survey, February 28, 1920, pp. 641–42.

Murray, Grace Peckham. "Health and Women's Work." Harper's Bazaar, January 1, 1901, pp. 390–92.

"My Cooks." Cornhill Magazine, August 1898, pp. 255–61.

National Urban League, Inc. Opportunity: Journal Life 7 (November 1929):335–36.

"Needed—A Domestic Union." Life and Labor Bulletin, December 1931, p. 3.

"News Notes." Journal of Home Economics 32 (February 1940):136.

"Nine-Hour Day for Domestic Help." Literary Digest, April 12, 1919, pp. 123–26.

O'Donnell, Edward. "Women as Bread Winners—The Error of the Ages." American Federationist 4 (October 1897): 186–87.

Offord, C. "Slave Markets in the Bronx." Nation, June 29, 1940, pp. 780–81.

"Our Own Times." Reader: An Illustrated Monthly Magazine, December 1907, pp. 107–10.

Peddler, D. C. "Service and Farm Service." Contemporary Review 123 (February 1903):269–77.

Peyser, Ethel. "That Servant Problem." North American Review 233 (January 1932):79–85.

"Plans for Improvement of Domestic Service." Monthly Labor Review 10 (May 1920):1186–90.

Plumb, J. N. "The Vanishing Servant." Horizon, Summer
    1973, pp. 10–11.

"Privileges of Servants." Outlook, March 17, 1900, pp.
    614–15.

Quimby, Alden W. "Housekeeper's Stone." Forum and Cen-
    tury, June 1901, pp. 453–61.

Ramsey, Annie R. "How a Bride Can Train a Cook."
    Ladies Home Journal, April 1909, p. 48.

Rawick, George. "Working–Class Self–Activity." Radical
    America 3 (March–April 1969):23–31.

Reid, Ira De A. "The Negro Woman Worker." Woman's
    Press, June 1930, p. 405; April 1932, pp. 204–6.

Richards, Ellen H. "The Eight Hour Day in Housekeeping:
    Conditions in the House Which Will Make It Possible."
    American Kitchen Magazine, January 1902, pp. 139–41.

_____. "The Eight Hour Day in Housekeeping: Condi-
    tions of Eight Hours a Day Work in the Trades."
    American Kitchen Magazine, November 1901, pp. 47–49.

Robb, Juliet Everts. "Our House in Order." Outlook, June
    18, 1910, pp. 353–60.

Roelofs, Henrietta. "The Minimum Wage Conference."
    Woman's Press, July 1923, pp. 401, 457.

_____. "The Problem of Women in Industry: A Report of
    the Women's Industrial Conference at Washington."
    Woman's Press, March 1923, pp. 143–45.

Roff, Katharine Metcalf. "A Plea for the Negro as Public
    Servant." New Outlook, September 27, 1916, pp. 223–24.

Roosevelt, Eleanor. "Servants." Forum and Century,
    January 1930, pp. 24–28.

Rorer, S. T., Mrs. "How to Train a Green Cook." Ladies
    Home Journal, January 1900, p. 24.

_____. "How to Treat and Keep a Servant." Ladies Home Journal, May 1900, p. 26.

"Rosie, Mary, and Adelaide." Scribner's Magazine, April 1911, pp. 506-7.

Rubinow, I. M. "Discussion of Women and Economic Dependence." American Journal of Sociology 14 (March 1909): 614-19.

_____. "Household Service as a Labor Problem." Journal of Home Economics 3 (April 1911):131-40.

_____. "The Problem of Domestic Service." Journal of Political Economy 14 (October 1906):502-19.

Rubinow, I. M., and Daniel Durant. "The Depth and Breadth of the Servant Problem." McClure's Magazine, March 1910, pp. 576-85.

Salifios-Rothschild, Constantina. "Dual Linkages between the Occupational and Family System: A Macrosociological Analysis." Signs: Journal of Women in Culture and Society 1, Part 2 (Spring 1976):51-52.

Salmon, Lucy M. "Democracy in the Household." American Journal of Sociology 17 (January 1912):437-57.

_____. "Recent Progress in the Study of Domestic Service." Atlantic Monthly, November 1905, pp. 628-35.

_____. "Some Historical Aspects of Domestic Service." New England Magazine, April 1893, pp. 175-84.

_____. "The Causes of Household Troubles." New Outlook, October 1, 1904, pp. 297-98.

Schatz, Ronald. "Union Pioneers: The Founders of Local Unions at General Electric and Westinghouse, 1933-37." Journal of American History 66 (December 1979):586-602.

Seeley, Evelyn. "Our Feudal Housewives." Nation, May 28, 1938, pp. 613-14.

Self, Edward. "Evils Incident to Immigration." North American Review 138 (1884):78-88.

"Servant's Library." Critic: A Weekly Review of Literature and the Arts, March 13, 1897, p. 188.

"Service without Servants." Good Housekeeping, September 1925, pp. 89, 220–24.

Sheldon, Charles M. "Servant and Mistress." Independent, December 20, 1900, pp. 3018–21.

Sherwood, M. E. W. "The Lack of Good Servants." North American Review 153 (November 1891):546–58.

Smith, Bertha H. "A Club for Maids." Ladies Home Journal, February 1916, p. 64.

Smith, Ethel M. "America's Domestic Servant Shortage." Current History 26 (May 1927):213–18.

Smith, Goldwin. "The Passing of the Household." Independent, August 24, 1905, pp. 422–24.

Smith, Mary Roberts. "Domestic Service: The Responsibility of Employers." Forum, August 1899, pp. 678–89.

Smith-Rosenberg, Carroll. "The Hysterical Woman: Sex Roles and Role Conflict in 19th Century America." Social Research 39 (Winter 1972):652–78.

Spectator, July 16, 1892; August 15, 1896.

Speed, John Gilmer. "Servants in the Country." Harper's Weekly, March 5, 1892, p. 235.

Sprague, Polly. "The Hired Girl in the Home." Ladies Home Journal, September 1916, p. 54.

"Standards for Women as Household Employers: Women's Bureau Investigation." Journal of Home Economics 34 (April 1939):350–51.

Strunsky, Simeon. "Help Wanted Female." Harper's Monthly, February 1919, pp. 402–7.

Taliaferro, Maybelle Cornell. "Philadelphia Council on Household Occupations." Journal of Home Economics 25 (February 1933):122–24.

Tarbell, Ida M. "Social Standing of Our Houseworkers."
Ladies Home Journal, March 1913, p. 26.

_____. "The Woman and Democracy." American Magazine,
June 1912, pp. 217-20.

_____. "What Shall We Do for Maids?" Good Housekeep-
ing, November 1917, pp. 22-23.

"Taxes, Servants--And Bliss." Nation, July 20, 1918, p. 61.

Thanet, Octave. "The People That We Serve: Sketches of
American Types." Scribner's Magazine, August 1894,
pp. 190-98.

"The American Aristocracy." Atlantic Monthly, June 1937,
pp. 702-6.

The Director. "Servants and Housekeepers." Good Housekeeping, May 1921, pp. 80, 125-26, 128.

"The Eight Hour Day in Housekeeping: From the Standpoint
of the Man of the House." American Kitchen Magazine,
March 1902, pp. 218-20.

"The Experiences of a 'Hired Girl.'" Outlook, April 6,
1912, pp. 778-80.

"The Home Club--The Servants' Side of the Servant Question." Outlook: A Family Paper, March 16, 1895, p.
440.

"The Servant Girl Problem." Independent, September 12,
1901, pp. 2193-95.

"The Servant's Right to Aesthetics." Harper's Bazaar,
June 1902, pp. 566-77.

"The Seven Weeks Experiment by the Committee on Household
Assistants." Journal of Home Economics 2 (December
1919):548-53.

"The Spectator." Outlook, January 11, 1902, pp. 117-19;
May 4, 1912, pp. 40-41.

"The Visiting Housekeeper." Good Housekeeping, March 1911, pp. 340-42; January 1912, pp. 60-63.

"The Young Women's Christian Association Commission on Household Employment." Journal of Home Economics 7 (December 1915): 522-549.

Thomas, Keith. "Work and Leisure in Pre-Industrial Society." Past and Present 29 (December 1964):50-60.

Thompson, E. P. "Time, Work-Discipline and Industrial Capitalism." Past and Present 37 (December 1967): 56-97.

Thompson, Flora McDonald. "The Servant Question." Cosmopolitan: A Monthly Illustrated Magazine, March 1900, pp. 521-28.

"To Save the Great American Home." Literary Digest, January 2, 1926, p. 11.

"Training for Household Employment." Journal of Home Economics 29 (October 1937):230-32.

"Training for Household Occupations." Journal of Home Economics 28 (September 1936):462-63.

"Training Unemployed Girls for Domestic Service." Monthly Labor Review 43 (August 1936):381-82.

Treiman, Donald J. "A Standard Occupational Prestige Scale for Use with Historical Data." Journal of Interdisciplinary History 7 (Autumn 1976):283-304.

Trueblood, Mary E. "Housework versus Shop and Factory." Independent, November 13, 1902, pp. 2691-93.

Tuttle, Margaretta. "Your Cook: Why She Hates Her Job." Ladies Home Journal, March 1915, p. 24.

Tyrell, M. A. "Fear in the Home and the Household." Nineteenth Century and After, March 1908, pp. 447-53.

Unger, Irwin. "The New Left and American History: Some Recent Trends in United States Historiography." American Historical Review 82 (July 1967):1237-63.

"Union in the Kitchen." Nation, September 5, 1901, pp. 182–83.

"Unionizing the Hired Girl." Literary Digest, May 9, 1931, p. 23.

Vrooman, Annie L. "Social Evolution of the Servant Question." Arena, June 1901, pp. 643–52.

Wallace, Eugenia. "The Servant and the New Democracy." North American Review 212 (October 1920):531–41.

Wallach, Isabel R. "The Staff of Employees." Cosmopolitan: A Monthly Illustrated Magazine, October 1903, pp. 696–98.

Wardel, Sara J. "Who'll Wash the Dishes?" New Outlook and Independent, January 30, 1929, pp. 168–70.

Watson, Amey E. "The Responsibility of the Home Economist for Improving Employer–Employee Relationships in the Home." Journal of Home Economics 28 (September 1936): 88–90.

Webb, Catherine. "An Unpopular Industry: The Results of an Inquiry Instituted by the Women's Industrial Council into the Cause of the Unpopularity of Domestic Service." Nineteenth Century and After, June 1903, pp. 989–1001.

Weber, Adna F. "Employer's Liability and Accident Insurance." Political Science Quarterly (June 1902):256–83.

Weed, Helena Hill. "The New Deal That Women Want." Current History 41 (November 1934):180–82.

Welch, Jessie L. "Help Wanted." Survey, January 15, 1927, pp. 520–22.

Wells, H. G. "Will There Be Servants in 2000 A.D.?" Current Literature 32 (April 1902):426–27.

Wells, Kate Gannett. "The Servant Girl of the Future." North American Review 157 (December 1893):716–21.

Welter, Barbara. "The Cult of True Womanhood." _American Quarterly_ 18 (Summer 1966):151-74.

Whiting, Isabel Kimball. "The General Housework Employee." _Outlook_, August 15, 1908, pp. 851-55.

"Who Is More to Blame: Servant or Mistress?" _Ladies Home Journal_, January 1909, p. 3.

Wilson, Thane. "How We Treat Servants and How They Treat Us: An Interview with Lida S. Seely." _American Magazine_, October 1923, pp. 64-65.

Wiltse, Sara E. "My Retinue." _Outlook: A Family Paper_, June 6, 1896, pp. 1105-7.

Wingate, Charles F. "Servants and Sanitation." _Country Life in America_, January 1909, p. 285.

Woodson, Carter G. "The Negro Washer Woman, A Vanishing Figure." _Journal of Negro History_ 15 (July 1930): 269-77.

Woodward, Ellen S. "Household Employment and the W.P.A." _Journal of Home Economics_ 28 (September 1936):439-42.

_____. "Making Housework a Skilled Occupation." _Journal of the American Association of University Women_ 30 (October 1936):23-25.

_____. "Women's and Professional Work in the W.P.A." _Journal of Home Economics_ 28 (November 1936):615-17.

_____. "W.P.A.'s Program of Training for Housework." _Journal of Home Economics_ 31 (February 1939):86-88.

Wright, Carroll D. "Why We Have Trouble with Our Servants." _Ladies Home Journal_, March 1904, p. 22.

Young, Stark. "The Lady's Looking Glass." _New Republic_, December 8, 1920, pp. 42-43.

Zieger, Robert H. "Workers and Scholars: Recent Trends in American Labor Historiography." _Labor History_ 13 (Spring 1972):245-66.

NEWSPAPERS

<u>Chicago Tribune</u>, 1870–1940.

<u>Cincinnati Enquirer</u>, 1 March 1982.

<u>Cleveland Gazette</u>, 1883–1940.

<u>Cleveland Plain Dealer</u>, 1870–1940.

<u>Duluth Tribune</u>, 9 May 1897.

<u>Freeman</u> (Indianapolis), 19 October 1889.

<u>John Swinton's Paper</u>, 1884–1887.

<u>New Orleans Picayune</u>, 1870–1914.

<u>New York Freeman</u>, 1 May, 18 December 1886.

<u>New York Herald</u>, 1870–1924.

<u>New York Herald-Tribune</u>, 1924–1940.

<u>New York Sun</u>, 26 June 1887.

<u>New York Times</u>, 1850–1940.

<u>New York Tribune</u>, 1845–1924.

<u>Solidarity</u>, 1910–1918.

<u>Washington Bee</u>, 3, 10 October 1885; 27 February, 20 March 1886.

<u>Weekly Pelican</u> (New Orleans), 18 December 1886; 26 February, 23 July 1887.

PUBLISHED REPORTS AND DOCUMENTS

Hill, Joseph H. <u>Women in Gainful Occupations 1870 to 1920</u>. Census Monographs, 11. Washington, D.C.: Government Printing Office, 1929; repr. ed., New York: Johnson Reprint, 1972.

Hooks, Janet M. Women's Occupations throughout Seven Decades. Women's Bureau Bulletin No. 218. U.S. Department of Labor. Washington, D.C.: Government Printing Office, 1951.

Johnson, B. Eleanor. Household Employment in Chicago. Women's Bureau Bulletin No. 106. U.S. Department of Labor. Washington, D.C.: Government Printing Office, 1951.

Pidgeon, Mary Elizabeth. Employment Fluctuations and Unemployment of Women: Certain Indications of Various Sources, 1928-31. Women's Bureau Bulletin No. 113. U.S. Department of Labor. Washington, D.C.: Government Printing Office, 1933.

Placement Standards for Household Employees. Works Progress Administration of California. Division of the Women's and Professional Projects. n.p., 1937.

Robinson, Mary V. Domestic Workers and Their Employment Relations. Women's Bureau Bulletin No. 39. U.S. Department of Labor. Washington, D.C.: Government Printing Office, 1924.

U.S. Bureau of the Census. Fifteenth Census of the United States: 1930. Vol. 4. Population and Occupations by States, Giving Statistics for Cities of 25,000 or More. Washington, D.C.: Government Printing Office, 1933.

_____. Fourteenth Census of the United States. Vol. 4. Population, 1920. Washington, D.C.: Government Printing office, 1923.

_____. Population of the United States at the Eleventh Census in 1890. Washington, D.C.: Government Printing Office, 1897.

_____. Social Statistics of Cities. Parts 1 and 2. Washington, D.C.: Government Printing Office, 1883.

_____. Statistics of the Population of the United States at the Tenth Census, 1890. Vol. 1. Washington, D.C.: Government Printing Office, 1883.

_____. Statistics of Women at Work. Washington, D.C.: Government Printing Office, 1907.

_____. Thirteenth Census of the United States. Vol. 3. Population, 1910. Washington, D.C.: Government Printing Office, 1913.

_____. Twelfth Census of the United States, 1900. Part 2. Population. Washington, D.C.: U.S. Government Printing Office, 1902.

U.S. Department of Commerce. Bureau of the Census. The Statistical History of the United States: From Colonial Times to the Present. With an Introduction and User's Guide by Ben J. Wattenberg. New York: Basic Books, 1976.

U.S. Congress. Senate. Report on Condition of Women and Child Wage-Earners in the United States. 19 vols. Doc. 645, 61st Cong., 2nd sess., 1911. History of Women in Trade Unions by John G. Andrews and W. D. P. Bliss. Vol. 10. Washington, D.C.: Government Printing Office, 1911.

_____. History of Women in Industry in the United States by Helen L. Sumner. Vol. 9. Washington, D.C.: Government Printing Office, 1911.

U.S. Department of the Interior. Office of Education. Household Employment Problems. Misc. Publications, 1971. Washington, D.C.: Government Printing Office, 1937.

U.S. Department of Labor. Bureau of Labor Statistics. Women in Domestic Work, Yesterday and Today by Allyson Sherman Grossman. Special Labor Force Report 242. Washington, D.C.: Government Printing Office, 1981.

U.S. Department of Labor. Women's Bureau. Family Status of Breadwinning Women in Four Selected Cities. Washington, D.C.: Government Printing Office, 1926.

_____. Bulletin No. 93. Household Employment in Philadelphia. Washington, D.C.: Government Printing Office, 1932.

_____. Bulletin No. 165. The Negro Woman Workers. Washington, D.C.: Government Printing Office, 1938.

_____. Bulletin No. 112. Standards of Placement Agencies for Household Employees. Washington, D.C.: Government Printing Office, 1934.

U.S. Industrial Commission Report. 19 vols. "Domestic Service" by Gail Laughlin. Vol. 14. Washington, D.C.: Government Printing Office, 1900–02.

Wright, Carroll D. The Working Girls of Boston: From the Fifteenth Annual Report of the Massachusetts Bureau of Labor for 1844. Boston: Wright & Potter, State Printers, 1889; repr. ed., New York: Arno Press and the New York Times, 1969.

UNPUBLISHED MATERIALS

Scharf, Lois. "'The Forgotten Woman': Women Workers, the New Deal and Feminism."

Van Raaphorst, Donna L. "I Won't Give Up, I Can't Give Up, I'll Never Give Up: The Motto of Geraldine Roberts, Founder of the Domestic Workers of America."

THESES AND DISSERTATIONS

Dublin, Thomas Louis. "Women at Work: The Transformation of Work and Community in Lowell, Massachusetts 1826–1860." Ph.D. dissertation, Columbia University, 1975.

Dye, Nancy Schrom. "The Women's Trade Union League of New York, 1903–1920." Ph.D. dissertation, University of Wisconsin, Madison, 1974.

Hartman, Heidi. "Capitalism and Women's Work in the Home, 1900–1930." Ph.D. dissertation, Yale University, 1974.

Haynes, Elizabeth Ross. "Negroes in Domestic Service in the United States." M.A. thesis, Columbia University, 1923.

Klazcynaska, Barbara. "Working Women in Philadelphia: 1900–1930." Ph.D. dissertation, Temple University, 1975.

McKinley, Blaine Edward. "'The Stranger in the Gates'": Employer Reactions toward Domestic Servants in America 1825–1875." Ph.D. dissertation, Michigan State University, 1969.

Pleck, Elizabeth Haflin. "Black Migration to Boston in the Late Nineteenth Century." Ph.D. dissertation, Brandeis University, 1973.

Rabinowitz, Howard N. "The Search for Social Control: Race Relations in the Urban South, 1865–1890." Ph.D. dissertation, University of Chicago, 1973.

MANUSCRIPT COLLECTIONS

Cleveland, Ohio. Western Reserve Historical Society, Florence Crittenden Papers.

_____. Western Reserve Historical Society. Phillis Wheatley Association Papers.

_____. Young Women's Christian Association Papers. Cleveland Chapter. Detroit, Michigan. Wayne State University. Archives of Labor and Urban Affairs. Mary Heaton Vorse Collection.

PROCEEDINGS

Knights of Labor. Proceedings of the General Assembly, 1881–1890. [Philadelphia].

INTERVIEWS

Roberts, Geraldine, founder of the Domestic Workers of America, Cleveland, Ohio. Interview, 25 February 1975.

Index

ABOUT THE AUTHOR

DONNA L. VAN RAAPHORST is an associate professor of history and social science at Cuyahoga Community College.
Professor Van Raaphorst holds a B.S. degree and an M.A.
degree from Eastern Michigan University and a Ph.D. from
Kent State University. Her research has focused on women,
minorities, and labor issues. She has been a National En-
dowment Fellow and the recipient of other academic administrative awards.
    She has recently completed a comprehensive package
of text materials to enhance undergraduate performance in
history and is working on an anthology on domestic workers
in the United States.